Anatomizing

The

Gang Culture

Adam R. Procell

Library of Congress Cataloging-in-Publication Data
Procell, Adam
Anatomizing the Gang Culture
ISBN 9780615870434
Front cover art by Daniel Procell

Printed in the USA
Beyond Reproach Publications

Table Of

Contents

For Robert

Foreword

The purpose of this curriculum is to educate the public as to all aspects of gang culture. This is a necessary and crucial step in understanding how to prevent future juvenile gang violence. As it stands now, our society really has a *mis*understanding as to why gangs "do what they do" or even why they exist.

It is because of this misunderstanding that the "war on gangs" has spiraled so out of control. This should come as no surprise to those who understand that no problem can be solved, resolved, or prevented without first understanding the foundation of said problem. As you read this book, I ask only that you keep an open mind and if possible, suppress any preconceived notions you might have about gangs and/or the gang culture. I ask this because many people create opinions based upon preconceived notions, thus never being able to fully understand certain realities that might conflict with said preconceived opinions. You may find some of what I say hard to believe, and while I encourage you to question what I state, I ask that you not dismiss it solely on the grounds that it conflicts with prior beliefs.

As you read, you will find that I often will use seemingly "off the beaten path" scenarios and "odd" references to help explain a point or issue. I will also speak on many topics that might at first glance seem to have nothing to do with the gang problem in America. I assure you that no tangent I use is without a purpose, though at times you might wonder where I am going. It is my goal to have you to think outside your normal preconceived parameters.

At the conclusion, please feel free to do as you wish with this information. Whether you use it to aid in the prevention of future juvenile gang violence, or disregard it as nonsense is your decision to make. Until the final page however, *please*, keep an open mind. After all, what do you/we have to lose at this point?

Chapter One

Gang members: a product off of our societal assembly line

It is becoming increasingly clear to see that there is an unofficial marketing campaign to create a product that no one wants. This product is coming off of the assembly line unsupervised, neglected, and uneducated faster than our society can pay the tab. Unfortunately these are the product's more humane qualities.

Even more worrisome, this product can come fully armed with military weaponry and a desensitized one-track mentality that fully intends to carry out any and all directives believed to further their cause.

Topics and questions elaborated on in this chapter will include:

- o What products are being produced?
- o How are they being produced?
- o Why they are being produced.
- o Why no one is talking about society's new product.

1 2345678910

*   *   *

The following is an excerpt from a sales brochure that I came across some time ago:

How many of you parents out there are always searching for a bargain, an offer too good to refuse? How many of you parents want the most for your money, a sale you can tell all of your friends about? With a sluggish economy, it is very practical to stretch a dollar as far as one can. Yes, who wouldn't want a product that costs very little money and is very low maintenance? Less money, less work, and more for your buck - sound interesting?

Is this what you want? You say to yourself, "Is this too good to be true? How can this be? Where can I buy whatever it is that you are selling?" Well, have I got a deal for you ladies and gentleman, a bargain too good to pass up. Most salesmen try to pressure you with such statements as "while supplies last" or, "for a limited time only." Well I am here to be honest with you my friends; I truly have an endless supply and an unlimited amount of time to sell my products.

Many of you have purchased and used my products in the past and are completely unaware that you have done so. Millions, yes millions of my products roll off of my assembly line so quickly to be used and abused. I have made a fortune in my business, making high-quality products for those who are always searching for a bargain. It is because of this that I can be so generous now. I am no longer in this business for the profit, the almighty dollar. I get satisfaction knowing that I have produced a product that I know you have asked for.

I also………………………….Oh, Excuse me, I have gotten so carried away that I have failed to introduce myself. Please accept my most sincere apologies for being so rude. I am Society. Yes you know who I am, you have heard of me. We meet all of the time and I can assure you that I know each and every last one of you. After all, it is my job to know who you are, what you are, what you say you want, as well as what you really want. Without this information, I would simply cease to exist. I am a culmination of you all.

I know what is wanted even when you think you haven't a clue. You are a tricky bunch however, because many times you truly want something you say or even think you don't want. I know otherwise however, because judging by your "actions" as a whole, you are getting just what those "actions" are asking for. I have been in this business since the day one person chose to exist with another.

I am able to see through all of your political correctness and fabricated morals.

Yes ladies and gentleman, parents and parent- to-be, I am so sure of my product that I won't even ask for payment in advance. I am so sure that I have produced exactly what your actions say that you want that I won't even ask for payment within the first year, or even five years for that matter. Now it differs from parent to parent, so I am willing to adapt to each and every one of your individual needs. Some may pay in eight years, some in twenty. I am so confident in my product that I will leave it up to you the consumer to decide when to pay.

Not many factories can offer a customer that type of leeway in their payment plan, but I am a firm believer in trusting my customers. The products that come off of my assembly line do not need parental supervision. In fact, the less the parents are involved in its personal care, the higher the odds become of you getting what you secretly desire. My product comes neglected and physically abused, battered, and bruised. Unlike many products, mine get better with wear and tear. You don't have to read to it at night or waste valuable time teaching it what is right and wrong. It just doesn't get any easier than that.

When you come home at night after a bad day, release your frustrations on my product. This is guaranteed to take all of your stress away. As a bonus, you are teaching it all of the essential survival skills that it will need later on as it grows and matures. (Two-for-the-price-of-one.) Why spend more of your hard-earned money on an already failing educational system when you can use that hard-earned money for what you really want; a new car, bigger house, or long vacation. What I am selling here today, my friends, thrives on run down schools with overcrowded classrooms. Why pay for one really good teacher when for the same price you can buy three mediocre ones and a new highway? After all, surely you need a nicely paved highway for that new SUV you want to purchase.

Have I captured your interest? It only gets better, I promise. The shelf life on my product is outstanding. You may get an unheard of twenty-one years of satisfaction out of it. If the individual expiration date starts to take effect, there is absolutely no need to worry. I would not dream of letting you purchase something that was not completely biodegradable and environmentally friendly. No need to have environmentalists picketing your home or place of employment, it's just not good for the reputation.

Another thing most manufacturers will not offer is this: when you purchase one of my products and then wish to purchase another in a few years, you do not need to worry about having to once again spend time programming your new purchase. The old will train the new; nothing at all is required from the parent whatsoever. You can now use your time getting drunk, partying whatever your hobby of choice is. Is that not the best news you have ever heard?

As I said before, I won't ask for payment in the near future. Some might say to themselves, "I bet a lot of people try and skip payment fifteen, twenty years down the road when you start demanding payment" I can assure you, my customers always pay. In fact, they beg me to take their payment, as will you.

When the time comes and I start to demand payment, I will demand death, I will demand murder, I will demand triple homicides and drive-by shootings. I will demand multiple stab victims. I demand children be fatherless. I demand that teenage souls perish inside the walls of your adult prison system. I demand that innocent children be caught in the crossfire of gang-related shootouts and die painful deaths. I demand that college honor students be mistaken for rival drug dealers and be executed! I demand that nine and ten-year-olds commit suicide because they are terrified to live in their own neighborhood. I demand that kids continue to kill one another because they chose to wear the wrong colored shirt to school that day. I demand utter chaos and mass genocide of today's youth! **I am SOCIETY!!!! WE** are in the business of manufacturing gang members............

Obviously by now you are quite aware that the "brochure" you just read was not "real." I am not trying to be overly dramatic, but if you really take a long hard look at the gang problem in America, you will find that it *is* a very dramatic problem.

Many people wish to run from the truth because the truth does not sugarcoat anything. The truth cannot be hid from forever. Sure, if we try hard enough, you, me, we -- society -- can temporarily blind ourselves to the crux of the problem but eventually the truth will rear its ugly little head from the depths of pain, chaos, and murder.

At some point, hopefully before the deaths of so many more occur, society will come to realize and understand that we as a whole are greatly responsible for much of the gang violence in America today. I do not intend to imply that society *consciously* wants gangs to exist, that society wants gang murders to occur every single day in this country. I want to show that our actions are sometimes in conflict with what we say we want. I will briefly give a few examples of what I am referring to and will get more in depth as I move forward in each chapter.

Take a child; say the age of twelve or so. His parents ask him if he feels getting good grades is important. The child replies "Yes."

This should come as no surprise given that most kids are told that an education is important in life. The child genuinely believes this; he is not just saying so for his parent's sake. The parent then asks why he feels getting good grades is important. The child states, "So that I can get a good job when I get old." The parent then asks why he wants a good job. To this the child replies, "So I can have money to buy a home, car, as well as the ability to take care of my family." The parents are satisfied with their child's answers and drop the subject.

A few weeks go by and it is a Monday. The little twelve-year-old finds out that he has an important exam on Friday and it will count for 75% of his grade. However, yesterday was his birthday and for a gift he received a new video game system he has been begging his parents for. The child comes home from school on Monday, study materials in hand and fully intending to study for his important exam. It is customary in this household to do one's homework and then play. The child goes to his room, pulls out his books but then sees the new video game system in the corner almost beckoning him.

At this very moment, a possible life changing set of events will begin in deciding what to do next. "Should I study for my exam, or play my new video game"? The child still believes without even knowing it that he wants to get a good grade on his exam. The child however, decides to study tomorrow so that he can play his game today. The child honestly believes that he will study tomorrow because good grades are after all, still important. This same set of events takes place on Tuesday, Wednesday, and Thursday with the same results. It is now Friday, exam day. The child fails the exam and brings the paper home to his parents who are understandably angry. The child is clearly distraught when he is again asked if grades are important. He exclaims nothing has changed, good grades are still important. What the child fails to understand is that actions can and often do supersede what one "thinks" they want, no matter how bad one thinks they want it. At the moment the child chose to play his video game rather than study, the child's actions stated that grades were *not* that important. At that particular moment a good job was *not* important. A nice home and new car were not important even though the child firmly believed at the time that they were.

It is possible in twenty years when that child has no job, education, or income, he can look back to those few decisions. The child will reap the rewards from that fateful decision for his entire life. Some, including that child are probably wondering how he will "reap the rewards" of that decision. Most when thinking of a reward think it is something one wishes to receive. It is. Unfortunately we really don't understand that our actions are telling the world that we want something else. (*On a side note, this same scenario doesn't have to end badly. Perhaps the child was so disgusted with himself for getting a failing grade that he never took the fun way out again and had a wonderful life. I also do not imply that one failed test can ruin a child's life; obviously other factors would come into play. I only use this scenario to make a point.)*

I'll explain further. Take me for example. If asked at the age of fourteen or so if I wanted to live the rest of my life in prison, I can assure you that I would have replied "Absolutely not." I firmly would have believed that as well. Not so fast however. My actions demonstrated something else entirely. When I chose to pick up and shoot a gun, my actions said to the world that I wanted to live my life in prison. I knew what I was doing was wrong, I knew it was illegal. Knowing all of that, right now today I am reaping the rewards of that decision. Apparently I really did want to spend the rest of my life in prison even though my thoughts, actions, and "wants" were obviously in conflict.

This same philosophy can be transferred onto to society "wanting" gangs to exist, "wanting" gang violence, and "wanting" to be terrified to drive through certain neighborhoods. On the surface, these statements I'm sure must sound completely insane, completely irrational. If you were to ask one million law-abiding citizens if they wanted gangs to exist, certainly they would say absolutely not. I also firmly believe that they truly believe this. No one could possibly "want" gangs to exist right? (*Not even gang members themselves want gangs to exist, as hard as this is to believe.*)

Well, let's take a brief look at what society's actions are telling the world they want. Remember, actions speak louder than words. Let's take a community at random, any inner-city community will do. We will begin at home. For many living within the inner city, home is a place with one parent. Not all, but a high number of families are single-parent households. Having a single-parent household creates a few problems: **1.** There is only one person to provide an income. This often leads to a status of poverty which will be discussed in a later chapter. **2.** While that single parent is working sometimes two jobs to support their household, their child or children are often left unsupervised. **3.** When the parent is at home, the parent is much of the time, exhausted from work. This can often lead to a very lazy parental attitude. The last thing a parent has the energy for is helping their child understand how to find the circumference of a 12-inch diameter circle. This comes not from being a bad parent, but rather an exhausted parent.

Also, much of the time there is not a set meal time if the parent is always at work. Studies have shown that families that eat together have children that are less likely to get into "trouble." Family dinner time often creates a relaxed atmosphere where the day's events can be discussed. This is where I believe a high portion of good parenting can be "inflicted." There are no televisions, video games, or phones to distract from whatever topics are being discussed. I do not believe that it is the dinner itself, but rather the structure this environment provides. **4.** Single parents are often either to strict when it comes to dealing with their child, or far too lenient with how discipline is carried out. There really is no middle ground I've come to find out. Many times two parents will balance each other out. (*If one is too strict, the other is nice.*) When a parent is too strict, a child will often get fed up and rebel. On the other end of the spectrum, if a parent is too lenient, a child will often be left to do what they want. This usually means they are allowed to stay out late, get bad grades, smoke, drink, etc. They quickly become the kid their friend's parents don't want their child associating with.

Finding the middle ground is very difficult for a single parent because even though "they" *are* the parent, there is an unmet need to be backed up when difficult decisions have to be made. It is very difficult for some parent's to tell their child "no." For some parents, it is too much to see the hurt, the disappointment, the anger in their child's eyes when they tell them they cannot do something, cannot have something, or cannot go somewhere. It is far easier to give in, let them do this *one* thing. After all, it will be OK to let them do this just once, right?

This begins a cycle, just like when a parent is teaching a newborn to sleep through the night. A parent when hearing their child crying in the middle of the night will want to go to them and offer comfort via singing, holding, talking, etc. This child is learning that crying equals mom/dad coming and making it better. Until that parent has the strength to resist getting up in the middle of the night when they hear crying, that cycle will continue. This is obviously not a healthy cycle to be in. There is no question that it is hard to resist going to one's crying child but most parents understand that it is necessary at times to do so.

Getting back to the "being too nice" cycle with older juveniles, it becomes even more difficult because you add in the element of detecting or understanding emotion. A baby cries and it is sometimes difficult to discern why they are crying. Is it out of fear, pain, or curiosity? Who knows at times? With a teenager, they are able to express to the parent exactly why they are mad, or "pissed off", or hurt. At heart, most parents do not want their child to feel "unhappy", so out of a weak sense of love often give in so that short term unhappiness, anger, or hurt can dissolve into happiness. Unfortunately, the longer this cycle continues the more difficult it will be to break.

Most likely, the cycle will not end until something so serious happens that fear will overpower the parent's willingness to "give in." Unfortunately, the "something serious" is often an event that is irreversible; whether it be killing someone while driving drunk, being killed by a drunk driver, hurting someone, killing someone, overdosing on drugs, or being murdered. After one of these many possible events takes place and it isn't irreversible, another problem arises. A parent will often be so overwhelmed by fear and anger that they will over compensate and do a 180° turn. They will now become so strict that it again can have a detrimental impact on their child's life. If a child was/is used to getting their way for months and/or years, they most likely are not going to react well to a complete change in parenting philosophy. Rebellion is likely to ensue. This rebellion can be even more difficult to break.

So what is a parent to do? Don't overreact. I know that this is an almost impossible thing to ask for, but you have to be strong. If a child makes a very bad decision, wait to react until cooler heads can prevail. Often when a child experiences a "close call", they on their own will take a breath; take a step back if you will. Sometimes this may only be a very short period of time, but it is a time they need to feel their parents aren't overreacting. This time is so unbelievably crucial. A parent's actions during this time can lead to two completely different outcomes. A parent has a chance if they do not overreact, to have their child come back to them. I speak not in the physical sense but rather the emotional. If a parent consoles, understands, and listens to what happened to their child, there is a high chance the child will gravitate back to their parent and away from the decisions and choices they were previously making.

Unfortunately, a large majority of the time the parent has a one-track mind set on punishment, (*Out of fear*) and squanders this once-in-a-life time opportunity to get their child back. Honestly, the parent cannot really be blamed for ruining this opportunity because they acted in a manner they thought would help their child. I am not at all trying to say that discipline should be abandoned. To the contrary, discipline is a necessity but only if used in appropriate form and severity.

One tactic that I'm sure will bring on scoffs would be asking a child what they believe their punishment should be; an opening of negotiations if you will. This automatically gives the child a feeling of both power and more importantly, responsibility. The feeling of having responsibility can be very empowering. It can lead to a high self-esteem which is something a lot of children/teenagers seem to lack. This low self-esteem is often the catalyst to hanging around "bad" friends, or trying to fit in with the wrong crowd. I believe many parents would be surprised at a child's first offer of self-punishment. If the parent thinks that the punishment is nowhere near severe enough, *do not overreact,* do not even offer a rebuttal punishment. Ask them if they feel their offered punishment fits the crime so to speak. Ask them what they the parent felt when whatever incident took place. Ask them if they can possibly understand how scared and hurt they (*The parent*) were. After this, ask them again what they feel their punishment should be. The child will often feel obligated to offer a stiffer self-punishment.

If the offer is still not to the parent's liking, then they counter offer until a resolution can be made. Granted, some incidents may require very little if any negotiation, but I think these times are rare. You can severely discipline your child with the negotiation tactic, as long as you go about it the right way. The goal of this tactic is to let the child think they have had a hand in what their punishment should be. They will more likely feel obligated to fulfill their punishment if they feel it was in part their idea. The child will often want to show their parent that they are dedicated to being more responsible. Many children are sorry, do want to change and are willing to "pay for their sins", so why not at the very least give them a chance to do so on their own?

Will this tactic work with every child? Absolutely not. One of the major problems in society today when it comes to juvenile gang prevention is this belief that what works with one child will work with another. The "blanket approach" and its detrimental effects will be discussed in detail in the chapters ahead. Every child needs to be treated different, needs to be treated as an individual. Many can be treated similar, but never exactly the same. It all depends on the situation.

Keep all of this in the back of your mind as you read further. Remember, I am speaking on what society's actions are saying they want.

We now move from the home to the "block." Unfortunately this same set of circumstances is rarely confined to one house on each block within the inner-city. The number of houses on a given block that are single-parent dwellings varies but the number is high. There are many "side-effects" that come with single-parent households that I will go into depth on in a later chapter. (*Not spending enough time with the child, being too strict, too nice, little supervision, etc.*) With many of these particular circumstances, a mentality takes shape for that particular block. You may think it is just one block, what's the big deal? As I will show later, remember that most gangs begin with a few kids on one block. All it takes is *one* block, one group of kids who are "similarly situated" (*Mentally*) with too much time on their hands.

These kids from this one block, many dealing with the effects of a single-parent household, are always hanging out with each other. Hanging out on "their block" can quickly turn into hanging out in their "hood." They now have something to lay a claim on. This is very similar if you think about it, to settlers laying claims to early western gold mines. I think perhaps America is a little in the dark about how fiercely men battled over little stakes of land, how many people were murdered for setting foot on another man's piece of land. Not unlike a rival drug dealer selling his/her drugs in another gang's neighborhood.

With this now staked claim by these juveniles, a mentality begins to form; a sense of ownership begins to take place over that one city block. Depending on the particular city and neighborhood, the lengths these juveniles will go to "protect" their neighborhood will vary. Some individuals in a "nicer" neighborhood might be content with simply hanging out, maybe spray painting here and there just to identify that block as belonging to them. On the other end of the spectrum, you take a walk in the wrong block in the heart of inner-city Chicago and you may pay with your life. There are many blocks in which you better not even think of entering. Wearing the wrong colors in these neighborhoods will quickly result in a loss of life with no questions being asked.

So, back to the one block with the group of teenagers that lay claim to it, a violent mentality will often arise to "protect" it. Other people on this block will see this mentality, know of its existence. For them another mentality begins to form, one of fear, distrust, and anger. They often say to themselves, "Let them kill each other off." This mentality transcends onto local businesses, whether it be the local corner store, barbershop, gas station, etc. The block is now divided mentally on a subconscious level which in the future will become quite devastating. How a block looks on the surface from an aesthetic perspective, i.e. clean/dirty, grass/no grass, boarded up houses, crumbling buildings, graffiti everywhere, and litter can create a mentality as well. A sense of anger and bitterness will become evident in many of the law-abiding citizens on that block. Now if this were just one block that had formed this mentality, it would be unfortunate but probably manageable. It isn't confined to just one block however. It begins to seep into the next block. This next block soon becomes a clone of the former. If containment is not successful, then block after block will share the same fate until the entire community, an entire side of town shares the same mentality.

Now you have an entire community that is in ruins, is divided on so many levels, has gangs everywhere, and is rampant with crime. Keep this community's mentality on a side burner while you think about how that mentality will affect the next local election. There are always referendums in an election, whether they are for new roads, a new community center, or additions to the local high school. All communities go through these passages or non-passages of referendums to better their community. In higher-income neighborhoods, the above-mentioned referendums are passed with much more frequency. The reasons for this can be many, but the most likely would be financial. Funding would probably be the biggest road block to passing many of these referendums. Another reason might be indignation. Many residents feel it is useless to put money into a community that they themselves deem forsaken. Why should they spend their hard earned money to build a new park where drugs will probably be sold at or some kid will be shot at anyway? Why should they vote to pay for a new computer lab in a school that is failing, has a horrible record, or "teaches" kids that terrorize the community? Why would these citizens pay for twenty more officers to patrol when there is nothing but distrust between them and the community?

Many of those in these "disenfranchised" communities simply do not vote. The reasons why at this point become irrelevant. What are their "*actions*" stating that they want? If they do not vote to better their schools, then their "*actions*" say that they want sub-par schools. If they "want" sub-par schools, what then comes out of sub-par schools? Juveniles with sub-par educations. What do people often turn to if they haven't an education to get a good job? Crime, because they have to support themselves somehow, right? What kinds of crime? Drugs, theft, robbery, etc. What groups are often involved with selling drugs or moving stolen merchandise? Gangs, of course. Are you beginning to see a correlation?

As unreasonable as it sounds when a voter chooses not to better a school in their community, their actions are saying by default in some way that they do want gangs to exist. This is true because as will be explained later, there is a direct correlation between failing schools and gang membership. Is this fair? Absolutely not. Should a person be able to live their own life, mind their own business, and not vote for any referendums? Of course, but life is not fair. We live in a *society*. What you do or don't do, for that matter, affects me in some way at some point. The effect may be minimal or life-altering, all depending on the situation.

For instance, let's say a voter from a violent neighborhood did not vote to pass a measure that would drastically improve a school on their block. A kid from that school goes on to fail in life because they do not receive a good education to get a good job. (*He*) decides that selling drugs is the only way he can support himself. He cannot by himself sell drugs in his neighborhood because the drug trade is owned by a gang on his block. He then joins that gang so that he may sell drugs without reprisal. One day he is selling cocaine on a street corner when "the deal goes bad." Let's say that he has a gun and shoots at whoever is trying to rob him of his drugs. Unfortunately a little girl is shot by accident with a stray bullet and dies. He did not intend for her to get hurt, but that is of little importance to her or her loved ones.

Now obviously that voter cannot be blamed for the little girl's death, correct? What if that vote was the deciding vote to improve the school the gang dealer failed out of? What if the measure *had* passed? What if the gang member had stayed in school, gotten an education, graduated, and gotten a good job? What if he didn't "need" to sell drugs to support himself, never had joined a gang or been involved in a drug deal gone bad, nor became the one who accidentally shot that little girl?

If that voter knew how his/her vote affected the future, do you think he/she would "feel" responsible somewhere deep inside? Or, depending on your particular belief system, whether it is atheism, agnostic, religious, etc., does free will for all human beings automatically release that voter from any and all responsibility? What about the individual who sold the gang member the gun? Does he suffer any responsibility for that little girl's death? If so, why? He didn't want that little girl to die; he didn't know she was going to die. What about the person on the other end of the drug deal gone bad? Do they have any responsibility? All they wanted to do was get high, appease an addiction. What is their role in that girl's death? Any?

Are these really such "laughable" questions, or is there some merit to them? Should there be merit? Who should receive some, partial, or all of the blame? Can it only be one person that gets all of the blame? What about all of the voters as a whole who voted down the school referendum? Most people I'm sure would absolve them of any blame. The gang member of his own free will took that little girl's life---accident or no accident. He deserves all of the blame. An argument can obviously be made for that belief, and no doubt the gang member is responsible no matter who else may or may not carry blame. Just because other people may be to blame, doesn't mean that the gang member should be absolved of even an ounce of blame, and subsequent punishment. Please understand that I am not in any way trying to mitigate punishment. To the contrary, I am merely trying to point out "why" the situation exists in the first place.

Blame is a fickle entity, with no set of rules of definition. Blame is rarely understood and can have many different faces; depending on how, why, or when a certain situation is viewed. It is easy to blame the gang member. (*Again, deservedly so*) Yet easy isn't all encompassing, or fair, and woe to those that say life is not fair. It is not, but this fact is not an excuse to stop looking deeper, to stop looking for the real problem. Sometimes our actions are in direct conflict with what we *say* we do not want.

There is a reason that the gang culture has exploded. It is because people have chosen to not understand the root of the problem. Society's emotions and anger have allowed us to take the easy way out and or offer short term solutions. How many more children have to die, have to be paralyzed before society says "hold on a minute, what are we doing?" "What have we been doing for so long?" How many more innocent people will have to live in fear of gangs before we understand that it will not get better until they/we as a whole completely change the way we think?

Discussed so far, are certain "ingredients" in assembling a future gang member and I have worded it as so because that is exactly what's being done. The inner city has become an assembly line, an assembly line that manufactures gang members. Think about it. An assembly line takes various parts, puts them together, and together they become a final product. Well, the "parts" of a gang member are often a single-parent household, (*And the mentality that often comes from that household*) a failing school system, a neighborhood with other like-minded juveniles, and a community to live in that has a bitter resentment towards them. These parts when "assembled" often create a gang member. Unfortunately the manufacturing process does not end at the creation of a gang member.

From a physical standpoint, certain available "bells and whistles", premiums, or additions can also be retrofitted to our newly assembled gang member. Military weaponry is an additional "add-on" that many gang members often acquire. The accessibility to not only hand guns and rifles exists, but machine guns and grenades are also easily accessible for many gang members.

From a mental aspect, a gang member can have many different "ways of thinking" wired into their brains, many different mentalities if you will. Children soak up what they see when they are growing up and often times try and emulate what they have seen. Or, they can despise what they have seen growing up so much that they become driven to never mirror what they have witnessed. Unfortunately, the latter is the rarer of the two. If a child has witnessed violence his/her entire life, how can they be expected to not refer back to those memories, perhaps even subconsciously when faced with certain situations in their lives? If they do become gang members, these prior memories of violence often become "training" to perpetuate the cycle. These memories and thoughts have become hardwired into their psyche, and like a virus; spread, mutate, and morph into the rationalization that it's OK to commit heinous acts of violence that we as a society see on TV, or read in the papers every day.

Society's approach to ending juvenile gang violence is akin to a doctor placing a tourniquet on a patient's *calf* when they were shot in the *thigh*. The tourniquet becomes counterproductive, and a device intended to save lives is now speeding up the process of taking a life. Any device/solution, no matter how genius, can become counterproductive if not used in the right place, time, or fashion.

In the case of preventing juvenile gang violence, society cannot presume to be effective in this endeavor if it does not start at the root of the problem. We must understand that as a society, we have let the problem get so severe, that we have turned a blind eye for so long, that understanding the root of the problem will show how unbelievably much will have to change for this problem to be solved.

It will be overwhelmingly daunting, this task of ending juvenile gang membership/violence. So many will have the desire to give in, and plenty will. In fact, many already have to be honest. Many more people as a result will die; unfortunately these deaths will often be children. How many more have to die before we quit taking the "easy way" out?

I'm sure some will say, "Just let them kill each other off. Why should I care what happens to 'them?" Well, I can assure you that you will care if it's *your* little girl that gets accidentally killed in the crossfire of a gang-related shooting. People don't buy car insurance because they expect to get into a car accident. They buy it just in case they are involved in one so they will not be riddled with debt when/if an accident does occur. Spending money to solve juvenile gang violence as a whole can be looked at in the same way as buying car insurance. Sure, you may never get into an accident, and all that money you spent on insurance will have been for naught, (*Except maybe your peace of mind*). Similarly sure, your son or daughter may never be accidentally caught in the crossfire of a gang-related shooting or be hurt by the hands of a gang member in any one of a thousand different ways, but why increase your odds? Millions everyday lessen their odds of having a huge financial burden by buying car insurance just in case they are involved in an accident. If asked however, these people would say with steadfast certainty that they will never be in an accident, yet they will continue to pay ridiculously high prices for car insurance, "just in case." Why these same millions don't want to spend a fraction of what they pay in car insurance to aid in juvenile gang prevention programs, I don't know. Maybe society thinks that it is a lost cause, that there is no hope, or that it is simply not their problem so why bother?

After all, it's not *their* problem correct? People often assume that life should be fair. It *should* were this a perfect world, but unfortunately it is not. So no, it is not fair that law-abiding citizens should have to pay for the types of programs that are needed to end juvenile gang violence. Many people will never be affected by gang violence but we will never know *who* won't be. It then becomes a two-fold issue, **1.** We should all as a society want to make said society better, **2.** How important is "peace of mind", at least in regards to *becoming* a victim of gang violence? This includes accidental and intentional acts of gang violence.

Unfortunately, I'm afraid that the "enough is enough" attitude will not become prevalent until some future act of gang violence occurs and this act is so heinous and grotesque that it shocks the senses. Maybe then we as a society will "bite the bullet" so to speak. (*Probably not the best use of an analogy, I know.*) So ask yourself: do your actions or rather *non*-actions contribute to the *possibility* of juvenile gang violence? Remember, *actions* always supersede *want*. Do you *want* juvenile gang violence to exist?

Do you think society or some sects of society <u>want</u> gangs to exist due to their inaction?

Chapter Two

Victims: a true definition

I hope that all of the chapters in this book will be taken seriously, but this chapter is especially important. At the end of the day, it is the victim that truly loses the gang violence war. For them, the problem is not someone else's. For them, the problem will not magically disappear over time. For them, sometimes there is no tomorrow. What *we* do as a society tomorrow to end juvenile gang violence will not bring them back. All they have is yesterday.

Unrecognizable to many hard-liners in society, there are many more casualties via gang violence than the individual victims of murder, robbery, and rape. It's easy to lose sight of the numerous other victims related to gang violence, understandably no doubt. They are often forgotten due to the 'get tough on crime' or as President Bush called it, "Tough Love" campaign that swept the nation in the 80's and 90's. Unfortunately many other victims were simply overshadowed. As I said, it is understandable because the more crimes committed by and for the benefit of a gang, the less tolerant the public becomes to the gang member who commits the crime, as well as any other party remotely linked to them. For instance, a gang member's family will often be vilified as a result of any crime that occurred, even if they had nothing to do with it. The mother and father are quickly labeled bad parents, (*And some are*). Many are not however. The communities where much of this gang violence occurs are labeled as "bad" communities, with that label encompassing everyone in it. Many of these citizens are themselves victims of gang violence but can't afford to live anywhere else.

It is very easy to criticize those on the other side of the fence but this criticizing in no way contributes to a solution. Even more excluded from the term "victim" are some gang members. I know, I know, "punish the sinners" you say; "if you do the crime you should do the time." I agree. This is where it gets dicey however. Yes, gang members need to be severely punished for their crimes, myself included. In no way, shape, or form am I trying to argue that point. However, kids do not exit the womb with bandanas and tattoos. They are not born gang members. They do not grow up with the sole intention of leading a self-destructive life. (*Contrary to popular belief, I know.*) Kids are very much like sponges, they soak up their surroundings. If *you* were to grow up surrounded by nothing but gangs, violence, crime, and poverty, how would you turn out? We can get into the whole human nature of "what is right and wrong" issue (*And I will later*), but that topic is widely debatable. So do you blame the kid? Perhaps. Do you blame the parent? Many do. What about a community? Can we charge a particular street with murder? "Mr. South 21st street, you are charged with 14 counts of intentional murder, how do you plead?" Is that really such a silly thought?

The importance of understanding why some young gang members are victims isn't so in determining a sentence "post crime", but rather is important to understand so similar crimes can be prevented in the first place. I cannot stress the importance of this issue. If we hope to end the juvenile gang violence issue, we have to understand *why* these kids become gang members in the first place. The sad reality is that many of them never really stood a chance. What then, would you define them as?

Topics and questions elaborated on in this chapter will include:

- o   The ripple effect.
- o   Defining a victim.
- o   Understanding who the non-politically correct victims are.
- o   Forgotten victims;
  - the family,
  - the community,
  - the *young* gang member.
- o   Why are victims in the eye of the beholder?
- o   Is it fair to criticize?

1234567891o

*   *   *

Vic·tim (Vik'tim) n. 1. One harmed or killed by another. 2. A living creature slain and offered to a deity as a sacrifice, 3. One harmed by an act, circumstance, or condition <victims of disaster>

Webster's II, New Riverside Dictionary Revised edition.

Vic·tim (Vik'tim) n. [Lat. Victima] 1. One harmed or killed by another. 2. A living creature slain and offered to a deity as a sacrifice or as part of a religious rite. 3. One harmed by or made to suffer from an act, circumstance, agency, or condition. <victims of disaster> 4. One who suffers injury, loss, or death because of a voluntary undertaking <victims of their own cunning> 5. One tricked, swindled, or taken advantage of. <the victim of a con game>

> Synonyms: victim, casualty, prey, n. core meaning: one harmed or killed by another. <victim of a street crime>

Webster's II New college dictionary, 3rd edition.

These are just a couple of definitions of the word "victim" from two dictionaries I had access to. The first definition would probably fit most people's view of what a victim should be defined as. Generally speaking, a victim would be defined to me as, *anyone* hurt by the actions of something or someone. To me, it makes no difference whether or not the actions were intentional or accidental.

Would it be reasonable to assume that most people would agree with definition #1, that anyone who was harmed should be defined as a victim? I do. You would think then, that this "class" of victim should be pretty straight forward to identify, correct? After some thought, I realized that this was not the case at all, that there are far too many variables that can be added or subtracted, possibly changing whether or not someone else could be considered a victim as well.

For instance, an example: (*Please follow me for a while, it will take a minute to see the point.*) Let us take two grown women, both of "average" weight and height. One of the ladies tells the other that she is overweight. The "overweight" woman's feelings are hurt. Is she a victim under any definition? Could this remark be defined as slanderous? What if the "overweight" woman was a model and the other woman out of jealousy told the media that she was overweight? There is a possibility that her job/reputation could take a hit. Does that "overweight" remark then rise to a slanderous level?

Slan·der (slân 'dər) n. A fake and malicious statement injurious to another's reputation. V. to spread or utter slander about: defame---slan'der-ous adj.

Webster's II New Riverside dictionary, revised edition

Is the woman a victim of slander if she really isn't "overweight" and the woman who made the remarks (*Also a model*) was trying to hurt her industry reputation out of jealousy? What if she never admits that? Can that ever really be proven unless she admits that her remarks were said maliciously to hurt the other woman's career? Then there is the whole argument about the definition of "overweight." Where is that line acceptably drawn? At what weight for what height? Must it be the scale used by the American Medical Association? Who determined those scales? I'm sure that those scales would not mirror what most people would define as overweight.

If the majority of people in this country "think" the woman is not overweight; does that nullify her title of victim? What if the jury she has at a potential "slander trial" are all moderately athletic and think she is overweight and find the other woman's remarks not to be slanderous? Now she is not "legally" a victim of slander or any *crime* per se, so would you still consider her to be a victim? (*I think the crime element is important here, because most people would define a victim as such; resulting from a crime.*) What if her jurors were "fat", and found her not to be overweight and as a result, found the other woman's remarks slanderous? She is now a legal victim of a crime and nothing at all changed in the scenario except for the weight of a few jurors' belt sizes. Does this mean whether or not someone can be labeled a victim possibly depends on a variable as ridiculous as a belt size?

Let's go a different route: What if the "slanderous" remarks came from a man? Do you think more people would consider the woman to be a victim if the remarks came from a man's mouth? Probably, at least in my opinion. What if the remarks came from a five-year-old little girl? Would more people without conscious thought, be more apt to think of the remarks as "harmless" if coming from the mouth of a five-year-old? I think so. If these remarks are harmless out of the mouth of a five-year-old, what about a six-year-old? Seven, eight, sixteen? Where is the line drawn, at what age do the remarks turn from harmless to malicious? We are speaking about the same exact words. I would assume that different people would define it differently.

So a victim would then have to be defined as what? In the eye of the beholder? A victim, is a victim, is a victim right? I guess I don't even think so anymore. How can the same statement; *"you are fat"*, victimize someone some of the time but not others, simply by the change of a single variable? I'm sure that there are countless other variables that could affect the scenario the same way that I haven't used. So who should make the determination of "who" a victim is? I am definitely not arrogant enough to make that decision.

I have merely used this example to show that a victim can be any number of people, depending on who they are, what they've done, and dependent upon the belt size of a juror. I want to show that just because "a majority" might believe only certain individuals can be labeled as victims, does not mean there are not other victims out there. There is I believe, no one definition of who can be a victim. Anyone can be a victim if the variables and circumstances are "correct."

I will get back to who "can" be a victim in a moment, but let's begin with the most widely accepted victim in the context of the gang lifestyle. Example: A car full of gang members does a drive-by shooting on a house they believe a rival gang member resides at. Unfortunately this is the wrong house. This house belongs to your typical family of four, with the children aged at six and eight. The six-year-old is tragically hit and killed by the gunfire.

I don't believe that there is a single sane person on this earth who would not classify that six-year-old as a victim of gang violence. The child was not in a gang. The child did nothing to provoke the shooting, and was simply at the wrong place at the wrong time. (*Or is it the "right" time? I've never really understood that phrase.*) That child was truly innocent of any wrong doing and can only simply be defined as a victim. Next, the other three family members who were in the house but were not physically harmed should in my opinion also be clearly defined as victims. The reason being should be viewed from two separate angles; **1.** The terror from being shot at, or having your life threatened by a stray bullet is terrifying. The psychological effects of a traumatic experience like this undoubtedly will affect different people in different ways for different periods of time. However, no matter the severity of mental trauma or how long the duration, it is trauma never the less, thereby deeming any who suffered said trauma a victim.

These three family members should all be labeled as victims for experiencing first hand, the trauma of being shot at and the trauma of possibly losing their own lives. Can I safely assume that you too would classify these three as victims of gang violence? **2.** The second reason these three family members should be considered victims is due to the 'ripple effect'. The ripple effect is a term used in programs such as Alcoholics Anonymous, Narcotics Anonymous, anger management etc. The ripple effect is a phrase that helps visualize how one's action to one person can create many more victims than the individual that was directly hurt.

It works like this: When you throw a rock into a pond, the place the rock enters the water is clearly affected. That disruption, "hole in the water", can be defined as "victim zero", or victim #1, however you wish to define it. When that rock enters the water, the space where the rock entered is not the only space disturbed, or agitated is it? No, of course not. The initial hole created by the rock impacting the water is essentially the victim a crime is being committed upon. Ripples immediately surround the impact zone. They begin very tight in circulation, gradually spreading out. The correlation here comes from when a person is on the receiving end of a crime, they are affected the most. The people closest to them however, are also affected by the crime. In the example of the family of four, the child who died would be the "impact zone" where the rock entered the water. The very first ripple could be viewed as the mother, or victim number two. (*I say mother in this example as the second victim to take nothing away from the father. Often times a mother will have a closer relationship with the child simply because she gave birth, therefore being more affected. I am obviously aware that there are plenty of horrible mothers out there that could not care less about their child, so in those situations the father might be victim number two, or a grandparent, brother, etc.*)

The mother is the first ripple in this scenario, with the second ripple representing the father, and the third being the other sibling. All three ripples are very close, very tightly encircling the impact zone because all of the family members were at home when the shooting took place. Every crime is different in both magnitude and circumstance, just like different sized and shaped rocks will create more or less ripples when thrown into a pond. In the aforementioned example of a murder, a very large rock was thrown into the water, a boulder if you will. There will be many ripples more than just the four I've mentioned. The fifth, sixth, and seventh ripples might be the grandparents, aunts, cousins, nieces, or nephews.

As the ripples lessen in tightness and height, so does the intensity of victimization felt by the affected parties. This in no way minimizes their status of victims or the pain that they may be suffering. The reality being that a second cousin twice removed who has never met victim zero is going to be affected less than the mother or father. Will they be affected? Absolutely. Also, I don't believe that family members are the only individuals that can be "ripples." Let's say that the next door neighbors have a child the same age as the child who died in this scenario and they happened to be best friends. I believe the next door neighbor child is instantly a victim of gang violence as well because it is due to said gang violence that he/she lost their best friend. Now they will not understand the whole gang violence concept, only that they no longer have a friend to play cops and robbers with, no one to hide from them while they seek. They will be hurt and not understand "why", and just because they don't understand "why" doesn't mean that they are not a victim. In fact, I would suggest that they are "more" of a victim than the second cousin twice removed. They may be the "eighth" ripple.

The neighbors themselves are also victims of gang violence because they were also close with the deceased child, not to mention the proximity of their house to the victims. They were essentially a stone throws away and I'm sure felt unsafe. I'm sure they felt like the sanctity of their home as well was compromised because it easily could have been their home that was hit. To feel unsafe on any level, I suppose could be the ultimate victimization in a way. If someone makes another feel unsafe, they are in my opinion victimizing them. It makes no difference if the one wielding the fear is doing so by shooting a gun or simply yelling threats in an aggressive tone. Either way, someone might feel unsafe. Either way, they have created a victim.

Just because the ripples spread out in relation to closeness with the victim, does not mean that the rest of the community does not also ripple with victimization. It varies on the community. Some are very close, some not so much. Either way, odds are everyone on that particular block will have been affected by the murder of a six-year-old. They too are all victims of gang violence. Again, some on that block will be more affected than others and the reasons for this are numerous. One example might be that someone didn't know the child while another did. Another example could be that someone themselves may have already been victimized by gang violence and either are affected more, or less because they are desensitized. If shootings are a frequent occurrence on this particular block, this particular shooting will have less of an impact (*At least consciously anyways*) via desensitization, than say a shooting that took place on a block that has never before experienced such an event. I say conscious impact because while some may feel unaffected or unmoved, the trauma on the subconscious level remains. Humans are not born in my opinion, to "be OK" with the concept of a child being murdered. I'm not saying that there are not plenty of atypical personalities out there that "get off" on such things; like witnessing and creating such carnage. I merely believe that they are not the norm.

As far as "normal" people thinking they are unaffected by shootings and/or murders due to desensitization, I wonder which is worse; being consciously traumatized by an event, in this case a child being murdered or, "seeing" this sort of thing happen so often that one "feels" unaffected? The latter scenario being two-fold: How would *you* feel if you witnessed a child being murdered and were conscious to the fact that you felt "unaffected"? You know that you obviously *should* be affected, so I wonder if that would make you feel like something is wrong with you. Though I guess you could argue that if one hasn't the emotion to feel anything when a child gets murdered, how could one then feel something when one realizes they are unaffected when they should in fact be greatly affected? Maybe it's a perpetually vicious emotionless circle, I don't know.

As the ripples lessen further in tightness, what of those on the next block and then the next who don't know the victim personally but hear the whispers of what happened? They too are affected in some way because it happened so close to home, again more or less so based upon life experiences.

I often wonder what "ripples" the homicide detectives, E.M.T.'s, nurses, doctors, and morticians are who deal with injured gang violence victims. I have to believe that it is highly unlikely that they are unaffected at the sight of a child's body riddled with bullet holes. How could they not be? These people are not standing a half block away or driving past getting only a quick mental snapshot of flashing lights and crime tape with wonderings of, "Oh my God, what happened?" For the doctors, detectives, nurses etc.; what they see doesn't disappear like a quick billboard of death as you drive by. They are forced to look; it is their job to dig out every bullet from that six-year-olds body lying there on cold stainless steel. I wonder what on earth is going through that crime scene investigators mind as they stretch open the wound to remove a bullet. It is their job to re-create exactly what happened to the child for the purposes of prosecution. Every last blood splatter and piece of flesh is painstakingly gone over. They can run from nothing mentally. Do you think that they are not affected by gang violence? I wonder if they aren't affected more than some family members, even though they never knew the victim. Even family members are not forced to inspect tediously for hours, every spec of blood, hair, dirt, etc. That has to take a toll mentally on the mind of any human being. As I really think about it, I don't know how some of them can sleep at night.

I would have to think that desensitization plays a major role in these individuals' lives as well, but still. It's interesting; I wonder if society ever thinks about *how* gang violence affects these types of people. Do you know any of these people; detectives, nurses, E.M.T.'s, etc.? I would suggest that you ask them. If you are reading this book, I would assume that you have some sort of vested interest in gangs and or gang violence, so would it not be appropriate to investigate all angles? (*After all, it is my goal with this book to open the eyes of society as to the gang culture in its entirety.*)

I wonder if these people *are* desensitized. I wonder if it ever gets more tolerable; viewing the corpses of so many youth who die as a result of gang violence. I don't see how it could, but something has to happen I would think to enable a person to continue to view such horrific images day after day. I wonder what their opinions of gang members are, if they have a loathing more so than the average person. I would guess it to be likely. What if one of their children became a gang member? Do you think they would be over passionate to a destructive level in trying to get their child out? I'm sure it has happened; I'm curious though of the final results.

I've always felt an effective tactic in the aid of prevention, (*Regardless of what is attempted to be prevented*) is showing an individual up close and personal, the results of their actions. For example; if a teenager has a habit of driving while drunk, take them to an emergency room during the wee hours of January 1st. *Make* them see the carnage they are likely to create. Let them see the blood, the fear in the doctors' eyes when they realize they cannot save someone. For those who say that, "those images are too graphic for a teenager to witness", to *you* I say, "Wake up!" Coddling will do nothing to help these teenagers. They are already *participating* in the act of driving while drunk; no more harm can come from witnessing what their drunk driving can cause. This same philosophy applies to overdoses and gang banging as well.

Teenagers are very visual beings; and the difference between hearing that people die from gang violence and seeing at the morgue a dead body with twenty bullet holes in it laying on a cold steel table is night and day. We need them to see what they are doing to people, "Here, look! This is what happens when your clip is empty; this is what you are running away from when you flee a crime scene. This is what will haunt you when you are old enough to understand what you are doing. No, don't look away now, stare death in the eyes, maybe it's you one day. Maybe you are not the killer, but rather the beneficiary of an emptied AK-47 clip. Maybe your brains will end up rotting in the gutter of some block." Let the teenager witness a mother identifying a body. Show them what their mother might look like as she attempts to identify *their* body, sobbing one small little word, "why?"

Such a small little word, only three letters, and yet who can answer such a question? What do you think the young gang member would answer to that question while standing before a bullet-riddled body? I wonder if they could give an answer, or if they are simply too young to understand the concept of death, the repercussions of their actions, or the finality of them. This is absolutely no justification to commit any act of violence. Just because they do not understand truly what taking someone's life means does not make the victim any less dead, or any less of a victim. I don't know that most adults understand the finality of death. I don't think any human being understands or can fully comprehend the finality of death. Yes, some might believe what their religious teachings promise after this life as we know it but even then, I don't think people can mentally comprehend the aspect of no longer existing. There is much I don't/can't understand in this world, but even though I cannot understand it, I can still *comprehend* that there are things I don't understand. I can't however, personally understand the concept of my mind, my thought process, my consciousness "not existing." Where do our thoughts go? To me, that is death; a cessation of thought. I personally couldn't comprehend that at fifteen years of age when I committed my crime, because I cannot comprehend it now. That fact changes not however, that my victim is dead as a result of my actions, nor do I believe it lessens my victims of such status.

I've always thought it interesting; one can acquire many things in life whether it be money, fame, love happiness, etc., all of which can be taken from you. Once you create a victim however, that person is *your* victim for all of eternity. There is not one single thing a person can do to "un-ring that bell." We can pay for our sins here on earth and invest all we are in making right that wrong. We can even be forgiven by those we victimize, but it still doesn't change the fact that they are and forever will be a victim of ours. I also understand the philosophy that many victims at a certain point do not consider themselves victims anymore, and I respect that with all of my being. I understand the act of taking the powerlessness of victimization away. In no way am I trying to infringe upon that right. I am more speaking along the lines of guilt. While it's true, time does *ease* pain, I don't believe time is the cure all. Time doesn't magically "un-make" a crime happen.

On the other end of the spectrum, at least from a guilt standpoint, time is the enemy I think. I can only speak for myself, but time is like a utopic breeding ground for guilt to fester and grow to overwhelming proportions. Time only aided in the understanding of what I've done, helped me understand who I've victimized. Victims I'm afraid, are the one class of people that will forever exist in life. They have always existed and always will—unfortunately for them, or us given that I'm sure everyone has been victimized at some point or another.

This made me ask myself if anyone deserves to be victimized. The easy answer would be to take someone like Jeffery Dahmer and say that he deserves everything he got. He I'm sure, got very little sympathy after he was murdered in the penitentiary. I remember being on the same tier at the newly opened "super-max" prison with the individual that killed Dahmer and I remember wondering if Jeffrey Dahmer were *his* only victim, would he be sent to hell by God given what Dahmer had done. Or, was Scarver "doing the world a favor" because Dahmer had sinned so greatly? I know that many people were sympathetic to Scarver for killing Dahmer because of what he had done. I wonder if these people condone consciously, the "eye for an eye" philosophy. Do they you think, believe that it is alright based upon circumstance to victimize someone? I'm genuinely curious, I am not judging at all. What about the victims in Jeffrey Dahmer's ripple effect? Do you think they condone the victimization of Dahmer? Prior to their victimization by Dahmer, if they believed no one was justified in being victimized but changed their philosophy after being victimized by Dahmer, are they justified? Is it simply human to want revenge on those who victimize you? If so, why? Is it the satisfaction in knowing he who hurt you now hurts, somehow lessens the pain? Why would knowing that the person who victimized you now hurts take your pain away? What bearing on your situation does, "yea, he got what he had coming" have? I wonder whether revenge is simply a temporary distraction from the pain of being victimized.

People say that they use drugs or drink to "get away", usually from something in their life that they find or feel is unpleasant. This could be a bad job, an abusive relationship, bitterness, etc. I believe they use drugs and alcohol as a distraction, a temporary distraction from what they perceive to be bad in their life. During this period of intoxication they are distracted by who knows what and in different ways, distracted from the pain they experience in a sober state of consciousness perhaps.

Revenge's distraction somewhat mirrors the distraction given by drug and alcohol use. If one's mind is focused on another's pain; for a period of minutes, days, hours, and years, they can be distracted from their own pain. Some might say a "football game" or a new hobby can be distracting, and for some it can be. If you are victimized severely however, it will take another huge emotion to be powerful enough to distract. So what are other emotions powerful enough? Love comes to mind, and while I personally believe that love is the strongest and purest emotion, it is so only if sincere and true. If it isn't 'true', then I'm sure it can feel good, but it is moving no mountains and it is not strong enough to distract oneself from victimization. Sorrow and sadness are very strong emotions as well but I don't know that they are necessarily aggressive enough to combat victimization in a "distracting" way. Bitterness is a tricky one I believe. Very strong, and capable of distraction, but I believe as with sadness, bitterness is spawned by pain as well. I think personally that bitterness is an emotion I pray I never experience. Most would probably say they hope to never experience hate and neither would I, but I have never been the "hateful" type so I really am not concerned with ever "hating" someone. I fear bitterness though, because I don't think many people overcome it, I think you die from bitterness. Bitterness is like a virus, there is no cure. Getting back to hate for a moment, I don't know that "hate" is necessarily an emotion, at least not in how most people use the word. I don't know that most people understand hate. Many people probably think that they do but I don't think they can honestly say that they truly "hate" someone. People overuse the word hate, lessening its meaning and strength. We say, "I *hate* the cold", or "I *hated* that movie." Is it really that cold, or was the movie really that bad to a point that it brought on hatred? Surely not, and most people would understand that they don't really hate whatever they say they hate. It still, I believe, has made people appreciate less, the power and emotional enormity of the word hate. Hate is the most impulsive emotion I believe. Very few things can stop a person from *re*-acting to a situation if they feel hate. This reaction could be mental, as in feeling good when someone else suffers, (*Revenge*) or the reaction can be physical, *("Crime of passion", or mass shootings like Columbine, Virginia Tech etc.*) Hate is triggered by rage, often from something that happened to a person. It can be done to them personally, as in a woman being raped. The woman will most likely hate her attacker. However, I don't believe that the attack has to be on one's self to hate, either. For instance, the rape victim's husband may hate the attacker just as much though nothing was actually done to him physically.

So yes, I think hate is powerful enough to distract from the pain one might be feeling via victimization because hate is in a sense, the mother of revenge; the perfect storm for distraction. I am not arrogant enough to claim either way whether or not someone is justified to feel it is all right for a victimizer to be victimized. On the surface I would like to think there is a simple answer and mine would be that no one "deserves" to be a victim. I believe the key word in that sentence however is "deserves" because who among us, of the flesh has the right to judge another of what he/she is deserving of? Seriously, think about it. Wouldn't that be the ultimate "judging", to give someone what they deserve? I think to give someone what they deserve, to *truly* give someone what they deserve, would require knowing *why* we are all here on this earth. Good luck with that one, I bow out at blasphemy, I do not have a clue what God's plan is. Let me give you another scenario:

It is the early 1900's and two young boys are at school, ages around thirteen. They get into an argument that escalates into a fight. One of the boys picks up a rock and hits the other in the head, killing him. He is rightfully charged with murder, but is sentenced to death. (*Sentencing juveniles to the death penalty in this country was allowable up until 2005, believe it or not. Don't believe me? Look up the case, Roper vs. Simmons, which ruled that an individual has to be eighteen years of age to be executed now.*) The juvenile is executed and life goes on because he "got what he deserved", right? It seems like a pretty easily understood set of events, and more likely than not has happened many times over the years. The circumstances may differ but the end result is/was the same. I know that there are some people that don't feel comfortable with the execution of a juvenile but outside of that, people would probably feel as though he got what he deserved. The victimizer got victimized due to his victimization of another. I'm sure that there were some family members of the victim that felt a sort of "distracted" revenge when the victimizer was executed. They were hurt after all, they just wanted justice and they got it right? Are they justified in wanting revenge? I think an argument can be made that without knowing God's plan, yes it seems as though the boy got what he deserved. However, I personally couldn't make a decision of that magnitude (*From a judging standpoint*), because I know if you add just *one* more piece of information to the scenario everything can change. This instantly makes me understand that there is nothing in life clear cut enough to make me feel OK with judging another human being. I'll explain. The one extra piece of information to the story is this; the little boy that died was Adolf Hitler. Nothing at all in the scenario changes with the exception of the "victim's" name, and what knowledge comes with that name though be it I'm sure, feelings of resentment, hate, disgust, etc.

There are a few ways to look at this situation. First, during the time when the little boy was killed, Hitler as we know him obviously did not exist so the people concerned in the scenario would get no extra meaning at the realization of the victims name. Their feelings will not change. You on the other hand do know who Hitler was, what he did and the pain that he wreaked upon this earth. What now are your feelings of the boy who "killed" Hitler by hitting him over the head with a rock? Because of that action, millions of people would now not die as a result of Hitler's future tyranny. Do you now feel the boy got what he deserved when he received the death penalty? Are *his* victims justified in seeking revenge, or do you think they would feel different if they knew the monster Hitler was to become? Do you think it would lessen their pain to know millions of people would now not suffer because Hitler *never became Hitler* so to speak, but rather only died a kid in a school yard fight? Again, I don't claim to have the answer. I try and put myself in their situation, wondering if someone I cared about most were murdered. I have never been the grudge holding type, at least not for any extended period of time and I unfortunately speak from experience. My best friend was murdered when I was thirteen years old. I was obviously angry and wanted the murderer to "get what he had coming" but those feelings quickly lessened and my anger turned to sadness. At the time I don't think I consciously thought it but as I look back, I have always been the type to understand that hate would not bring my best friend back. Revenge wouldn't bring him back, so there was no reason to perpetuate the cycle.

However, that was one situation and I reacted in a certain way due to who was taken from me. I think about whether or not I would react the same if the one I loved most was taken from me. How would I fare? Perhaps not so well and I hope to never know. Perhaps I would be so consumed with hate that I too would seek the distracted comfort from revenges embrace. Now I take that same scenario and ask myself if I would still seek revenge if I magically could peer into the future and see that my loved one would have killed millions of lives had they been left to live. Would that fact lessen my desire to hate? Up until this very moment when I asked myself that question, I thought surely I could rationally convince myself that my desire for revenge would lessen; knowing x-amount of lives would be saved. Now I don't know. Interesting, I wonder if it's like that for everyone. Does everyone have a certain someone that they simply can't bear losing regardless of what they would have possibly done in the future?

I understand that I have gone on a tangent but there is a point to all of these "what if" scenarios. It goes to the fact that as much as we think we know how we would react in a particular situation, there are countless variables to that situation. I am not saying that because we don't know God's plan or what someone "might" have done if they weren't murdered, that justice shouldn't be handed down when a crime is committed. I personally don't believe that justice and giving someone what they "deserve" have anything to do with one another. There has to be law and order and we as a people have to make decisions based upon what has happened to us in our own lives as well as what has transpired throughout history. True, we will never know with any degree of certainty whether or not we are giving people what they deserve but that cannot stop us as human beings from trying to do what is best for humanity.

We have to be careful though. For instance, in old world England when people committed certain crimes, they were thrown into a river and "floating" determined guilt/innocence. That is insanely barbaric as we look back on it but at the time this practice was viewed as justice by God fearing people. I wonder what became of the people that pushed the accused into the river. At the time they were doing what they believed was right, what was "just", what was logical. I wonder if God would deem those people as murderers, at least those that pushed innocent people into the river. In that case, I wonder if the individual who "flipped" the switch on an electric chair execution goes to hell if the person was really innocent. Thou shall not kill, correct? Beyond that, I find it hard to believe that in this countries racist prime that there was not a single black man who was convicted at some spectacle of a trial for a crime he wasn't guilty of.

I wonder if God takes into account, the executioners "blindness" to the truth or the fact that he was just doing his job before he would "sentence" him to wallow in the depths of hell for all of eternity. I have no clue and no one else can possibly know that either which is exactly my point. Let us not be so quick to think we know for sure how we would feel about a situation and react to that situation without looking at it carefully from every angle. I am not naïve to the fact that when something horrible happens, sound judgment or reasoning skills are not the quickest to step forward in our minds. I don't exclude myself from that category either. I know consciously that there is always "another side" to the story, but I still sometimes react in a counterproductive manner.

I raise all of these seemingly absurd "what if" scenarios to soften the blow of the final group of people that I believe can *potentially* be victims as well. I can hear the masses scoff at the audacity of my labeling certain gang members as victims. Let me be clear, not all gang members should be labeled as victims. In fact, most should never deserve to be called such. I definitely do not put myself in the category of victim either. Would I love to have an excuse for what I did? Sure, but alas, I do not have the luxury. I am 100% responsible for my actions; I have no one to blame but myself.

As politically incorrect or insensitive as it may sound, the logic behind the statement, "gang members can be victims too", makes a lot of sense if you really take a look at the situation as a whole. I will do my best to explain to those who care to understand, but I know that there are many victims of gang violence that will not want to under any circumstance, believe that a gang member could be a victim. They might not even care if I can prove that what I am saying is true. Believe it or not, understanding this concept will in the long run help end gang violence. I know I have a long way to go in hoping to help you understand this concept but I assure you it is true. Were my son taken via gang violence, I too would likely not wish to hear these statements but I can only hope that you are starting to see that I am genuinely concerned with ending juvenile gang violence and would not tell you something that would be counterproductive.

This concept hinges on the "what is human nature?" argument. I'm curious to see your feelings on the following bizarre scenario. Let's say that a child was born into a Twilight Zone-esque science experiment if you will. Immediately after the child is born he is taken from his mother because she wanted to give him up for adoption. The child is taken to his new home but the home is really a science lab fashioned to look like a child's bedroom. However, there are no teddy bears, bright colors or cozy soft blankets. (*Remember, this is an odd scenario to help make a point.*) The room is painted in typical army camouflage. The pictures hanging on the wall are of various weapons such as knives, guns, bows and arrows, etc. The crib is stainless steel, the bedding no different than what a newly recruited soldier would receive upon enlistment to boot camp. The child is placed in this room to grow up. One man and one woman who also wear fatigues interact with the child as the years progress. They essentially play the role of mother and father with a few minor tweaks to those roles. For one, they show little to no emotion. They don't coddle him when he cries; they don't play "peak-a-boo" or anything of that nature. They feed the child and change him until he grows old enough to do it himself. They read to him at night sometimes but they are not books such as Winnie the Pooh or Clifford the big red dog. They read such titles as the Art of War, 48 Laws of Power, and Behold a Pale Horse; books that teach cunning, skepticism, and paranoia. Obviously during his younger years these books will hold no true meaning to the child but as he ages and learns, they begin to "make sense" to him. The child is taught to read, write, and problem solve via top notch home schooling from his faux parents. He is also taught how to use all of the weapons he sees pictures of as well as become very proficient in various forms of martial arts. It is instilled in him that essentially he is a weapon. He is taught to trust no one, that everyone he will ever meet will want to take his life so he must strike first to save himself.

He wonders what is behind the door his parent's always come through and is told that it is a dangerous place and not to ask about it anymore. He grows into a teenager, very smart, very strong, and very believing in all that he has been taught over his life. After all, why would he expect to think anything he has seen, been told, or experienced is anything outside of "normal" parameters? As far as he is aware, everyone is raised like this so he should have no reason to think anything at all is amiss. Then one day when he is fourteen years of age, some tranquilizers are slipped into his food and he falls asleep. While sleeping, he is taken from "the home" he has lived every day of his life in and is placed on a bench in central park New York, or any other place where there is high human traffic. He is laid there at night while no one is around. He is left there and when he wakes up, finds that he is all alone. What do you think will happen? Put some thought into it, please.

What happens when he sees his first human being, his first "enemy target" based upon what he was taught as a child? Remember, he was taught that everyone was out to kill him, and that he has to strike first in order to save his own life. I've thought about this sort of scenario many times and I have come up with many different outcomes. Obviously he could go and kill the first person he sees, or he could run and hide from that same person because he is afraid, I don't know. I guess I hope to never know what would happen because that would mean that this scenario would have been enacted because I don't think there is any true way of knowing what could possibly happen. For the sake of this argument, let us say he did kill the first individual that he saw. He was quickly apprehended because he did not know where to go and hide. The particulars of the crime or apprehension are of no importance to this scenario. After being taken into custody and after countless hours of interrogation, interviews with psychiatrists and the like, everyone believes the child was born into a bizarre experiment. They believe him because the "mother" could not with clear conscience; let what happened stay a secret. She essentially blew the whistle on the whole experiment. The "lab" was found, as was all else the child told investigators. So…The facts are that someone was murdered. They are obviously a victim as are all of their loved ones. What about the teenager? Would *you* consider him to be a victim? If you do, what does that mitigate in the area of punishment for the murder of an innocent person? The child truly felt that he did nothing wrong, that his actions were 100% justified as a result of his upbringing. I think I would characterize him as a victim without question, and I do believe that his upbringing should in fact be a mitigating factor in regards to punishment. With that said however, I cannot say what my feelings would be if the person that he killed were the one I loved most. I am not naïve enough to think that I would with any degree of certainty, feel the same way that I do now.

Punishment in this case is a tough one. You would automatically think that because someone was murdered, there has to be severe punishment. An eye for an eye maybe? There are some people out there that do not care about any mitigating circumstances. If you kill someone, they want you to suffer the same fate. They do not believe that age, background, or any other factor has any bearing on punishment. Many of these people are the ultra-conservatives who have a right to feel this way I suppose. I honestly don't know how I feel about this scenario. The "human nature" concept would have to come into play for me and as I said earlier, but there is no way to ever know whether there is such a thing as "human nature." If there is, what is it? What are humans inclined to naturally do? The young boy in the scenario was not really treated as a human, at least how we would define "humanely treated." There will I'm sure be at least two general sides to the argument concerning punishment. On one side there will be those who will say "he knew what he was doing, *he had to know*. These people are probably the God fearing conservatives that believe in the eye for an eye philosophy. On the other side will be the ultra-liberal lefties who will view the boy as a victim and be reluctant to administer any harsh punishment. They would probably ask that the boy be sent to a mental institution for treatment, sort of like when a person is found not guilty due to a mental disease or defect. These individuals are committed for an indeterminate period of time until they are believed to no longer be a threat to society. How long that will be I don't think can be truly known.

Maybe it will be impossible to unlearn everything he was taught in his science experiment of a life. Can you imagine if everything you have ever known up to this point was a lie? How would I cope with that I wonder? I think I would question whether what I as being told "now" was the lie. It reminds me of a movie entitled "The Truman Show." How would you cope do you think? Regardless of political associations, the more I think about it the more understanding I think people would be to the boy's plight. How could you not feel sympathy? How could you in some sense not view him as a victim? So if he is now a victim, you do what to/for him? You help him. You don't tell him, "Too bad, that's the breaks" or "tough cookies", or any other to bad so sad statement. You feel compassion, a sense of responsibility to help someone who has been victimized. You don't forget his crime but you don't act as if there was no reason behind it. Again, I understand that mitigating circumstances don't revive the victim. They are still deceased. We need to understand however, in order to prevent the same set of events from taking place again.

I'm sure you are wondering why the weird /crazy scenario and I'm sure I would be thinking the same thing. Just keep that scenario in the back of your mind as a reference while I raise the next one. Don't forget how you felt about certain aspects from the last scenario while you think about the following. This one is also heart wrenching and to some might not seem so extreme, but to me it is actually more so because this one is a sad reality for many children.

Let's take any major metropolitan city; Chicago for instance. There are two gang members: a mother and father whom have a child together. Neither one of them has a job but they do own their own apartment. Its location is in the heart of their particular gang's neighborhood. I'm not referring to some small little street gang where people simply talk tough, but rather a gang that is deadly violent, where respect is demanded and anything less leaves you lifeless. Both mother and father are completely immersed in the gang culture to a sickening degree. Their furniture, bed sheets, towels, etc. all bear their gang's colors and are representations of what they believe in. They are both violent and their violence is directed at all comers not excluding each other. They pay rent by selling drugs, robbing, and with other miscellaneous criminal endeavors. They believe in the gang lifestyle with all that they are to the point that they are convinced death will come via the hands of a rival gang member. That is their gangland destiny. Unfortunately this mentality breeds the, "I don't give a fuck" attitude. (*Please accept my apologies for the language, but sometimes reality is not so proper.*)

This attitude creates a conscience suppressing mentality that allows them free reign emotionally to inflict unspeakable acts of violence without the slightest hesitation or feelings of remorse after such violence is inflicted. They both use drugs and drink almost daily. There are often house parties thrown in their home where there is a plethora of violence, sex, drugs, and alcohol. After learning that they were pregnant, they viewed their child as heir to their position in the gang. They wanted their child to be blessed in from birth. (*Join at birth.*) The child is born and they bring him home. (*Yes, it is a boy.*) From the onset they treat the child very rough. They spank him when he cries and constantly yell at him as well as each other. The father beats the mother in front of the child as he grows up. She hits him back and uses weapons but that only intensifies her beatings. As the child ages, he witnesses all of the violence and pain you would expect to see in a violent neighborhood. Very early on it is clear that the boy is a little "hellion", always tearing stuff up and hitting people. He swears and is taught all of the gang's signs and yells them at anyone who will pay him any attention. He is obviously too young to understand the meaning behind his actions but that is of little matter. In fact, the only times they are not violent are when they are teaching him the ways of their gang, the literature behind it, and the ways of the streets. The kill or be killed mentality is hardwired into his brain. This "get them before they get you" thought process is the birth child of the "I don't give a fuck attitude." Believing everyone else is the enemy makes it easier to victimize. It stifles that little voice in the back of your head that says, "This is wrong." It allows one to inflict pain without reaping the guilt from a humane mindset. It is the ultimate justification to do whatever is needed to acquire whatever it is one might want.

The child goes to school, or at least he goes to a building with a school name written on the front. As will be discussed in an upcoming chapter, the schools some of our kids are attending are in name only. They are truly despicable. He starts skipping in elementary school. When he does go he is always being suspended for fighting; with both teacher and other students. He is eventually expelled with the streets quickly becoming his new classroom as the cliché goes. He does not hang around with kids his own age, but rather the older ones aged fifteen and up. He is now eleven years of age and wants desperately to be accepted by his older friends. They often tease him for being so young with taunts intended to emasculate. This infuriates him for many reasons. The gang lifestyle is all he has ever known, it is what he was born into. He thinks; "How dare they" tease his masculinity, his honor simply because he is so young. "I'm a killa" he thinks to himself. He often postures aggressively in both body language and word, claiming he better never catch a rival gang member or he'll do this and that to them.

An older boy calls his bluff one day, telling him if he's not scared that he should take this here Glock 9mm pistol and prove it.

"You know where the enemy lives; *show* us you're not scared." The eleven-year-old quickly takes the gun, still aggressive in bravado and rises to the challenge. He goes and gets his bike and is off to the neighborhood of some rival gang to "earn his stripes" so to speak. Whether or not he's scared I do not know. You would think he would be nervous or scared, but he has been around violence for so long that he may be unaffected via desensitization. He might very well be too young to understand the gravity of his actions. The boy rides into the neighborhood of his most hated rivals. He knows exactly the house they are always hanging out at and sure enough there are numerous individuals on the porch with hats tilted the "wrong way." They are wearing colors they would gladly die for. (*On a side note, I don't know why it struck me now as I was writing this last sentence, but I was reminded of a memory when I saw my first color wheel in school. It had to be in kindergarten and the color wheel seemed so innocent. Who knew the eventuality of how deadly those colors could become? Who could have imagined that if you liked the red circle on that color wheel, those who liked the blue circle would surely kill you? How do you think gangs would identify themselves if the human eye could only identify the world in shades of grey?*) (*And no, not in fifty shades.*)

The eleven-year-old has his victims in sight. He pulls the Glock 9mm from his waistband, checks that it is ready to take a life and create a victim. He quickly rides to the front of a rival's house where there are some rival gang members sitting on the porch. They spot him but it is too late. His arm is already raised, his mouth already moving; yelling death to their set and proudly exclaiming it is at the behest of his. As he pulls the trigger, bodies scatter and before the copper jackets even hit the ground, he becomes a father three times over; for borne with three bullets, three victims that day. As fast as it began it was over. (*I've always been amazed at how quickly shootings take place, but how long the grieving lasts. It almost seems impossible that an event that takes a few seconds to run its course will forever change the lives of so many that were not even present at the scene of the crime. How unbelievably unfair it is that one can do the right thing their entire life and have the rest of their life shattered due to an event that occurred where they were never present at. It is humbling.*)

It makes me think about a certain aspect of life. Or at least one of many "why's" in life I would love to have answered. Unfortunately or fortunately, these "why's" can usually only be answered by God. In life, most people want the same thing when you get right down to it. They want a way to earn a living, preferably from a job they love---someone to share life's ups and downs with---a couple of children to further their family---and a place to call home. I think most would agree that these are all good things that are possible as long as we work for them, correct? Why does it take so long to achieve "good" things? For most of the aforementioned "wants", it takes nearly a lifetime of hard work and sacrifice to see them come to fruition. When one's dreams are finally realized, it is often times close to that "eternal slumber" all our bodies will eventually take. On the other hand, how quickly a bullet can come and take a life and create countless victims. In an instant, a drunk driver can shatter the lives of an entire family with a split second sober-less lapse of concentration. What if a husband and father of three has a few minute tryst with a female coworker? His marriage is ruined, his kids caught in a custody battle for years---the family shattered forever by an act that lasted mere moments. A tornado lasts but a few moments but can destroy an entire community for years. Terrorists changed the course of the world for years on 9/11 in a moment. You would think that most people are inherently "good" by nature because there clearly isn't a lot of incentive to sacrifice and work hard your entire life just to reap the rewards shortly prior to death, when in a single moment usually by "chance", your entire life's work can be taken. It is essentially the backwards lottery of sorts. You just have to hope that you are never chosen. It is the truest "life isn't fair" statement. Why isn't it fair? Why do we play life's backwards lottery our entire existence knowing it can all be taken in a flash? People must somehow put this out of their minds or everyone would be hermits or shut-ins, afraid of everything and anything. I guess we play because we haven't any other choice. You have to play to "win" correct?

Getting back to the eleven-year-old, he pedals back to his neighborhood after creating "his" victims. He returns to those "friends" that so willingly sent him off to destroy so many lives, including his own. They accept him with open arms and seem impressed that he didn't get scared. Later that day his parent's find out what he did and they shower him with praise. The eleven-year-old genuinely feels as though he did right. Why wouldn't he, based upon the reactions from everyone that he has ever known? As is expected however, it isn't long before authorities find out who is responsible for the shooting that took the lives of three teenagers. It makes little difference to them that the suspect is only eleven years old. They eventually bring him in, question him and believe he is guilty. This is in large part due to his confession.

So...Obviously the deceased gang members are victims correct? I'm sure there are sects of society out there that don't believe the deceased are necessarily victims per se, having a mindset of "they got what they deserved." I can understand that argument.

Now that I think about it though, I wonder how some of those people would feel if they read the following tickertape scrolling across your average newscast: (*Pretend you had never read the previous scenario and were just watching the news one day.*)

Three teenage boys killed....... (*And stop right there for a moment.*) In that split second after they read the word "killed", most everyone who read just those four words probably felt empathy without even knowing it. I doubt they had time in that split

second to wonder who they were and/or why they were killed before the next words scrolled by. These three teenage boys were probably labeled as victims in the minds of those who read just those first four words. Alright, a few more words scroll by on the ticker: ....by an eleven-year-old...... (*OK, stop again.*) What would you be thinking now? Would you still be viewing the three deceased boys as victims? Would the killing seem that much more senseless now that you know it came at the hands of an eleven-year-old? After reading the first nine words on the ticker tape, I'm sure the wonderings of "why" would be forming in your brain. I would have instantly wondered why or how could an eleven-year-old kill three other teenagers. Consider this as well, do you think anyone who read just the first nine words so far felt any compassion for the eleven-year-old, knowing that he has essentially squandered his life at such a young age? Do you think people would have assumed that something must have happened to him in a negative fashion to take three lives? I guess it would depend on the person reading the ticker tape and personal life experience. Alright, now the rest of the story scrolls by:....boy believed to be in a rival gang...Now what emotions do you suppose would be fleeting from the average citizen reading that story? Any? Compassion? Any feelings of victimization concerning the three boys at the realization that they were in a gang and died at the hands of a rival gang member? I'm genuinely curious now. If I had to guess I would say that yes, normal citizens would in fact view the three deceased boys less as victim's after all seventeen words were read compared to the first four. I wonder if I myself would have viewed them as victims. I cannot "un" know what I already know, but perhaps I would have as well. What about you? If so, is that right? I would say no, but only because I have had the time to rationally view the situation.

The whole point of this was to examine the thought process at each individual moment a set of particular words scrolled by. I wanted to know what the mind thinks at each moment before we have the luxury of time to think rationally. I think much can be gleaned from instant gut reactions to something because in those very brief moments, our reactions are without filter. In that I mean we as humans in a society growing up have created filters so to speak, in how we process what we see and hear. Over time without even knowing it, we react based solely upon how society has "taught" us to react. Here is a very crude example: Let's say you hear a forty-year-old man married a thirteen-year-old girl. You almost surely immediately feel that this is sick and or wrong. *I* would say that it is because I was raised in a society where that is unacceptable and immoral. However, there are many cultures that do not believe that concept is sick or wrong because young girls are bequeathed to older men all the time. Someone living in one of these cultures when hearing about a forty-year-old man marrying a thirteen-year-old girl might not find it sick at all. They might wonder about dowries and or status instead. Their societal filter of what is socially acceptable is different than ours and so an argument could clearly be made about who is right. I obviously believe we are right but I'm sure they may feel the same way about their own culture, otherwise I'm sure they wouldn't accept a practice they view as a whole, immoral.

I bring this up because I believe there are very brief windows where our emotions or reactions to something are not filtered as a result of what we have been taught to believe, and instead are feelings from a "human nature" perspective. So back to questioning whether or not the three boys would be viewed less as victims because they were gang members; I think that some might still consider them as such, but with almost a mental asterisk next to that feeling. What about their ripple effect? Would you consider their mothers and fathers, sisters and cousins victims of gang violence? They did nothing wrong, they simply lost loved ones that just happened to be gang members. As for the seemingly forgotten eleven-year-old in the scenario, he was tried as an adult and sentenced to life in prison without the possibility of parole. For those who think young juveniles are never given life without parole sentences, I offer the internet as a way to learn just how many there are. As of 2012, there were over 2,600 juveniles serving life without parole sentences. This *does not* include the thousands of other juveniles serving life *with* parole sentences. Just because they have a parole date by the way, does not mean that they will get out one day. Some parole dates are set beyond the expectancy of one's life, but are still considered legally to have the possibility of parole. I think society will be shocked to know how many young kids are serving life sentences in the adult prison system. Please, do not take my word for it, investigate.

So what of the eleven-year-old in the scenario? Do you define him simply as a killer? Do you also feel he should never be considered a victim? I'm sure many would not view him as such. Do you consider how he was treated by his parents a mitigating factor? This is a tough one, even for me because I think I could make an argument both ways. I think most people would take the easy way out and simply say "he killed, so he is no victim and throw away the key." I believe most do not want to deeply delve into all of the factors in the eleven-year-old's short life that led him to a place mentally that allowed him to murder. I think it is easier for society to pretend that there are not millions of homeless people in this country, millions of starving children in third world countries, or little kids that grow up in violence so severe that they were essentially never given a fair chance at life. What if however, you were forced to look at every element in the situation or you were the sentencing judge? Could you sleep at night knowing you had to hand out a *de facto* death sentence upon an eleven-year-old that never had a chance to succeed in life? Essentially you would be saying that there is no hope of rehabilitation because he will take his final breath behind the walls of a maximum security prison. I'm sure it might be "easy" to sentence some criminals to a life sentence or the death penalty because they might be guilty of some heinous and grotesque crime. For the record, it is my opinion that every murder is heinous and grotesque, including mine, but realistically I do think some are viler than others. For many of these men, they lived a life that gave them a chance so to speak, to be humane, unlike the eleven-year-old in the scenario. What sentence would you hand down upon the eleven-year-old? Due to mandatory sentencing laws, you won't have much if any leeway other than maybe deciding a parole date. For instance, my judge had no discretion in sentencing me to life in prison. Life was a mandatory sentence for my crime. He was only allowed to decide whether or not I would receive a parole date.

Can you hold the eleven-year-old completely culpable? I can't help but think about how kids are like sponges and often soak up what they see as they grow up. Children are mimickers. This doesn't always hold true, in fact some of the best human beings I have ever met or heard of grew up in horrible environments and turned out great. On the other hand, I have definitely met some pretty sorry excuses for human beings that grew up with great families, communities, and schools. There are always exceptions to the rule and it is to that fact, the point I am trying to make. Could that eleven-year-old really have been expected to become anything other than what he became? Why *wouldn't* he become a violent gang member when that is all he knew? When you raise a child to be polite, non-violent, trustworthy, and good; you expect them to do what? Rob and steal? No, absolutely not. You instill in them the values you wish for them to carry with them throughout life.

If on the other hand, the values you instill are like the ones the eleven-year-olds parents instilled in him, you would expect him to become what exactly? Nonviolent, honest, and polite? As crazy as it may sound at first glance, could you make the argument that because kids soak up their surroundings, had the eleven-year-old turned out to be a nice, non-violent polite individual, something "went wrong"? Look at it the other way; if a kid was raised by the president for example, and was surrounded by nothing but the best of values but ended up becoming a serial killer. You would say that something "went wrong" correct? So why wouldn't it work the other way? It has to I'm afraid, much to the chagrin of all kids out there that grow up without a fair chance at life. The only way around this argument is that you believe humans are innately born to be good. There goes that whole human nature thing again though. Life would be so much simpler if we could prove what human nature consists of or if it even exists. We can deduce and essentially make educated guesses, but the sad reality is that no one knows whether or not all human beings are born good or whether some are born evil rather. There are some studies being released that show certain similarities in brain patterns in those of "heinous criminals" as opposed to those of "average" citizens. The goal is to determine whether there is a "criminological gene" in a sense, in the hopes of trying to locate those who might be higher at-risk to commit a crime than others. This kind of reminds me of the movie "Minority Report", in which people are convicted of murder prior to even committing the murder. Slippery slope stuff there I think.

With this line of thinking, can you see why I would suggest that the eleven-year-old might in fact be a victim as well? Yes, he is a convicted murderer but does that absolve him of any chance of being labeled a victim? Let me be 100% clear, just because I believe the eleven-year-old is in fact a victim does not mean that I don't believe he should be held accountable for his actions. To the contrary, I feel he should be held accountable for the three lives he took. Just because someone is a victim does not give them the right or authority to victimize someone else. If victims were allowed to victimize, it would open the door to countless other painful situations. There has to be some middle ground however; a place between punishment and rehabilitation. I think it would depend on the individual in question as to how far to one side the sentence/punishment should go. Some people might need more punitive sentences, some more treatment in nature. I'm sure that many of you are thinking, "Well, isn't that what happens when you come to prison?" The short answer is no. Unfortunately with mass overcrowding in prisons, the budget has skyrocketed for corrections. The result is a cessation of many rehabilitative programs and for those left, a lack of staff to ensure all inmates get into said programs until they are almost at release. The end result is that some don't receive their programs and others refuse them because they couldn't get into them earlier. This occurs because inmates will not be allowed to be released on parole until all required programs are completed. Programs such as AODA, Anger Management, Domestic violence, etc. need to be completed prior to release, but many inmates are not let into their programs until the last months of their sentence, thereby forfeiting any real chance by no fault of their own, of a chance to be released early. When they are finally offered their program they refuse out of bitterness because when their release date comes, they have to be released regardless of program completion. End result? Many don't get the help that they need prior to release and are soon to become a statistic of recidivism.

I think giving a juvenile a life without parole sentence is the cruelest sentence in existence, even more so than giving an adult the death penalty. I'm sure some might scoff at that notion but think about it. Starting off with giving an adult the death penalty as opposed to giving a juvenile life without parole; the juvenile will spend considerable more years in prison than the adult due to the simple math of life expectancy. Both will die in prison. There is no hope for either to be released. The adult's life in prison is shortened by an execution date. The juvenile on the other hand is subjected to spend the next 60-plus years in a world rampant with rape, murder, disease, degradation, and despair. The hopelessness of knowing that this "world" he/she lives in will never be anything other than one of rape, murder, and degradation, is torturous. I can promise you that many juveniles would pray for an execution date rather than to live without hope. To do something at age eleven, twelve, thirteen and be told you will never become anyone other than the person who committed that act, is a punishment that I believe has no rival.

There are of course numerous people for a fact that I believe don't care whether or not a killer is an adult or juvenile, both deserve to die in prison. That is your right if that is what you believe. It is *much easier* to make no distinction between the two. I think that is the philosophy that created the mandatory minimum sentence trends. I feel many now believe that mandatory sentences are a horrible idea, most notably the judges that hand them down. It is they after all, who have to live with sentencing someone to life in prison because they stole a piece of pizza. This was a result of the three strikes law. I wonder if those who wish to punish juveniles as adults were in a situation where their own child was the driver in a getaway car from a bank robbery in which someone was killed. Would they change their tune? Many states would charge that juvenile with murder as an adult and sentence them to a mandatory life sentence even though they did not kill anyone or weren't even in the bank when the person was killed. That is the reality of the law today and you can choose to believe me or do some quick research on the internet to ensure that I am speaking the truth. I don't think society knows how the law works when it comes to how juveniles are treated. I speak from experience. My family was shocked to learn the way the law works as it relates to juveniles. They could not have imagined it was the way it is. Again, I think society would be shocked to learn how many juveniles are serving life sentences for murder, when they did not in fact murder anyone but rather were convicted via party to a crime, often to an adult.

I completely understand that there needs to be a get tough on crime attitude when it comes to juveniles committing serious crimes. I get that, I really do. I don't however believe that locking them all up in adult prisons for the rest of their lives is the answer. Beyond just my opinion, there are many studies being released bringing to light the fact that the juvenile brain is not fully developed until around the age of twenty-five. It is due to these studies that have led the United States Supreme Court to repeal the juvenile death penalty, as well as dictate new guidelines when it comes to sentencing juveniles as adults. Without getting into the tedious aspects of "why this is", it can essentially be understood by looking at another legal issue relating to adults. Prior to the juvenile issues being decided by the Supreme Court, the issue of executing the mentally ill was brought before the Court. The Court found it to be unconstitutional to execute adults who are considered ill by mental disease or defect. It was reasoned that it would be cruel and unusual to execute someone for something they could not mentally comprehend doing. Those in question were not released, but rather given life without parole sentences. This same line of reasoning was raised by proxy, but applied to juveniles. Essentially the Court found that it was cruel and unusual to execute a juvenile when the brain has not developed enough to allow them to appreciate fully, that in which they have done. Again, the juveniles in question were not released but were given life without parole sentences.

I understand that this seems to be way off the path of the eleven-year-old in question but I assure you it is not. That eleven-year-old, age aside, was raised in a way so that he now lacks the fundamental "sane" reasoning skills needed to cope in a society. If an adult had his same lack of education, same lack of reasoning and comprehension skills, that adult from a *legal* standpoint would be labeled mentally ill. There is increasing pressure from juvenile advocacy groups with the belief that juveniles are not adults just because the crimes are "adult" in nature. (*Whatever that means, anyway.*) Juveniles cannot think like adults so they shouldn't be held to a higher standard than an adult but believe it or not, that is exactly what is being done.

I want to be clear on something else as well. I gave the scenario of the eleven-year-old and how he was raised to make an argument to show that a gang member can be a victim too. While I do feel that there are numerous gang members that have been raised in an environment like the eleven-year-old, I do not believe all gang members grow up in an environment so extreme. I also don't believe that being raised in such an environment gives one an excuse to murder or hurt, only that one's upbringing should be a mitigating circumstance for *some*. I am also not naïve to the fact that if these doors were opened, countless gang members would say that their crimes are a direct result of horrible childhoods. There will be no easy fix, and or answer to weeding out the imposters. This is also my point. Whenever there is no easy answer or cheap answer rather, those in the powers that be class, simply resort back to "just lock 'em up and throw away the key." They think this is cheaper, and it is; at least in the short run. Unfortunately society is starting to see the consequences of that short sidedness as many states are being bankrupted by correctional budgets. States are being forced to release thousands of inmates, (*Many who have completed no programs*) back into society. Many of these inmates have simply been warehoused and have nothing to help them be anything other than what they were when they came to prison in the first place. What do you think is going to happen? More victims will be created! This is what happens when society takes the easy way out. This is why the gang problem is so out of control because society chose to simply lock up every gang member without putting funding into determining "why" there is so much gang violence in the first place. "One" of the reasons relates directly to the scenario involving the eleven-year-old. I don't intend to label him a victim to gain sympathy for him, but rather to help understand why it got to that point in order to prevent the next eleven-year-old from doing the same thing. Now are you starting to see why it is important to understand *how* some gang members are victims? If we can help them from being victimized at such a young age, (*Growing up in certain extreme environments*) then we can begin eliminating from the roots; the juvenile gang epidemic. This obviously as a result equals fewer juvenile gang members which equals fewer adult gang members which in turn equals fewer victims. Is this not the point we are aiming for?

I understand the gang problem and even I am often at a loss for how much it will take for society to "fix" it. Just because it is daunting does not mean that we give up. We can no longer try and work backwards. We have to strike at the roots and the only way to do that is to relearn everything we think about gangs. A victim is a victim is a victim. No one deserves to become one, but I am afraid many more will become so if we do not change the way we think.

Chapter Three

The problem: understanding the foundation

The problem is "clear." Living within the inner-city where there is less parental involvement, poorer schools, and violent neighborhoods, many kids are raised with the expectation that failure is very much an option and that the odds of success are slim to none. Does society want a solution to this problem? They say that they do, but actions speak louder than words.

Before any solution can be implemented, we first need to examine it closely so that we may understand it. Right now this is the biggest problem; not understanding what the gang problem really consists of. Most politicians and legislators who are implementing these new laws like mandatory minimums or lowering the age in which juveniles can be tried as juveniles are not doing so because it is effective in preventing future gang violence. True, I'm sure it has prevented some "repeat" gang violence from occurring, but that does not go to the root of the issue. These laws are nothing more than political redirect, something to fill their campaign commercial's with. Politicians know that there are term limits and that what might work in the short term won't work to solve the problem, but who cares right? That's for the next politician to worry about. For many years an area that a politician could always count on for votes was showing that they were tough on crime. It began with President Nixon, and became a fundamental pillar of the Republican Party. It was quite ingenious actually. The Democrats had nothing to offer in response, because appearing "soft on crime" was political suicide. The prison boom was on. The eighties and nineties saw prison expansion like no country has ever seen before. Inmates were the new "black gold", with prison creation expanding into billion dollar private corporations. Society is always tired of crime within the inner-city, and the inner city always wants to believe that it will get better. It very well may too, at least for a while. Short term is simply that, short term, lacking any future value. Again, who cares though because come next election, "I'm voting for the candidate who says he is tough on crime, and he means it!" Once again the public, tired of crime within the inner-city, welcomes with open arms the next politician who claims to be "tough on crime." As the saying goes, 25th times the charm. And the cycle continues.

It's interesting to note that while I was writing this, some very conservative Republicans have come out recently, stating that the lock 'em up and throw away the key approach was perhaps not a good idea. Texas of all states is leading the way to cut back on prison spending, with relocation of funds going to preventative type programs. There was a study I saw recently that showed it would cost taxpayers $9,000 in preventative type programs a year to keep someone out of prison, as opposed to $32,000 a year to warehouse a healthy inmate for a single year. I am happy to see that politicians are finally starting to take a look at alternatives to incarceration because believe it or not, these alternatives can have a direct impact on eliminating adult gang members.

Topics and questions elaborated on in this chapter will include:

- o Identifying the real problem.
- o Who, if anyone is to blame?
- o Why is there such a gang problem now?
- o Understanding how massive the gang problem is.
- o Explaining the stress of inner-city youths.
- o Accepting that there is a problem.
- o Explaining why the negative approach will never work.
- o Explaining why no one wants to ask for help.
- o Why is pride so destructive?

12345678910

*   *   *

In theory the obvious first question should be, "What is the Problem?" There seems like such an obvious answer: Juveniles are joining or forming groups that more likely than not, eventually victimize the community or another human being. This victimization can be via spray painting graffiti on a garage, sentencing a community to live in fear, or killing someone in a gang-related shooting.

Essentially at its core, the problem is that juveniles are joining gangs. It is unfortunately much more complicated than this however. I feel the most productive way of evaluating the situation is to break everything down into its most simple state. It may seem that I am making "obvious" observations, however I think in this case it is necessary to do so to ensure we are all on the same page. In all things, the foundation *must* be solid---in this case, the simple understanding of what a gang really is. So to ensure everyone has the same basic fundamental foundation to these and other similar questions, we have to break everything down and separate fact from myth and assumption.

If I asked you: What is a gang? What would your definition be? Seems like a simple enough question right? Please, humor me and define it out loud or by writing your definition down on a piece of paper. I'm trying to remember my definition prior to my joining a gang at the age of fourteen. It was definitely a different definition compared to the one I would give now. At thirteen, I would have stated that a gang is a bunch of teenagers that dressed similarly, hung out in a certain area, and sold drugs. If pressed further I would have stated that they had a particular name and committed acts of violence to uphold a certain image. Looking back, I don't think I was necessarily wrong "per se", more so that my definition was very generic and stereotypical. Did your definition sound like mine? Was yours simply, "some young punks who cause mischief?" I picked out a dictionary at random that I found and looked up the word gang.

> gang (găng) n. 1. A group of persons who work together or socialize regularly. 2. A group of criminals or adolescent hoodlums.

> Webster's II New Riverside Dictionary, revised office edition

I am assuming you do not find the first definition to be appropriate given the nature of this book, but rather the second. I'm sure that there are many situations where the first definition is a correct statement for a group of individuals. I'm sure if a group of law-abiding citizens is out having a drink at their local bar and they regularly do so, the bartender might make the statement, "I see the gang's all here," upon bringing the "gang" their drinks. I highly doubt that anyone, including those labeled generically as gang members, felt any connotations of the second definition; "a group of criminals or adolescent hoodlums." (*To ensure we stay on the same page, the definition of "hoodlum" is 1. a ruffian or gangster, 2. a tough, wild, or destructive young man.*) I remember being in the newly opened super-max prison and a program we were allowed to watch upon reaching a certain level was entitled the "Capitol Gang." It was a show on CNN that discussed politics. I remember sort of laughing to myself, wondering why a group of intellectual adults would label themselves a "gang." I obviously knew that they were not intending to label themselves as a gang under definition #2 but I still found it odd. I know I'm clearly over thinking it, but that is the point.

To over think it even further, let's take that "Capitol Gang" for instance. What if they all were stopped and given speeding tickets one day? I don't know that technically, speeding is a "criminal" offense from a legal perspective; I suppose it varies from state to state. In any event, they are breaking the law or at least an ordinance. Could they be considered a group of criminals? What if a similar group of adults all had driving under the influence arrests?

Aside from those arrests, they are "pillars in their community"; doctors, lawyers, mayor, etc. Driving under the influence *is* a criminal offense.

They all hang out together as a group, so would you consider them to be a gang? Strictly from a definitional standpoint, wouldn't you have to? Are they not because they do not have a name like the Bloods or Crips? If so, let us take six or so teenagers that hang out with one another all day. They sell drugs, rob people, and vandalize property but do not "have a name." They do not call themselves anything nor do they identify themselves as a group. Would you consider them to be a gang? Seriously, if you get right down to it, what would be the difference? How could you consider one group a gang and not the other? Is it because society lives in a blinded reality in which drunk driving is somehow not "criminal"? Do you think more people die each year from being hit by a drunk driver, or from the bullets of a rival gang member's gun? It is really "bass ackwards" if you think about it. I've met countless inmates in here on revocation for their third, fourth, and fifth drunk driving offense. I guess I don't see how the deaths of so many innocent people can be taken so lightly. Drunk driving should be as criminal as it gets for the amount of victims it creates and how many families it destroys. I guess that is another subject however.

Getting back on track, I raised those scenarios to show that one individual's definition of a gang may be different than another's. I'm not trying to insist that the group of friends whom all were arrested for drunk driving should be labeled as gang members either. I want to show that by definition, there are many different types of groups that theoretically can be defined as a gang. I cannot stress enough how important it is for everyone concerned with juvenile gang prevention to be on the same page, even with the simplest of things like; "what is a gang?"

Defining the word "gang" in the context of this book will take some time because it is not as easy to understand as one might think. Generically, the word "gang" can apply to what I am speaking about in this book, but I feel it is necessary to break it down further. What society would probably define as a gang, would in reality be one of the following: gangs, street gangs, prison gangs, organizations, biker gangs, sets, crews, neighborhoods, blocks, hate groups, crime families, and organized crime families just to name a few. The word "gang" is vague. To the lay person, there would be no distinction between any of the previously mentioned classifications, but there is clearly a difference in the mindset of each and every one of these groups when compared to one-another. This is important because as I stated before, in order to successfully deter juvenile gang violence, we have to understand all aspects of gang culture from top to bottom. You have to at the very least be able to distinguish or separate one group from another to better understand "why" it is that they do what they do. As a whole I will refer to them as groups because in reality, all of these groups are not "gangs" in how society generalizes them. It is somewhat of a daunting task to understand all of the sometimes subtle differences of each particular group, I know. It is so however, because we have let it get to this point.

I will start with the smallest of the groups from a numbers standpoint. I would like to be clear however, that small numbers do not necessarily mean that they are less of a threat or shed less blood. Sometimes the opposite is true. From a gang standpoint, the United States is for the most part broken down into four quadrants: the West Coast, East Coast, Midwest, and the South. The gang culture in each of these quadrants is different. I've often wondered why this is, why groups on the West Coast think and act differently than those on the East. I will break down the differences between a few major groups in the Midwest. I say Midwest specifically because these same groups might act completely different in the East or West. It makes no difference if they are the same group.

There are groups that represent a particular "**block**" or street. There could be a couple of blocks connected together as well. Sometimes they will identify themselves by the numbered street they are on; like 3rd street, or they may go by the name of the street. Their numbers are relatively small, usually less than fifty. Sometimes this block will associate itself in some way with a larger organization. In the Midwest, there are essentially two sides that *most* groups affiliate themselves with in some way or form. On one side you have Folks; on the other you have People, or Almighty. There are always exceptions to the rule. There are many groups that identify only with themselves, but even they to some extent have a partiality toward either Folks or People. As this relates back to a particular block, it could be that they represent Folks or People in some way, or even have different members of opposing gangs that claim the same "block." This often happens when the individuals involved are into making major money over everything else and aren't going to let an affiliation of some sort get in the way of making a bigger profit.

One example would be if a member from one group needed to buy a large quantity of narcotics and as luck would have it, the cheapest seller happens to be a rival gang member. Things often get dicey in these situations because there are a lot of different things that can take place. There is an obvious mistrust involved, not to mention pure paranoia. If however, large amounts of money can be made by both parties, the obligatory hatred for each other will be set aside for the sake of business. Over time, a faux-trust is formed, but true trust never really materializes. There is often backstabbing over time, thus ending that particular blocks run. I would say that this relationship is very high stress.

"Crime families" that are un-organized, (*non-"mafia"*) usually don't affiliate themselves generally or specifically with a particular "side of the fence", at least not in the beginning. There might be one or two *family members* that belong to, or associate closely with a larger group. These families are often into selling narcotics and making money. Having a particular allegiance creates unnecessary drama, unnecessary risk, not to mention would cut their potential customers in half. They would also not be able to sell their drugs in half of a city. Losing fifty percent of a market "off top" is not smart business. The numbers for these families are probably the smallest of any group, but the propensity for violence is very high. They have no organization "backing" them, so they must show a high degree of force to minimize those who might think of taking advantage of them. At the beginning of this paragraph, I stated that unorganized crime families *begin* with no allegiance to a larger organization or group. As life goes on, this will often change when a drug war happens between the family and one of the larger organizations for various reasons. They are too small to take on one of these mega organizations so they will often then align themselves with that particular organizations rival until pretty soon; they are members of the rival organization.

"Crews" are similar to unorganized crime families but without the blood relation. They are often together for the purpose of making money, whether it is by selling narcotics, guns, stolen cars, or by committing home invasions/armed robberies. There is a lot of unnecessary violence, but that violence isn't always fatal. They understand that murder leads to life sentences, but still needs to inflict fear to get what they want.

"**Sets**" are somewhat like blocks, but are very much affiliated with a larger organization. There is no mixing of particular groups for the purposes of profit like with "blocks." The interesting aspect of sets is that sometimes they will have a prefix or suffix added on to the existing overall organization name. For instance, there is a set that calls itself the "two-threes." They consider themselves to be Latin Kings, but apply the added "two-three", to distinguish themselves from other Latin Kings. You can almost look at it like AOL-Time Warner when they merged. They are the same company, but they combine names. This can happen for many different reasons. For example, let's say you have a small group that hangs out. They are like a little version of a gang, and even claim to be part of that larger group, but are not sanctioned. I can recall many times when two "sets", both from the same organization will go to war with one another for a short period of time. Sometimes the war can be so violent that one set will branch off entirely and become something else completely; a new rival so to speak of the larger organization. For instance, in Milwaukee there was an organization called the Spanish Cobras. One member killed another, leading some to branch off and call themselves La Familia, a new gang. They then became bitter rivals to the Spanish Cobras even though just a short time earlier they were all Spanish Cobras. One interesting thing about "sets" is that while they usually claim that they are a "set" of a larger organization, their existence is rarely if ever, sanctioned by the larger organization. To the larger Organization, there can be no words placed before or after their name to distinguish them apart. They are what they are, like the Latin Kings. I can remember a time when the Latin Kings told the "two–threes" that they could no longer identify themselves as "two-threes." If they continued, they risked being slaughtered.

"**Street Gangs**" are larger versions of sets. They usually start off as a set, but for various reasons branch off and become a street gang; like "La Familia" or "2-1's" in the Midwest. Sometimes they morph into organizations. The "old school" 2-1's used to be Latin Kings but are now one of their biggest rivals in Milwaukee. They went from being "People" to being "Folks." Their numbers usually start off small but can grow in fad like fashion. A "Street Gang" is usually located in only one neighborhood in one city of one state. They usually pick a "side of the fence" to align themselves with; in the Midwest, Folks or People. Even though they are a separate entity, they still tend to be partial to one side or the other. Sometimes they stay on the same side of the fence from whom they branched off from, but often the reasons *for* branching off were too severe to overcome and choose to cross the street so to speak.

"Biker gangs" (or Clubs) can be criminal or non-criminal. Predominately they are white, but there is a growing number of minority biker gangs, especially considering the "crotch rocket" revolution. (*Japanese or imported bikes.*) Some biker gangs have a name, wear insignias or their "colors", look menacing, but as a whole are actually upstanding citizens with no criminal records. They love to ride and are often members of the military or law enforcement. Biker gangs as most people think of them can be very large in number or be quite small, but usually fall under five major factions. The Hells Angels, Mongols, Outlaws, Banditos and Pagans are the main five. Biker gangs can sometimes blur the line between some race based groups or "hate groups." Many of them are created within the walls of the western prison system, as well as the Federal prison system. Some "Bikers" will claim allegiance to both biker and hate group. This is one of the few areas where it is accepted to claim more than one group. Usually this is forbidden.

"Tagger Crews" are kind of like "crews" but don't so much get involved with the violent aspects; the home invasions, armed robbery etc. They obviously damage property, probably more so than any other group with their graffiti. They often smoke marijuana and drink, do ecstasy (X) and or acid. They like to throw house parties and otherwise just like to "have fun." They began by being pretty non-violent, choosing to take any skirmishes "to the wall." (*Two individuals from opposing crews that get into an altercation will instead of fighting, go find a wall and duel it out via mural or* *"tag off."*) You can kind of look at it like the battle of the bands down south between Grambling and Southern University. These marching bands spend millions of dollars to be the best. On Thanksgiving, they are given national air time to show what they got, to "serve or be served" as it were. I have seen a growing violence between tagging crews though, to the point that I really saw no difference between them and some small Street Gangs. In fact, some small crews were eventually absorbed by new or existing Street Gangs. It's ironic, because some of the tagger crews I knew couldn't stand gangs or the gang life and yet eventually became what they loathed.

Those associated with **"Organized Crime"** could be by definition, at the top of the evolutionary tree concerning the "gang world." I've noticed however, that the word "gang" is rarely used these days to describe organized crime. I wonder if that is by design and if so, by design of organized crime families that don't want to be associated with the "lowly street gang", or by law enforcement that wishes to distinguish the two. Descriptive words such as "Mafia", "Mob", "Crime Family", are used instead. I believe the word "gangster" originated from organized crime, but I would assume that if you knew someone who admitted to being a member of an organized crime family, they would take offense to being called a "gang" member. Ironic. It is as though being a gang member is beneath them, like being a two-bit petty thug so to speak. I wonder as a whole, if society feels organized crime members or gang members are a bigger threat to the safety of said society. I wonder if Hollywood's glamorization of the "Mafia" plays a role in how we view organized crime compared to how gang members are viewed. I would say so. I can see the distinction between low level street gangs, sets, crews, etc. compared to organized crime, but I see no distinction between organized crime and certain prison gangs and organizations. They are all criminal in nature, all can enact extreme violence, and are all organized. I would argue that some prison gangs are much more "organized" than some crime families. The reason is that those incarcerated have infinite periods of time to strategize and plan. They have far less distraction to deal with than those living in the free world. If I had to distinguish the two, I would say that organized crime has a much higher propensity to become involved with non-criminal business; meaning that the profits from criminal enterprises will be used to create non-criminal businesses. I generally don't see as much of that with the smaller groups. Some of the larger organizations however, are attempting to do this as well.

Of the last groups I will discuss, are "**Organizations**" and "**Prison gangs**." "Organizations" transcend penitentiary walls and fences. Sometimes the same organization will have one philosophy within the walls of a prison but will have a different one on the "outside." Understanding these groups will help understand where the power lies, because they are at the top of the totem pole so to speak.

"Organizations" are what society thinks they are referring to when they use the word "gang" to identify a group. When those in society refer to "gang members", they are often referring to those who they see in the movies, on the news, and even in shows like Law And Order; Bloods, Crips, Latin Kings, Gangster Disciples, Vice Lords, Spanish Cobras, Maniac Latin Disciples, Mexican Mafia, Sureños, etc. They are all organizations. Their numbers and locations dwarf those of your average "Street Gang" *by the thousands*. These mega-organizations are located in almost every state and penitentiary. I have grouped "Organizations" and "Prison Gangs" together loosely because for the majority of "Organizations", their leaders are incarcerated. They are usually serving life sentences in the Federal Correctional System. It is from within these walls that certain orders are given, the general direction taken.

Organizations have their own neighborhoods, blocks, parks, etc., just like "Street Gangs", but on a larger scale. Some of them own small businesses that they use to funnel funds through, some to become legit citizens. To become a member of one of these "Organizations" differs greatly. On one end of the spectrum, you can be "blessed in." This can mean that you simply recite various words, the organizations creed if you will. To some, being "blessed in" means to get beat in. This physical beating can come in multiple fashions as well, from a couple of punches thrown by one person, to 130 second rounds of rotating people throwing punches. These beatings can last anywhere from one to ten minutes. Some "Organizations" need a showing of violence, (*Bravery*) whether it be going to fight a rival gang member, or killing a rival gang member. Upon completion of the initiation, the "new recruit" is officially "on count." (*A term I will explain in a moment.*) One major difference between other groups and "Organizations", is the fact that all members of an "Organization" will be accounted for. Take Street Gangs for example; they are pretty much unofficial members, meaning that there are those that simply claim to be a member when in fact they are not truly accounted for. They were not "blessed in", or beat in. Street Gangs want to increase their numbers as much as possible so they don't necessarily mind that people claim their fame so to speak. They are often not too particular about who they recruit, so long as their numbers grow. Their philosophy reminds me of the inscription emblazoned on the Statute of Liberty's tablet that speaks upon accepting all of "your" huddled masses.

Organizations believe it or not, are not as liberal with their welcome mat. It is true, they have their "wannabees" and posers who try and claim they are legit members, but they usually only last until they run across a real member. A few things can happen when this occurs; they can be told to stop claiming allegiance, beaten up for claiming that they are something they are not, or placed on "probation" in a sense, to see if they are worthy of becoming a true member. Where this really becomes an issue is in the penitentiary. "On the street" one can run and hide, or avoid meeting a real member if they are claiming to be a member of an "Organization" unjustly. You may be found out or you may get away with just claiming it. The prison world is very different however because there is nowhere to hide. Prison is a very difficult "entity" to explain because so much of prison life is wrought with unspoken rules and laws. I guess one example via sports analogy would be as follows; when a batter in baseball hits a home run, he does not have to run fast around the bases because there is no threat of being thrown out if he doesn't make it to home base fast enough. However, it is *known* that the batter shouldn't "show up" the pitcher by doing something that isn't in any official "rules of the game" manual. If the batter were to simply stare at the pitcher as he ran the bases, I can almost guarantee that the benches would clear. At the very least, the next time he comes up to bat, I can assure you that he might very well get hit by a pitch. For those that don't know baseball, they would see nothing wrong with a batter looking at a pitcher after hitting a home run but to those in the know, know that behavior is unacceptable. Yes it seems silly or stupid but sometimes life doesn't make sense, it just is the way it is.

The penitentiary is a world filled with a thousand rules; some given by officers that should be followed, but the rules the majority abide by are all unwritten. As it relates to gang life, again, different prisons have different sets of unwritten rules. The biggest difference is how prisons on the West Coast for instance; differ from those in the Midwest. The difference is really night and day. For example, West Coast inmates for the most part segregate themselves by race rather than by "gang", *but not completely*. Take Latinos for instance; there are those that come from northern California and those that come from the southern portion of California. They do not get along whatsoever. In the prisons down south, there is also a race based division, but instead of the northern and southern division, the division is between the Texas Syndicate and the Mexican Mafia. They are split up by prison officials and housed at different prisons, or segregated at the same prison because they will kill each other if they get a chance. After that initial separation, and other similar cases with other races, people "put on the back burner", what they were claiming in the free world and become one with their race. There could be and often are many rival gang members that are forced to "be cool" with one another and leave old skirmishes behind. This is done because prison supremacy is a numbers game. Each race wishes to have the largest numbers because to them numbers equates to power, which equates to money. Different illegal activities are controlled by different races. For the most part, you have the "Blacks", "Whites", "Latinos", "Mexicans" (Northern/Southern-----Mexican mafia/Texas syndicate), and the "Natives" (Native American). The numbers for the Natives are very high in the federal system because any crimes committed on the lands of a reservation are considered to be a federal offense. The federal system is also a "race segregated" rather than "gang segregated" system. In the Federal System, there is also a large "black" concentration from Washington D.C. because crimes committed there are also considered "federal offenses". Technically Washington D.C. is not a *state* from a legal standpoint. They call themselves the D.C. Boys and are extremely notorious.

When it comes to state prison in the upper Midwest, there is more of a gang-based segregation rather than one of race. The rivalries from the street usually transcend the razor wire and concrete. Differences are much more difficult to put aside just because one comes to prison. Life gets so much more serious behind the walls of the adult prison system. Street Gangs are rarely allowed to exist in the prison system. The same goes for crews, sets, unorganized crime families, etc. They are often absorbed by the bigger "Organizations." There are always a few exceptions, but for the most part, the numbers by these smaller groups are not large enough to war with larger "Organizations." As I was explaining earlier; in the free world anyone can claim they are affiliated with whomever as long as they know who to claim in the presence of. In prison, every "Organization" has a count. The phrase in here is "being on count" if one is a sanctioned member. There is absolutely no claiming allegiance to an "Organization" if you are not "on count." Violence will strike you quickly and often if you *try* and claim you are a member of one of these larger "Organizations."

Every single member is accounted for. Unlike the Federal system and the West Coast prison system where race divides the inmates, in the Midwest the following "Organizations" are largest in numbers: Gangster Disciples, Vice Lords, Latin Kings, Spanish Cobras, Maniac Latin Disciples, Sureños, Imperial Gangsters, Simon City Royals & Black Stones. Bloods and Crips are smaller in this system but you have a few of them here and there. The smaller "Street Gangs" will still claim to be what they are, but will often be on the count of one of the larger "Organizations."

Sometimes it gets dicey because there are "Street Gangs" that don't really get along with any of the larger "Organizations" on the street, but are forced to take orders from them upon incarceration. When an individual is on count, they are required to follow any and all orders given by the individual who is "calling the shots" for their particular section. If they are told to go beat up a rival gang member or violate a fellow gang member who broke a rule, they have to do it or risk worse happening to them. I have seen some truly crazy situations that make me thank God that I am no longer involved with that lifestyle. One such occasion involved a guy that I knew who was ordered to go violate another member that he personally thought he was friends with. They were in the library sitting at a table together when the would-be violator told the soon to be violated that he had to "handle his business" but it was nothing personal. He felt bad because they were "cool" with one another. As soon as the would-be violator informed the other why he was there, the one who was supposed to get the violation started hitting the guy that was supposed to give it. At the end of the day, there is little honor in this world it would seem. I always felt bad for the guy who didn't want to violate his "guy", but that's what happens in this world. On a side note, it was not very long after that incident that the would-be violator renounced his gang affiliation as well. That incident was the final straw for him and I can't say that I blame him. As it were, he is one of the few people that I consider to be a friend of mine in here.

For the most part, this chapter thus far has been about various groups that I feel are important to distinguish. There are many other groups that also exist that I haven't covered, like cartels, syndicates, hate groups, anarchists, and terrorists. They could all be labeled as "gangs" at least in the eyes of the layman, but that would not be accurate. Just like I have shown you the difference between say a "crew" and a "street gang", so too are the differences between a "cartel" and a "set."

As it stands now, you should have a very basic understanding of the differences between the various previously mentioned groups, why you shouldn't lump them all together as "gangs." Understanding the difference will become crucial when we get into understanding how to prevent juveniles from joining these particular groups. I will stress over and over why it is so important not to use the blanket approach when it comes to juvenile gang prevention. Each group has a very different mentality, so logically it should not be hard to understand that to deter juveniles from each of these groups will require a different approach each time.

So, the problem today is that all of these different groups exist. They all exist and society can no longer pretend that they don't. Their numbers are huge and they are not just going to disappear as much as some would love to believe. Gangs are not just a phase that today's youth are going through. You can kind of look at it the same way alcoholics look at it; you have to admit that there is a problem. Admitting that there is a problem isn't done by just saying "there is a problem." Obviously most people would say "we" in America have a gang problem. I think however, most say it with veiled consciousness, almost as if saying yes we have a problem but it is not my problem. Gangs are everyone's problem. To understand this, just think; in every single major city in America, there is a huge gang presence. In 100% of major U.S. cities, there is a gang presence, not 50%, 60%, 70%, but rather **100%**. Beyond that, thousands of cities smaller in size are finding that they have a growing gang presence.

It's funny, when I was a kid I used to be amazed at how many cans of "Mountain Dew" there must be on this earth because I knew that if I walked into any gas station, I could buy a can of soda. It did not matter if it were in New York City or some backwater small town. I remember wondering how it was possible for there to be so many cans of soda, so many that I could go get one anywhere at any time. Do you know how many small gas stations there are in this country? Every one of them has Mountain Dew. I know this must seem silly, but I think it helps to paint a visual concerning the number of gangs in existence. You can go to nearly every city in this country and find a gang member. That is a lot of gang members. Just think, every single one of those gang members are in a gang for a reason, in that their circumstances in life have led them to that point. Some may share certain circumstances but no two are alike. Every single one of them has their own beliefs, their own thought processes and whether they are outside of normal societal parameters is a separate issue. Take some of the people that you know, do any of them think exactly the same way? Some may act similar, but can you say that any two people you have ever met in your life act and think exactly the same? Obviously not. Because of this, we treat people different correct? We all, based upon our core values, treat different people in different ways. With all of that being "common sense", why then does society seem to want to treat all juveniles *the same* when it comes to preventing juvenile gang violence? It baffles me when society wonders why their particular prevention programs are not effective. How can we expect positive results? No one on earth reacts well to being treated exactly like someone else. We wish to keep our sense of individuality and as a result do not respond in a way as productive as some would hope when we are lumped together with a bunch of other people. Why then would juveniles who are going through all of the emotional turmoil of adolescence respond well to the blanket prevention approach? They don't and won't.

I believe one of the main aspects of a juvenile's growing pains are the feelings of, "no one understands me." We all at some point during adolescence feel like our parents, friends, teachers, etc., cannot possibly understand what we are going through. It makes no difference whether it is an honor student who is stressed out about getting straight A's, or a teenage girl that just found out she was pregnant and the father just received a life sentence. I think juveniles lash out when they believe no one understands when in fact it is often they themselves who do not understand. This probably comes from the fear of trying to figure life out. The worst possible thing to do to help any teenager in that situation is to treat them in an *un-individualistic* way. They need to feel as though they are being understood and the only way to accomplish this is to focus on their needs individually, to show that you are *willing* to understand their problems that obviously no one else in the history of time has had. Let's be honest, this is what teenagers think; that their problems are so bad, so unique that no one could possibly understand them. Yes, the ramifications of what I am saying are enormous; to treat every single potential juvenile gang member different seems impossible. Sometimes even I think there is no way this can be accomplished; that there is no way society has the will power to do this.

The sheer numbers involved alone almost makes one's knees want to buckle. Unfortunately however, it is like this now because society has let it become so. It seems like America has this disease that makes us believe if we pull the wool over our own eyes, surely the problem will fix itself. This is why the gang problem is as severe as it is now, why the thought of fixing it seems next to impossible. Israel and Palestine seem to have better odds of becoming BFF's (*Best friends forever*) than for us to solve the gang epidemic any time soon. Another human trait/curse is that whenever there is a problem we *always* have to find someone to blame. Why is this? Why does there always have to be someone to blame? If there is a problem, does this mean there has to be someone to blame? Maybe someone does have to be to blame because problems don't just materialize out of thin air, right? Can't we just chalk some things up to learning how to exist? I mean there is no manual to life; no sure "one right way" to evolve as humans is there? If there is, I must not have received my copy.

I guess my issue isn't so much with the blaming itself, but rather what comes from it. When people search for blame they are often without consciously being aware of it, alleviating themselves of any wrongdoing. They/we are not looking to take responsibility for our own problems/actions. Don't get me wrong, clearly we are not at fault for all of our problems, but I think we bring many upon ourselves. The biggest issue I have with this is the amount of time it takes to find a solution because people are so concerned with finding someone to blame, some small sect of society to blame. Yes, it's true that sometimes the solution will come when we find "the culprit" but this is not always the case. At the end of the day, does it always matter whose *fault* it is? I believe that in order to solve a problem one has to understand *why* there is a problem, which is why I write this book. I don't feel like we need to blame anyone for it, other than saying we are *all* responsible for this problem. In upcoming chapters I will explain why bad parenting, failing schools, and forsaken neighborhoods are "to blame" for the gang problem in America. No one wants to be accused of anything, so we have to be careful not to alienate those whose help we will need. We need to shine the light on various aspects of life that I'm sure some will bristle at, but that's just the way it goes sometimes. We have to do this because if we don't, kids will continue to kill one another. The problem will not solve itself.

The first step of many is asking for help. Pride is a powerful beast and it is pride that often times prevents us from asking for help. In a large number of cases, it is the "who" we have to ask for help *from* that prevents us from asking for said help. This needs to be done on a community by community basis. In many communities the public would rather die than ask the police for help. How would you define the word "community" by the way? Would you say that you live in a "community" based solely on your definition of the word? I will speak on communities because I think again; we need to be on the same page. Communities are hugely responsible for the gang problem and as a result, need to be fully involved in fixing said gang problem. Here is one definition of the word community:

> com·mu·ni·ty (kə-myōō-nĭ-tē) n. pl. –ties
> 1a. A group of people residing in the same region and under the same government. B. The region in which they reside. 2. a A class or group with common interests. 3. Likeness or identity. 4. Society in general.

My definition prior to looking up the word in the dictionary would have resembled 2.a if I had to pick one. I guess taking it a step further I would agree that it would be those common interests that would give that community "their identity." In my own words I would have defined community as a small gathering of homes where everyone's names are known and there is a general caring for one's neighbors. It would go beyond borrowing a cup of brown sugar or preventing a "tagger" from spray painting on your neighbor's garage. I believe there has to be trust and a sense of caring that sadly seems to have become a thing of the past in many communities. I wonder why this is. Is it because the once small communities have exploded into these huge metropolises that have seemingly endless rows of similarly looking homes? Has society in general become less friendly? Perhaps crime has eroded neighborly trust. As much as people do not want to ask for help, they have to even if at first it comes from asking each other. One family on one block cannot do it alone but if one more and then one more come together and make a stand and ask for help, there is hope. When families begin to make a stand and help each other, people with the powers that be *will* take notice. It may not come in the ways we want at first or in the desired time, but it will come. It's sad, all people have to do is show that they care just a little bit. So much good can come from this; families can take their neighborhoods back from the violence that gangs wreak upon their "community." Unfortunately, everyone feels so hopeless as a result of how big the problem has become. People cannot seem to understand that change *always* begins with *one*. At first there seems to be no impact of one's actions and so people give up. Today's generation seems to need instant gratification. Unfortunately the winds of change blow like a midsummer night's breeze: lazily. Its seconds feel like hours and days, but I believe this is our punishment for allowing things to get as they are. Everything in life we need to make this planet better will take time and energy----in this instance I speak of gang prevention. There's an old saying we have all heard and probably hate hearing; "Rome wasn't built in a day." It's amusing to me as I think about it; every time we have heard that statement, it probably came at a time when we were frustrated and being impatient, to which we thought to ourselves "Yea, no shit Rome wasn't built in a day, how does hearing that help me now?" If you actually think about it however, the connotations behind that statement are very apt. I wonder who first uttered that statement.

I will detail each element of the problem in upcoming chapters and at the conclusion will try and show what can be done to implement the changes needed. At the end of the day however, it will come down to whether or not individual communities will say enough is enough. Change can come by implementing preventative measures or as a result of losing everything and having no other option but to change. How much death are communities willing to accept before they change?

Chapter Four

Families: unconventional and failing

One of the biggest disconnects between adults and teenagers today is the fact that parents are trying to raise them the same way they were raised. Society has become so fast paced today. The way society viewed morality, violence, sex, and drugs even ten years ago is completely different than it was viewed when many parents were growing up; compare that to today.

Parents are simply not changing with the times. Being unaware as to the world their child lives in today prohibits them from making the correct decisions on how they *should* raise their child. The end result is the teenager loses faith in the parent, to which the parent becomes frustrated with the teenager. The consequences of this are the parent either takes out their frustration on their child, or does the opposite and lets their child run wild. Both contribute to the gang problem.

Of the thousands of former and active gang members that I interviewed for this book, an overwhelming number said that their father was not involved in their life. When the father is not around, the mother is stuck working sometimes two jobs just to support her family. This leaves many potential gang members completely unsupervised all day long. With no constant positive influence, it should come as no surprise that teenagers start leaving home mad and feeling emotionally neglected. Within the inner city, these teenagers are not alone, but unfortunately many who share their circumstance are gang members.

The most important aspect in a juvenile's life is how they are treated by their parents or guardians. Without a positive role model in their life, how can they realistically be expected to act in positive manner, or not end up living the same type of life they grew up surrounded by? It begs the recently asked question of whether parents should be punished for their child's actions. I personally don't think so in most cases, but there has to be more responsibility taken by many parents because clearly many have all but given up. Actions always supersede want, correct? These problems and answers are one of the key links to first understanding why there is such a juvenile gang problem, and then solving said problem.

Topics and questions elaborated on in this chapter will include:

- Trying to understand why there is such a generational divide.

- Why are there so many one parent households?

- Understanding why communication, or lack thereof rather, is so detrimental.

- Compromise is the only solution.

- Like father like son.

- The downside of bringing job related stress home from work.

- "Distancing"; and why it is so dangerous.

- Why do parents give up so quickly?

1234 5678910

*　　*　　*

Do you think every generation has thought to themselves, "My parents don't know what it's like to be a kid/teenager in this day and age?" There are a couple of ways that I want to look at this topic. First, is that statement in fact true? If you take a look at it, I think there is some truth that parents do not know what it's like to be a kid in "this day and age", whatever this day and age may be. Any juvenile who utters that statement would be correct because I don't care how knowledgeable, "hip" or "cool" the parent is, they actually do not know what it is like to be a kid "today." As society evolves, so do the elements in a juvenile's surroundings as they grow up.

The reverse can be said as well, because we will never understand what it was like for our parents when they grew up. We won't understand the issues that they had to deal with, the problems they faced. I remember looking at my dad when I was a child, trying so hard to picture him as a young boy, wondering what his juvenile mind would have thought about whatever I was facing at the time. No matter how hard I tried however, I just couldn't picture him as a kid. It's like my mind was unable to picture him as anything other than an adult. It just wouldn't compute in my brain, kind of like when I try and think about the whole "what came first, the chicken or the egg?" concept. I wonder if it's like that for all people no matter the generation. Can you picture your parents as teenagers? I would guess it will be different for future generations with the advent of video and the prevalence of it. Now a child will be able to watch their parent doing whatever. That has got to be a little weird though.

If we can understand that there will always be a generational divide, we have to understand why. If I had to assess why in two words, my two words would be human ingenuity. I'll explain. As an example, let's say it's a year before electricity was invented. What if the fire of human ingenuity simply faded at this point? No electricity, no TV, no internet, no anything like that. Let's also say that no internal combustion engine was created either; just for good measure. With electricity and the combustion engine nowhere in our minds, so many things would be different. There are two major problems/issues that juveniles wouldn't face today, which are a direct result of electricity and the internal combustion engine. No teenager will ever have killed another as a result of driving drunk, and no teenager would ever have committed suicide as a result of cyber bullying. Underage drunk driving and cyber bullying are huge issues that exist solely because electricity and the internal combustion engine were invented. Let me be clear, I'm not saying that electricity and the combustion engine are *"to blame"*, rather simply stating that these particular issues would not exist without their invention.

I'm sure there are many who will say that if drunk driving and cyber bullying were never issues, then some other issue would have taken their place. This is exactly my point. For those born in the days prior to each invention, those issues did not exist. For the subsequent generation after their initial existence, they are now parents of children for whom those issues now exist but they have no true frame of reference in regards to dealing with said issues. Sure, there were other problems faced by them that for all intents and purposes created an equivalent amount of victims, but they still have no idea concerning what their child is going through. This does not make them bad parents per se. I say per se because what comes next does in some instances create bad parents. It's the way of life; each generation is going to face hard issues never before faced by previous generations as a result of human ingenuity. Unfortunately; when a child is faced with an issue that has never before been faced by the parent, communication is likely to break down out of frustration. The child will be frustrated because they feel the parent cannot understand what they are going through, and the parent out of fear of what to do because they truly can't understand certain issues, might over or under compensate with their parental duties.

Communication is one of the most important elements in existence and unfortunately most people suck at it. It's ironic, all of the electronic devices these days are created to help us better communicate with one another, and yet they have essentially done the opposite. The communication skills of today's youth are alarming. I have really noticed it because of my current place of residence. I have been incarcerated since the age of fifteen. I am now going on thirty-three years old, and haven't had the luxury of growing up with the internet, I pods, MP3 players, etc. For years, I have spoken with at-risk youth via different preventative type programs utilized by the adult prison system. Many of these kids are the same age as me when I was arrested, and yet their communication skills are deplorable. Perhaps it sticks out more to me because I haven't been around technology as much as they have. You know when you go without seeing someone for years and they lose a little bit of weight, to you it looks like they lost a ton of weight simply because you haven't seen them for a while? To those that interact with that person everyday however, might not even have noticed that they lost weight because they see them on a daily basis, and don't see change as clearly from gradual observation.

One of the most important aspects of a juvenile's life is how they communicate with their parents/caretakers. If a juvenile feels like they cannot talk with their parent, there is the potential for some serious harm to arise. You would think that it is an issue of trust, or lack thereof that would keep a juvenile from speaking to their parent but I don't necessarily think that is the case. It wasn't for me at least. I trusted both of my parents immensely. They always made me feel as though I could talk to them about anything. They would always listen, no matter what I wanted to talk about. I initially felt as though I could come to my parents about anything, but that began to change as I got older and it had nothing to do with anything they did. I began to feel like they couldn't understand my issues, like many kids I'm sure feel at some time. The reasons for this vary I'm sure, but for me it was because I felt my parents grew up in a different social circle than I did. I'm referring to the different labels kids use to distinguish one group of kids from another: the jocks, nerds, emo's, cutters, gang bangers etc. The odd aspect is that I had absolutely no idea what group my parents belonged to when they were young because I never asked. I guess I just assumed they couldn't possibly have hung out with the same types of kids that I did. I wonder why that was now that I think about it. I suppose I could just go with the obvious assumption that my parents didn't hang around gang members which would be true, but I think there is more to it than that. I wonder if it came from the thought I'm sure most kids have about their parents being "cool" or not. I didn't even give them a chance to understand my issues. I don't know that I thought I had any issues I couldn't handle myself. Where this arrogance came from I don't know. It's ironic, I think my arrogance was somewhat born out of "being such a good kid" at an early age. I think it instilled in me this belief that I could accomplish anything, that I didn't need help, and I could handle everything. That was clearly the biggest mistake I ever made.

When a parent and child find themselves in the grips of feeling misunderstood, there usually comes a distancing from the child. A parent can distance themselves too, but out of the two it will usually be the child to do so first. I believe most juveniles at some time as a teenager will distance themselves from their parents, even those living the purest of lives. There are many different reasons for this, most notably in my opinion the issue of teenagers trying to find their own identity. This is one of the most crucial times in a human beings life I believe, because any path can be taken regardless of the path they have thus far followed. I think this crossroads as I will call it, is a time that we don't really figure out what we want or who we are, but rather the opposite holds true. I think we answer these questions by default, by figuring out who we are *not.* Curiosity is at an all-time high, almost a subconscious injection of rocket fuel wonder. With that trial and error comes the foundation of who we are *not*, if that makes any sense to you. I always found it interesting; I've met people raised by ultra-conservative Christians who rebel at a rate that would scare anyone. In many of these households, the child's identity has been given to them. It would be suffocating don't you think, to have one's parents tell you who you are going to be?

Out of that rebellion often comes a period of actions that one regrets for the rest of their life; perpetually emotionally damaging.

On the other end of the spectrum, I've met individuals raised by super-liberal tree-hugging hippies with an anarchist philosophy who have not fared any better. I raise this to say that the middle ground is the only viable solution in my opinion. I think if you pressed most people, they would have to admit that you cannot be one sided in life. It just doesn't work, we have to compromise. I get it however, that one cannot compromise on certain issues, or certain beliefs. I mean you either believe in abortion or you don't. Or do you? You either believe in the death penalty or you don't. Maybe you can find certain little nuances of those issues that you can go either way on, but for the most part this isn't the case. For example, I personally don't "believe" in abortion per se, but I also don't think I have any right to tell a woman what to do with her body. Who am I? What *right* do I have to tell a woman what to do with her body? If I am the father, then obviously other issues come into play but again, at the end of the day a child grows in the mother and not the father for a reason. Would I try and convince her to not have an abortion? Absolutely, but again it is her right to choose. I have my opinions as to the morality of abortion. I do often wonder when "life begins" and I go back and forth on this in my head. Is it when the heart makes its first beat? When the brain makes its first "wave"? I guess that's the central issue for me, in that once "life begins", is anything done to extinguish it after that point murder, regardless of whether the child is within the womb or out? I think by the way, that there are two different issues here; one being whether or not abortion is murder and two, whether murder can be *justifiable* under the guise of abortion. It's interesting, in 1980 the question would have been, "Do you believe in abortion?", but in 2010 the question has morphed into one of, "Do you believe in a woman's right to choose?" Personally I think women have changed the focus because they do not want to deal with the emotional enormity of abortion. "A woman's right to choose" is the softer, gentler way of discussing the issue of abortion. Women are a clever bunch are they not? I think they had to change the issue from one of "child murder" to one of "rights for women"; otherwise abortion's legality surely would have faltered by now.

As to the death penalty, it's interesting to me because everyone has an opinion one way or another, with very little middle ground because you cannot "half" execute someone. For those who believe in the death penalty, I think many of their opinions would change if they were the one that had to "pull the switch" on an electric chair. For those that do not believe in the death penalty, I think some would change their mind if the one they loved most were brutally murdered. I believe the death penalty is one of the biggest "stick your head in the sand" issues in America today. I feel people take a very cursory look at this issue, *thinking* they know how they feel. I wonder if people want to understand these issues or rather wish to blind themselves to the tough aspects of the death penalty. I think most people don't want to face anything tough. I don't like this, but I can understand that philosophy. There are a couple of different ways to look at this and I think after doing so, many people will change the way they view the death penalty. I know, I know, what could I possibly say that could change your mind one way or another on such an issue? I am not trying to "change" your opinion about anything, but rather only want you to look at the situation from a different angle before you decide whatever it is that you decide.

Let's start with those that believe in the death penalty. If this is your belief, that's fine, everyone is entitled to their own opinion. What most people close their eyes to without even knowing it, is the fact that someone has to carry out the order to execute a condemned man/woman. Someone has to physically take the life of every living being that is executed, whether it be by pulling the switch that sends an electric current through a human body, or pushing a button that sends heart stopping chemicals through the veins of another human. No matter which way you look at it, one human being is taking the life of another. I initially found it interesting when I learned that in the cases of death by firing squad; only one person has live ammunition. There are a number of people that have guns and shoot, however, all but one of the individual has blanks. No one knows who has the live round in their chamber. Who do you think thought of that idea, and why do you think that is? In my opinion this is done to lessen the emotional toll executions must leave on the psyche. I wonder what the thought process is for those people that volunteer to execute someone. They obviously believe in the death penalty or they wouldn't volunteer, and if they believe in it, why then wouldn't they be OK with knowing the death came from their bullet? If the death penalty is "Kosher", why then should there be a need to mask the emotional enormity of taking a life legally? I think the same scenario applies to lethal injection and the electric chair when it was in use, in that more than one person pulled the lever or pushed the button, none of them knowing who delivered the lethal action. I'm not certain of this however.

I'm sure that some people would have no qualms about being the one to deliver justice in its purist and most final form. (*At least here on this earth*) I want to add another element to this discussion. What if one day no one wanted to be the one to execute the condemned? The placebo switches and buttons no longer were effective and there were simply no more volunteers for this "job"? As a result, the government passed legislation that worked in a way similar to jury duty. If you vote that the death penalty should be legal, then you are placed on a list and put into a pool. Whenever there is an execution, a name is chosen from the pool of voters who voted in favor of the death penalty. It will be this person that "pulls the switch", or "pushes the button." It will be this voter, this citizen who takes the life of a condemned man. Now that I think about it, I think that would be an excellent idea. What are you thinking? Do you feel that would be fair? If not, why? This would be one way of truly understanding someone's position on the death penalty.

When people voted to allow the death penalty, they did not do so thinking about every individual case; the evidence presented, or whether there was a reasonable doubt of guilt or not. I think most assume the system works the way it should, that if someone is sentenced to death, they deserve to die. I don't think that there is anything wrong with that philosophy per se. I believe that is how you would have to rationalize it to vote in favor of the death penalty. Do you think however, that if you believed in the death penalty and were the one chosen to execute the condemned, that you would want to view the evidence yourself, "just to make sure" they are guilty? Would this give you peace of mind? Let's be honest, there are essentially two major aspects in the battle for the death penalties existence: **1.** The fear of executing someone who is innocent, and **2.** If they *are* guilty, is it alright morally to execute another human soul? I believe the first question is far easier than the second, but I believe most people don't really delve into the second. I feel most people place more emphasis on the first. I guess it makes sense now that I think about it, because if you execute an innocent human being, not only would you have to live with that on your conscience, but I'm sure God would take issue with it as well.

Let me ask you this, and I touched on it in an earlier chapter; what if the person that was executed was eventually proven to be innocent post execution? What of the people, then, who voted for the death penalty? Are *they* responsible for an innocent human losing their life? Should they be responsible? Why or why not? A vote is a vote, is it not? Every vote counts, right? Does it really matter that 50-million or so other people voted for the death penalty as well? Do a certain number of votes absolve *one*, of responsibility? Should they not be held responsible because they voted in favor of the death penalty under the guise of "the system will always work"? You would think people would always understand that when it comes to humans, there is always a risk of getting things wrong once in a blue moon. Is one innocent life worth executing ten thousand guilty lives? I know you have heard that question before, and I think it is a pretty good question. I guess it depends on the value you place on an individual life. I also wonder if that one innocent life that was to be executed were your loved one, would that "life value" increase? Would people be so willing to look the other way if it were the one they loved most being wrongfully executed? I say *look the other way* not to imply that any are OK with executing an innocent human being, but rather because as I stated earlier, actions supersede "want", and so I think people who vote in favor of the death penalty have the responsibility to educate themselves as to the legal system. You are free to vote however you wish in my opinion, but at least make it an "informed" vote.

Let's add another twist to the scenario; what if the United States was a monarchy? The president was king and had the final say on what laws were passed. He voted in favor of the death penalty just as it is today, but an innocent man was executed. Would the king be responsible for the death of an innocent man? There was not 50-million other votes in favor of the death penalty, but rather just one; the kings. There then can be no great volume of votes to lessens one own responsibility, it was only the king himself whom allowed the death penalty to exist. Does this change anything for you yet?

I don't know if you are aware, but when a person is sentenced to death they are not given that sentence by a judge but rather by a jury who recommends a sentence of death to the judge. A jury can decide to hand down a death sentence, or a sentence of life without parole. If the jury sentences the individual to life without parole, the judge cannot set aside that sentence and impose the death penalty. So again, with the execution of someone innocent, are those 12-15 jurors responsible for taking an innocent man's life? Do you think God will punish them? Remember, it is their vote that green lighted the execution. Obviously no one can know what God would think, but does it not make you wonder? So often you hear about these men who have served twenty or thirty years on death row and are found to be innocent via DNA evidence. What do you think those jurors feel knowing they took X amount of years from an innocent man's life? What if the law student/organization had either given up or never taken the case, and no "12th hour" stay of execution came?

I most certainly believe in punishment if you commit a crime, and I have met some people that I have felt should never be released from prison. Society can probably make that argument for many people, including myself for what we have done. However, to take a life because of what someone may have done; who are we to decide whether another soul should perish? I believe that there is too much we don't understand to take someone's life, legally. That is only my opinion however. I also believe that for those who are in favor of the death penalty, that opinion might change if it were you who were forced to "pull the switch" or administer the lethal injection via a "jury pool." I don't feel it is unfair to force anyone who votes in favor of the death penalty to administer what they voted for, do you? Why or why not? What if that person executed an innocent man? What responsibility do they have, any? I think if you cannot do it yourselves, then obviously you have some issue with the death penalty not being just. People simply choose not to truly face these issues because they can simply check *yes* with their voting stylus and give it no more thought.

On the flipside of this argument, there are those that obviously believe the death penalty is wrong, mainly for the two reasons discussed earlier: **1.** The fear of executing someone innocent, and **2.** The morality of executing another human being.

Many of these people are steadfast in their belief that the death penalty is wrong, sometimes being even more zealous than those in favor of the death penalty. For those, if the one they loved most were murdered in an unimaginably heinous fashion, would their philosophy change? Would their doctrine change to an "eye for an eye"? What about you, if you don't believe in the death penalty? What if your entire family were murdered by a serial killer? Would you yourself say they should not pay the ultimate price? Wouldn't rage so consume you that your belief in the death penalty being wrong would change? Would you want to administer the lethal injection while looking the SOB in the eyes?

If you are saying you don't know, there is no way to know how you would feel, then you see exactly the point I am trying to make. We *don't know* how we would feel. Compassion is such a fickle entity. It is easy to have it when your family is alive and well, but if they are taken from you at the hands of a murderer, compassion sometimes becomes harder to find than a shadow on the dark side of the moon. I have experienced true compassion, and it is humbling beyond words. Out of respect for them, I won't delve into details but I can only hope to be the type of human beings they are one day. Their compassion changed the entire way I viewed life. You know who you are, and I thank you D.B.

We do not know how we would fare given a certain situation. I have raised the topics of abortion and the death penalty because they are two of the issues that seem to have very little middle ground, very little compromise. I want to show that we might feel different about something if we look at it from just a slightly different angle. When these issues are debated, there is usually a heated debate whereupon communication breaks down. This is so because people are so steadfast in their beliefs. Throughout this book I raise seemingly odd scenarios for a reason; in life you may never know how you would feel about a situation or issue unless you face it or look at from numerous angles. The importance of understanding this seemingly obvious fact is this; when you truly understand this, you will be able to communicate with anyone about anything. Communication is not simply opening one's mouth to get across an opinion, and then listening to who you are speaking with only long enough to think about what you wish to say next. That is not communication. We need to understand all aspects from all angles, even if we don't want to or care about the particular issue. True, the death penalty and abortion don't really have anything to do with juvenile gang prevention, but if you can become more than one sided via any of the scenarios I've raised, then you should be able to do so with less heated topics. We have to train ourselves to think loosely. It takes time to not think so within a box, but if we ever hope to communicate well, we have to be able to see things from a perspective we may not understand at first. Essentially it is compromise, not in one's belief, but rather in feeling confident enough in one's own beliefs to try and understand where someone else may be coming from.

As this relates to a parents interaction with a child, when a situation arises that the parent has never faced when they were a child, the parent needs to be able to see the problem through the child's eyes and not overreact. I touched on this earlier; the worst thing a parent can do is overreact. Many parents take the position that there is nothing their child could go through that they themselves didn't go through when they were young. This is simply not the case, but is one of the leading reasons communication breaks down between parent and teenager. Why wouldn't it break down? When a teenager is facing some tough issues, why would they *want* to interact with a parent who in their mind doesn't have a clue, who is overreacting with punishment out of fear? For the parent, why *wouldn't* they become frustrated because it seems like their child won't talk to them, won't believe they want to help, can't understand that punishment is given out of not knowing what else to do?

This is when distancing usually begins to occur. There is a difference however, between distancing and taking a step back from the situation so that everyone can "take a breath" and evaluate things clearly. I think taking a step back is hugely important, but again needs to be communicated that this is what is occurring so that the child or parent doesn't feel the other is throwing in the towel. You would be surprised how effective it is to say to a teenager; "listen, we obviously are at an impasse here, I cannot understand where you are coming from and you cannot understand where I am coming from, so let's agree on that for now. Let's take some time to gather our thoughts for a few days and really think about what it is we need each other to understand." Is this the cure all? Absolutely not. All this does is verbalize the obvious, state that communication has broken down with the reason not now being of any importance. What can be hurt from doing this? How can taking a few days to think after something happens make the situation worse? The reason I am even broaching this topic is because for many of the juveniles who are in a gang or are hanging out with gang members; communication has probably been broken down for some time. Now it's all about acting out and being punished. Everyone is frustrated, waiting for the next inevitable "mess up." It then turns into a self-fulfilling prophecy for all parties at this point.

Once it gets to that stage, it is extremely difficult to right the ship so to speak. It feels hopeless and many parents give up without even knowing they are giving up. Teenagers especially need to know that their parents/guardians have not given up. The key as common sense would dictate is not letting it get to this point. As to why it gets to this point, there are a number of elements involved.

Many of the gang members that I have spoken with have grown up without their fathers. A huge number of those whom I interviewed did not have any "*positive*" male role model in their lives. Obviously all gang members are not "fatherless." I for example had a very positive father whom I lived with for the majority of my free life. For those that did not have a father in their life, there is an old saying that I think is very apt; "like father like son." I wonder why you never hear "like mother like daughter." It has to be more than it never caught on or simply doesn't have a "good ring to it." With all of the single-parent households in the U.S., the phrase "like father like son" should bring on a sense of panic if this saying is true. Let's be honest, these one parent households consist mainly of mother and child, not father and child. If these sons are going to end up like their fathers, then we as a society are in for some serious trouble. In fact, we *are* in trouble, more so than anyone I think can understand. So many more juveniles are growing up in fatherless homes compared to even ten years ago. Think about it; think of the millions of teenage boys across this country who have deadbeat fathers. They are the fatherless generation. It seems as though everyone I meet in prison has *numerous* children and are/were not involved in their lives when they were free. Are we ignorant enough to believe that somehow this fatherless generation will as a whole, not be like their fathers? Why would they *not* be like their fathers? You have an entire generation of essentially fatherless teenagers that lack positive male role models; what do you think is going to happen? Common sense would dictate that the conditions for assembling future gang members could be no riper. Why will there not be *more* gang members if the leading commonality between gang members of all races is that most of them grew up in single-parent households? There are obviously other factors that contribute to gang membership that I have or will speak upon; like poverty and failing schools. I will get to them later, but I will note that the economy is in shambles and the American education system is not what it once was.

As I write this book, today is December 9th, 2011. I think it will be another ten to fifteen years before we begin to see the effects of the fatherless generation. If I am to be 100% honest, I don't see how we as a society won't reap what we've sown. I don't see how society will not be inundated with so many young gang members. I make this statement believe it or not, with a glass half full philosophy, though I'm sure it doesn't sound like it. If my glass were half empty, you would not now be reading a book aimed at preventing juvenile gang membership. If I felt the war on juvenile gang membership were a lost one, I would be spending the rest of my life doing what I wanted to do prior to coming to prison. I most certainly wouldn't be dedicating the rest of my days to a cause if I felt it were pointless, or hopeless for that matter.

I make the statements about how bad the problem is, how hopeless it may seem when you take a close look at it to show you the reality. We can no longer keep our heads submerged within the sand. The gang problem is going to get worse because so many have had their heads in the sand for an entire generation. Hopefully it hasn't gotten to a point that it won't bankrupt America to fix it. Unfortunately the effects are already being seen throughout this country where the corrections budgets in many states have surpassed education. If that is not an alarming fact, I don't know what is. States are being forced to release thousands of prisoners because they simply cannot afford to house them any longer. As stated earlier, many of these inmates are being released with no real skill set because many programs have been cut due to the growing debt. This is the result of being reactive rather than proactive.

So when they get released, they are often pissed off from being warehoused essentially, and have no viable way to support themselves. What do you think is going to happen? Many of them are going to rob, steal, and sell drugs. Who has their hands in many of these rackets? Gangs, of course. There you have it, and the cycle will continue; society will wonder why the recidivism rate is so high. Why wouldn't it be? I'm actually surprised it is not higher.

If society wants to lock everyone up and throw away all of the keys, fine. If they could pay for it, it would certainly reduce crime. I think it would be an inhumane strategy, but effective nonetheless for reducing crime. Unfortunately society cannot pay this tab and in knowing that, must know that many people are going to get out of prison one day. If we keep cutting the funding to almost all rehabilitative type programs for budgetary reasons, why would the people being released "get better"? It makes no sense.

Getting back to single-parent families and their contribution to creating the ripest conditions for the next gang member; when are we going to say enough? It seems like so many families are content to just let things be as they are, with thoughts of, "I can't make a difference!" It is this self-defeating attitude that is crippling the effort to say enough. As long as individual families continue to essentially look upon their communities with veiled eyes, nothing will change. This is the sad reality of the situation. There is no responsibility being taken among families. It is always someone else's problem, someone else's fault. When a single-parent works all day and brings home that stress, pushing their child away; the results will unfortunately likely become society's problem. Yes, it is just one family, one teenager that will have free reign to run the streets right? Last I checked, many single grains of sand make a beach, similar to the many individual teenagers that make up the gang problem.

Yes, it is unfair that many single mothers have to work all day to support their kids, and when they come home are no doubt exhausted and in no mood to "parent." That's life however, that is the situation they put themselves in. I know this is a harsh thing to say but someone needs to say it, it is reality. These teenagers didn't ask to be created, didn't ask to grow up in single-parent households where the father exists in name only. It is the fault of both the mother and father for bringing so many juveniles into this world without being ready to do so. Unfortunately, it falls on the mother to "remedy" the situation because the fathers care about no one but themselves; care about nothing but sleeping around. Some might say that women should know the types of men they are getting involved with; knowing that if a man already has four kids and is not taking care of them, why would they do anything different with theirs? There is some truth to this, and they need to take responsibility as well. I know single mothers do not want to hear this, but if we have to hurt a few feelings to stop this madness then so be it. No one wants to face reality and it is a lack of facing reality that contributes to so many juveniles killing one another as a result of gang violence. Males today seem to care nothing about "being a man." Yes, we are all going to make mistakes and I don't absolve myself from making them as well, but many of today's "men" don't seem to care about raising their child, being there for their wife, supporting them both emotionally and financially. I think it is alarming. Count to yourself, the number of single-parent households you can think of. Any? A lot? A few? How many households can you think of that still consist of the same mother and father for all their children? I can only think of a few personally. I am sure that there is a plethora of books written about why there are so many one parent families and I'm sure they go into depths most care not to understand. Whether they are correct in their diagnosis, who knows? Why do you think that there are so many single-parent households? I ask this because I think single-parent households are the single leading cause from a root level, in leading juveniles towards gangs.

I want to be clear once again however, that I don't believe kids join gangs because they are searching for a family. As I have stated before, many in society like to use this as the sole reason for why juveniles joining gangs. I think this is a cop-out, a reason given by those with their heads still in the sand. When I say single-parent households are in my opinion a huge factor in why so many teens join gangs, I do not say so with the implication that membership somehow fills the void of a true family. Rather, it is what comes from growing up in many single-parent households that leads to eventual gang membership. For those who have grown up in single-parent households and never once thought about joining a gang, relax; I know that only a small portion of single-parent households yield gang members. (*Small when you look at the nations single family households as a whole, but not so small when you look at families that have a juvenile gang member*) I do think there is a reason as to why so many single-parent households exist. Once again I might look at things different than you, but I feel I am correct. I am just going to be blunt, because I don't think there is really anyway to word it differently. So many single-parent households exist simply because we as humans are horny. I know this is a crude way of putting it, but think about it. I'm all about getting down to the root of the problem, not what most want to believe the root is. Sometimes the root isn't always so pretty to look at. That is what this book is about, trying to help people see all of the societal factors that affect the gang problem. It baffles me to think how many people think the gang problem isn't complex. People are so surface orientated when it comes to problem solving. Most people out of pure laziness, ignorance, or genuine stupidity seem not to even be aware of how some of their views could change with just a little mental investigation. I will give an example that is completely unrelated to anything in this book, just to show you what I am trying to explain.

What race are you? Seems like a simple enough question right? For the sake of this example, let's say that you said you were Irish. I will explain why this does not make sense to me but please bear with me. Saying one is Irish, Italian, German, etc. is like randomly picking a place in history and saying, "I come from here." I'll explain. You claim to be Irish, right? Why? Because your great, great, great, grandparents were from Ireland? Most would probably say something to this extent, and it makes sense right? What if your great, great, great, *great* grandparents were born in *England*, but migrated to Ireland for reasons that are not important in this scenario? Are you still Irish? Are you now British? How can you claim Irish origin from your great, great, great, grandparents, when if you go back *one* more generation, you would be British? Beyond that, what if their parents were born in France? Would you now consider yourself French? This point in history that people seem to just pluck out of thin air seems so arbitrary to me. Your fifth generation predecessors did not just "poof" into existence without parents that came from somewhere. Am I making any sense? I cannot be the only one who thinks like this. How does one choose to pick ancestors from only four generations ago, why not five, six, ten? If you really get into depth and follow the evolutionists' theory of origin, wouldn't we all have to say that we are African? Science would suggest that we all came from a single "human" who is believed to have evolved from modern day Africa. Perhaps you are of the "Garden Of Eden" variety instead, would you consider yourself then, as an "Edenite"? Many believe the Garden of Eden to be in northern Africa or the southern section of the Middle East. On a similar note, maps of the world were not precise until recently. There were no satellites or planes to map the borders of the world, only man. The border of each country most likely "floated" within an area of who knows how many miles. I'm sure little towns and villages that were located near the borders of certain countries claimed allegiance to each country at different points in history. What if your ancestors were born in one of these villages when they were thought to be occupied by Ireland, when it is clear on the maps of today that your village was clearly within the borders of Great Britain? Would you say that you are English or Irish? My whole way of looking at race began when I found out that my father was born in Venezuela. My father is "Caucasian" however, as am I. Should my father say that he is Venezuelan because he was born there? Should I say that I am Venezuelan because my ancestor[s] was born there? What if my father was born there *only* because his mother was on vacation, or living there for the winter? Should he call himself Venezuelan? He did not grow up there so what does that mean for him, for me? I guess I cannot for logical reasons, just randomly pick a point in history to claim origin from. Perhaps I am crazy for thinking this way, but I think it actually makes sense when you think about it. So what do I say when someone asks what race I am? I simply say that I am American. Am I wrong for saying so? I was born here, so why can't I say that I'm American? Four hundred years from now, when my great, great, great, grandchildren are alive, perhaps someone will ask them what race they are. If they pick *my place* in history to claim origin from, would they be wrong to say that they are American? Why? Because America is considered to be the "New World"? So too was Ireland and every other country at some point throughout history.

I'm clearly off topic it would seem, but I used this example to show you how issues can be viewed differently if you put some thought into them. How I break down the issue of race below a superficial level, is how I view the issue of understanding the reasons for so many single-parent households. Yes it may sound crazy at first glance, but if you really think about it, it makes perfect sense. I stated that there are so many single-parent households because we as humans are horny. Think about it; if you really get down to it, sexual satisfaction over the history of time has led to empires being crumbled, wars being created. In "early humanity", sexuality for the most part was suppressed and labeled as taboo. Yes, there were certain cultures that were extremely sexual, but for the most part, sexual satisfaction has widely been publicly suppressed. Whether this was right or wrong I have no idea, and really don't care for the purposes of what I am writing about. Over the last couple of decades, almost everything has been sexualized. Movies, TV, commercials etc. all have a sexual element to them do they not? As they say, sex sells. The amount of money spent on porn these days could finance some countries. Advertising to younger and younger in a sexual way has become much more acceptable than it ever used to be. Why? It used to be that in earlier societies, a man and a woman were to be "together" only for the purposes of procreation, not recreation. Lust was a sin, and the fear of being labeled as lustful or an adulterer kept much *open* sexual desire in check. Adulterers in some cultures were stoned to death or ostracized forever. As the years progressed however, the "sexual revolution" in the world began. Europe was a major contributing factor in that regard. They are still very tolerant with nudity and sexual situations. What they show on broadcast television would surely get any U.S. TV station shut down. It's weird, though everything in America seems to promote sexuality; America at the same time seems to have a suppressive attitude towards it "publicly." As all of the sexual scandals would prove, it is obvious that Americans have a huge sexual appetite, regardless of what we say publicly. It is because of this blasé attitude these days about sex that I believe has led to people choosing so many sexual partners without any care of whether they are compatible *if* a child is born. So when a child is borne by two individuals that have absolutely nothing in common, why would anyone expect them to stay together to raise a child? It would make no sense. It is socially acceptable these days to have a child out of wedlock. Let me be clear, I cast no stones, believe me. I merely state the obvious. To each their own.

When a child is borne by two individuals that have nothing in common with one another, they "split up." (*Not that they were ever together in the first place.*) As if out of thin air, a single mother is instantly born. (*Or single father.*) The troubling aspect, as if that isn't troubling enough, is that there are usually multiple children by multiple fathers and none of them in my opinion get a fair shot at life. It is quite sad if you think about it.

Out of that desire to satisfy a physical sexual desire, the numbers of single mothers has grown and grown beyond belief. There is obviously so much that could be dissected on this topic, but for the purposes of this book, that cursory look will have to suffice. In short, people these days are less careful with whom they sleep with and as a result, create a child with. I don't believe there is a desire to become pregnant, but careless actions speak louder than words. So now you have all of these children living in single-parent households, usually with their mother. The father is indebted forever by child support. Many have their checks garnished and feel like a "regular" job cannot support them. Many times they will turn to less than Kosher means of work so to speak. Many sell drugs and we know gangs have their hands all over the drug market. Others turn to under the counter paying jobs which may not individually affect the economy, but as a whole very much so. Are you starting to see how so many things are connected?

I haven't even gotten to how these teenagers are feeling emotionally about growing up without a steady father figure. Yes, they could say to themselves that they will never become like their father, and perhaps they won't. They could grow up resenting their fathers and any other man their mother brings into their life; good or bad. What results from this is many times a sense of resentment to authority figures because to a teenage boy, a father is the ultimate "authority figure." For better or worse. I think it is something we are born with. The troubling aspect is that the "authority figure" is a figure we resent—whether it is because they were not there, or really just didn't care. That boy will often grow up not respecting authority without even being consciously aware of doing so. What is the biggest side effect of resenting authority, the easiest way to "stick it to authority"? REBELLION! What is often the easiest way to rebel? To hang out with the "wrong crowd." To associate with the "friends" your parents, teachers, police don't want you hanging around. What group would be tops on any parents list of people they don't want their kids hanging around? You guessed it, gang members.

It all makes so much sense if you look at it just a little differently. It is unfortunate however, that most in society don't take the time to think about every single angle of the gang problem. They often give up after learning how many different things can lead to gang membership. They think it is a problem with only a few contributing factors. It is my goal to show that that this line of thought is actually a *contributing* factor to promoting a far bigger problem. Take this for example; say a patient walks into a hospital with an unknown infection. The doctor isn't going to just give the patient some penicillin because penicillin is known to cure *some* infections. Who knows, the patient could be allergic to penicillin. The hospital will run numerous tests, ask many questions before they ever consider administering any medications. You would view this as common sense, correct? The hospital has rules in place so that the patient does not leave worse than when they came via any maltreatment administered by doctors. Why shouldn't this same approach be taken with the gang problem in America? Convince me that gang membership is not a cancer upon today's youth. I doubt that you could convince me that it is not. Single-parent households are a major *contributing* factor towards juvenile gang membership. It may appear on the surface that there is only a small correlation, but all you have to do is view the situation from every angle to see the direct correlation.

As I've explained thus far, there are many different elements that contribute to juvenile gang membership; more so than I or anyone can really begin to imagine. Unfortunately, I think single-parent households will be the single most difficult element to "fix." It is the single issue that keeps me from sleep at night, simply because of the sheer numbers involved, and the time needed to make an impact. There are so many fatherless teens out there. I guess with any massive problem, all we can do is start with one. We cannot save two without first saving one.

Chapter Five

Education: a lack thereof

So many gang members fail to receive their high school diploma by the age of twenty-one. Within the laws of gang membership, an education is surprisingly a must. However it is obvious with the high percentage of uneducated gang members that there is something of a discrepancy here. To understand, you have to look first at the gangs in society, then the gangs inside the walls of the adult prison system. They are very different in the way that they act, even though they may be the same gang. In society it is all about perception. Gang members, whether consciously or subconsciously keep up a certain image. If a gang member is going to school, they have an image to uphold. (*To the surprise of many, most do go to school. They usually just don't finish, with the reasons varying from lack of interest to imprisonment.*) There are many different social classes in today's schools: "jocks", "preps", "nerds", "taggers", "gang bangers", "gang banger wannabees", "emo's", "skaters", "goths", just to name a few. You also have a few kids that don't really fit into any of the aforementioned groups but share almost the same social status as the "in-crowd." These kids are usually into sports, are "attractive", get good grades but are not considered nerds. They are in a sense respected for their "God given abilities." (*Athletic and aesthetic.*)

Many young gang members don't want to risk losing their status by carrying around school books, doing their homework, or being known as the teacher's pet. Even though there is an education is a must attitude, there is also many times an "I won't tell if you don't attitude as well." Once you come to prison, the entire situation takes a 180 degree turn. Again, the gang is once again broken down into two different classes. On the one side you have those that suffer from the same image crisis that they did on the street, afraid to be seen learning anything. On the other you have those that take every free second they have to study, get their H.S.E.D., get into college classes and or any other offered classes. In prison society, the knowledge seeker carries the higher social status in the world of "gangdom." Those who suffer from their own image crisis are quickly shunned or forced to get with the program.

Topics and questions elaborated on in this chapter will include:

- o Why do kids go to school and yet learn so little?
- o "Nobody suspects the butterfly"; are inner-city schools the enemy?

- o You get what you pay for, concerning teachers.
- o Where is the money being spent?
- o Is school just another social club?
- o Sex, drugs, and a lack of understanding.
- o Expulsion equals a future gang member.

*1234**5**678910*

*   *   *

When most in society hear the word "school", what do you suppose they think? To be more precise, when people are just taking a cursory glance at schools not putting much thought into anything specific, do you believe most think schools are good for our kids? I do. I believe that most would think that, at least under the assumption that the schools are doing what they are supposed to.

Like much of everything over the last couple of decades, schools as an institution throughout the United States have changed drastically. In the early to middle part of the last century, schools in my opinion were used almost as a third parent. Teachers were trusted to do so many things with their students at the time. Discipline was/is a huge difference between then and now. Back then, some of the tactics used to enforce discipline if done today, would have the entire school district mired in lawsuits. Physical discipline was not viewed necessarily as a bad thing in some areas of the country. This probably held true in most areas now that I think about it.

Many parents would give the teacher permission to spank, or crack across the knuckles any unruly child. It's as though there were a trust between parent and teacher. When the child was at home, the parent would teach the child what they needed to be successful in life; respect, honesty, discipline, etc. When the child was in school, it became the teachers responsibility to ensure those same values were enforced. If you look at the education system as a whole now compared to last century, there are almost no similarities. How can they be so different? We are the same people, in the same country, in relatively the same era of history, so how can the difference be so drastic? When did it become so different and why? More importantly, have some schools of today essentially become a *contributing* component to assembling future gang members? I believe they have in some parts of the country. I believe some schools are breeding grounds for the creation of gang members. These buildings, (*I say buildings because using the word school to describe some of these institutions does not seem accurate*) are sorry excuses for learning centers. You may think that I am being overly dramatic, but if you take a serious look at some of these schools and how they function, you would absolutely be in shock. Again, once you start to look below the surface, it should come as absolutely no surprise that these schools are the way they are. Like I said many times before in this book, why wouldn't they be as they are when you consider all of the factors that come into play? There are in my opinion, three major reasons why many schools are the way they are. There are many other elements that also contribute to the state of so many schools, but too many to name here. I shall touch on the ones that relate to the gang problem.

The first issue, and in no particular order of ascension, is funding. The second and third are tied somewhat together, with the second being how children are being raised at home. The third is the attitude that many juveniles have today; an "I don't care' attitude that is often bred at home. I spoke on families in the last chapter, and a lot of those arguments are the root of two of the three problems discussed in this chapter. That old adage, "it begins at home" is so apt in almost any situation. In earlier chapters I discussed a few issues that eventually relate to the education system. I spoke on single-parent families and their effect on many of today's youth. I said in previous generations that parents used schools as a third parent. Well that same philosophy is being used with one minor exception. Today's parents are using ill-equipped schools to be the *only* parent. This would be bad in any generation, but not as bad in generations past because as I said before, schools were much different. They were not nearly as crowded and were filled with teachers that had all the available resources they needed to teach and *parent*.

Essentially in a single-parent household, many parents send their kids off to school in hopes they will get what they need because they are often so overwhelmed with being a single parent of X-amount of children. I in no way imply that any of these mothers are bad mothers; to the contrary many of them are great. The reality of the situation is however, that it is hard to be a single-parent and the stress of being one often is not healthy. There are those also that should not be a parent because they are so young and immature. That really cannot be changed at this point however. I'm sure these parents love their children but it is almost as though they are pawning them off on the school system. There are many that don't have a choice at this point because they cannot afford day care and have to work three jobs to support their family.

It is so easy to judge and label them as bad parents for letting the school system essentially raise their child, but what would you rather them do? What would you do if you had three kids, two jobs, and no significant other to help raise your children? It offers no solution to say that you wouldn't create three kids in that type of environment in the first place. We are beyond that point. Of course the obvious answer is not letting it get to that point, but then it becomes a proactive rather than reactive philosophy. I think this is the philosophy we should take, but that philosophy costs money, and society hates to spend money it seems, on anything preventative. We as a society need to admit that many parents are letting the school system raise their children. If so, then maybe school districts need to acknowledge this and offer assistance in this regard for teachers. These "amenities" will cost money though, and the school system is already starving for funds, so what do we do?

I have been looking at the education system as a whole from so many different angles and it seems like such a huge problem because the education system is such a huge infrastructure. It is massive, and there is a part of me that doesn't understand how it won't one day collapse under the weight of its own enormity. It is not so much that the education "system" is completely flawed, to the contrary I think some of it is the best in the world, or at least it used to be. The parts that are flawed now aren't pieces of the whole that can just be quickly fixed and made better. So where to begin? Good question.

I suppose in this instance funding is almost the cure all, because so many programs are dependent upon funding for existence. Many things cost money, whether it be the building itself, the desks, lockers, computers, gym equipment, etc. Most importantly you have the teachers and their salaries. In my opinion, teachers are the single most underpaid workers on this planet. It is not so much for what they have to put up with, but for the impression they leave on their students. The future will in large part, depend upon how teachers paint the picture of life. It is scary to see how much influence teachers have upon our future given how little they are given to do so, at least from a monetary standpoint. It is analogous to never changing the tires on a school bus. Eventually one of the tires is going to burst, it is just inevitable. Why would we not ensure that those tires aren't the most reliable in the world? After all, the state of the world's future hangs in the balance. You may think I am being overly dramatic, but just think about it. Teachers have such a lasting impression on their students. Do you remember your favorite teacher as a child? Why do you think that is? I do, mine was named Mrs. B. in fourth grade. I will never forget her. Why do you remember yours? Is it because they made learning fun? Did they make you want to learn? What if every single one of your teachers throughout school taught exactly like your favorite teacher? Would you be the same person you are today? Would you have the same job do you think, the same ambition, same family? What if every single teacher in the United States taught exactly like our best teacher? Imagine that for a moment. How different do you think the United States would be? Yes, it is impossible to know, but wouldn't it have to be better?

I did very well in school as a child. I was always on the Honor Roll and would have been devastated if I didn't make it. I actually enjoyed school. I do remember a couple of teachers that I just dreaded. They were so mean and I did not want to be in their classes. I was also very fortunate to go to a very good school. I think in large part because it was on a military base. It was a public school, but was located on a military base. It was a well-funded school with classrooms that were not overcrowded. Were I not a good student and hated school, I can see how I might have used those dreaded teachers as an excuse to drop out of school if I had been unlucky enough to be stuck in their classes. Looking back, even as a good student I didn't really let myself learn from those teachers that I did not like. I had a wall up before I even entered their classroom. It made no difference what was actually being taught in the class. I couldn't wait to get out of those classes.

Now that I examine the situation, what if I wasn't a really good student, but rather just an average one whom just happened to be fortunate to get really good teachers? Did they make me into a good student, make me want to learn, want to be smart? I guess it is a little like the chicken and egg question; would the student be good with a bad teacher? I guess it is impossible to know. I can remember my teachers from a very young age and as I said, was very fortunate with all but two. Now I'm questioning myself, I wonder if I was just an average kid fortunate enough to be blessed with great teachers that motivated me to learn. I don't know how I feel about that now. (*Don't you just love certain trains of thought that seek to discredit one's entire foundation?*)

A large percent of students if asked, would probably say that they don't like school. Would you agree? If pressed as to why, I'm sure that there would be a few different answers given. Near the top however, I'm sure would come, "because I hate my teachers." I'm sure they don't literally hate their teachers, but the end result might be the same. Let's face it, while there are some teachers that are smart and can teach the required curriculum also have the social skills of a cold sore. I would differentiate those teachers from another group of teachers kids "hate", and those are the strict ones. Now I don't know that the next thought comes with age, but I believe we all had teachers we couldn't stand because they were so strict, but looking back they were just what we needed. I clearly didn't buy into this reasoning as a child, but now that I am older I can see things a bit more clearly.

If you asked a thousand teachers if they were happy, what do you think you would get in response? Would there be a difference in region, state, city, or school district? I think so. I believe that a teacher's happiness is very important in the context of ensuring children like their teachers. I know it sounds cliché, but doesn't a happy teacher have a better chance at becoming a good teacher than an unhappy one? I cannot help but think of some older movies like "Dangerous Minds" and "The Principal." Do you think there are not schools like that in America? What of those teachers? Ask a thousand of those teachers if they are happy, if they feel respected by their students. As crazy and unfair as this may sound, I believe that it is a two way street; that the student needs to respect the teacher as well. I believe that if the student respects the teacher, the teacher can better teach the student. Should it be that way? Probably not; a teacher should be the same good teacher to the well-mannered student as well as the smart mouthed young punk of a student. This is not reality however, teachers are human as well. I don't care how strong one is, one can only take so much. By this I don't mean that the teacher will become outwardly disrespectful or belligerent, (*Some unfortunately do as cell phones have recently captured*) but rather will become less patient, less apt to go that extra mile for someone who has absolutely no respect for them or what they are trying to accomplish.

Here is an odd prison example of how human beings become different by way of negative interaction with those they supervise. In prison, at least in Wisconsin, most guards have their assigned areas or units that they work in each day. There are some that are called floaters and they have no assigned area to work in each day, but rather are essentially fill-ins when the regulars have their days off. Early on in my incarceration, there were a couple of guards that worked in the cell hall that I lived in. They were in my opinion, very respectful and treated us like human beings rather than inmates. I know that there is usually an "us against them" mentality, (*Between guard and inmate, and vice versa.*) but some guards didn't believe in holding our past against us. These guards were always respectful, tried to help you out if you had various issues, but would also write you up if you broke the rules. Because they were so respectful however, many inmates gave them the same respect in return. One day for reasons I don't know, they were transferred to work in the segregation unit. For those of you that don't know what segregation is, (*The hole*) it is where an inmate is sent when they break certain rules within the prison. The rule infractions could be fighting, using drugs, or being involved with some type of gang activity. If found guilty of an offense, the inmate can be sentenced anywhere from 1 to 360 days in segregation. It is like a prison within a prison. Most property is taken from the inmate, how much depending on the particular prison or level the inmate is on during their segregation stay. Some may only get a bar of soap, writing materials, toothpaste, and religious texts.

I will be honest; segregation would be a horrible place to work if you are an officer. Many inmates housed in segregation simply do not care about anything, so they no longer are afraid to get written up for rule infractions. This is a dangerous mentality because anything goes. It is the guards who bring the food, medication, and mail. They are often bombarded with disrespectful remarks every single time they walk down the hallway. They can have urine and feces thrown on them and sometimes are forced to clean up cells where inmates wipe feces all over the walls. This goes on day after day. Imagine coming to work every single day to that type of environment for weeks, months, and years. Would it not take a toll on you? It was about two years later when I saw those same two officers again that had been so respectful to inmates. They were completely different human beings. They were miserable. This was really the first time that I saw such a drastic transformation from any human being. They were disrespectful and quick to instigate a negative situation so that they could write someone up.

While I don't condone the type of human beings they turned into, it does not surprise me considering the environment they worked in for those two years. I think many of us as human beings, somewhat mirror our environment to some extent. There can be good instances or bad. I think this happens without us even realizing it until someone else finally says something. To this point, I think many people in society are unaware from a self-point of view. There are too many distractions in life for most to be consciously self-aware, consciously aware of whom they are becoming. I've always thought that because many people mirror their environment, how cruel it is that some people are born into environments that aren't fit for any human being. I'm sure it is this train of thought that breeds the "why me?" syndrome, or why not me rather, I don't know which is more apt. I'm speaking about when you see someone who was born to such unlucky circumstance, and you wonder why you were lucky enough to be born "not there." I suffer greatly from this wonder. How can you not?

Getting back to the two guards, I think they became a product of their environment: mean, nasty, disrespectful etc. They were no longer very professional or cared about doing their job in a productive manner. They were eventually let go, fired, or transferred. As this relates to a larger number of teachers than we as a society care to admit, teachers also can become mirrors of the environment they teach in. Imagine, you are a teacher and your classroom is in one of the worst neighborhoods in a major city. The school is severely underfunded and understaffed, with huge class sizes. Many of your students are extremely disrespectful and care nothing about receiving an education. You are in this situation, obviously not for the money, but because you have a passion to teach, a passion to make this world a better place. You teach in this environment for fifteen years. After fifteen years, will you still be the same *effective* teacher you were when you began? I'm sure that there are many who still are as effective, and it is these teachers that have steered countless youths from almost certain self-destruction. These teachers are the great ones that will never be rewarded, at least in this life for what they have done. For all of the great ones however, the reality is that there are some not so great ones as well. It's so sad, and not just for the obvious reasons. They too could have possibly been great, but simply were not strong enough to withstand the tough environment they taught in. It is them that eventually hurt young people today I'm afraid to say. Not intentionally, but at this point intent is irrelevant. I think many people don't want to admit that there are some bad teachers out there. Personally, I think you're either a good teacher or you are not. There is in my opinion very little middle ground in defining a teacher as good or bad. Yes, teachers as I said are greatly underappreciated, underpaid, and undervalued. Everyone knows this, so it's as though no one wants to cast an accusatory stone at a teacher. This again, is a product of sticking one's head in the sand.

Honestly, how good of an education are some of these kids getting in a school district that cannot even afford to hold school five days a week? There are thirty plus kids in many of these classrooms. Do you honestly believe that a classroom full of thirty kids, many of whom don't care about receiving an education, is a good environment for creating great teachers? Earlier, I spoke on great teachers being good for students, but I think it works both ways. I think many teachers need to have a lot of good students to create a positive "mirrored environment", so that in fifteen years they are still effective teachers. More has to be provided for these teachers to give them a fighting chance at loving their job for more than just a couple of years. I think many teachers are just simply overextended and burnt out. They are human; it is going to happen if they are placed in an environment that is negative.

Speaking of the overall environment, many of these same schools don't have the funding to provide new books, or at least up to date books and computers. I think it is very important to have up to date materials, not for the materialistic or aesthetic aspect, but rather for the psychological. I'll explain. I remember taking one of the many offered self-betterment programs we as prisoners have to take before we can be released. When I received the study materials, they were old not only in appearance, but the material was created in the 1970's. The very first thought that came to my mind without me even being conscious of it was, "this old stuff can't teach me anything because it couldn't possibly relate to me." Obviously this probably wasn't true, that it couldn't relate to me because of the year it was written, but I didn't think about that at the time. As soon as my first thought was formed, my wall went up. I was already without even knowing it, giving myself less of a chance to learn something because my eyes saw materials that were old. Now let me be clear, had the material been up to date and brand new, I still might not have been very gung-ho about learning what was being taught. At least though, there would not have been that initial wall put up by me. How do you think some kids feel when they get these 1960 text books that smell of dust and old age? This is the age of technology, and whether right or wrong, some kids won't give anything smelling of the past a chance.

Many of these issues that I am raising may on the surface seem like small trivial issues and looking at them individually they might very well be. If you look at the totality of circumstances however, the culmination of all these issues creates a very large problem. I would look at it like this; let's say your house is made out of bricks and one day you are hooking up the hose to water your lawn. You notice that a brick next to the spigot is cracked but are in a hurry to water your lawn so you give it little thought. You really pay it no mind because after all, you have a huge brick house and one small cracked brick cannot possibly be cause for alarm. Some days later, you are taking out the trash when you notice a little piece of broken brick on the ground. You pick it up and look at your house to see where it came from. As you take a close look, you notice nearly all of the bricks have cracks and chips in them. You can't believe it. From a distance your house looks great, but upon closer inspection there are cracks everywhere. All of those cracked bricks when looked at individually didn't cause alarm. Now you can see that all of the cracked bricks are putting pressure on other bricks, causing them to weaken. Stress fractures take the path of least resistance and eventually the collapse will come. It may take a few years, but it will come. So too, the collapse of the teacher teaching in a negative environment.

Yes, how insignificant a couple of added students to a class, how insignificant the older curriculum, how insignificant the lack of wanting to learn by some students. These factors are all stress fractures as well, and will take the path of weakest resistance. This path is often via an overworked, underpaid, unappreciated teacher. What do you think is going to transpire?

As I am writing this particular chapter, a big issue in the news lately is the billion dollar cut in education for Wisconsin. A billion dollars! Collective bargaining rights for teachers have been next to eliminated. I won't delve into whether unions are good or bad because they are not my area of "expertise." Don't get me wrong, I have quite a few opinions on the subject, but that is all I can label them as. Regardless of all this, I know that for better or worse, unions try and get the most money and best conditions for teachers. Eliminating their collective bargaining rights then aims to do what? The only logical answer would be to reduce any increase in pay and or benefits. If everyone on this planet knows that teachers are underpaid for what they do, what possibly good reason is there to make it more difficult to increase their pay? I don't understand this concept. I understand the economy is very bad, and cuts need to be made. I am all for that; but making cuts to education should be the very last thing cut. Teachers as I said are so important for the future, and a happy teacher is an effective teacher. Maybe it will take the entire education system collapsing before we will wake up, to take our heads out of the sand.

Funding is so important, and more has to be done to better fund all school districts, but especially the already under funded inner-city schools. At the time of this writing, I have spent eighteen years in prison. I have been in a few prisons over the years, most all of which have been located in very small cities. (*I've always wondered why prisons are built in smaller communities, far from larger cities in the state*) I have a small television, no cable just normal over-air stations. I remember living through many local elections and they were pretty much the same as I remember from the elections in larger cities as I grew up. There was one difference though. On Election Day, the bottom of the TV will scroll election information as the station gets results from each precinct coming in. Some of the information includes various referendums and whether or not they passed. In the smaller towns there were always it seemed, various referendums to add on to an existing school, or build a new and better school. Some of the upgrades would cost millions of dollars, all paid for by citizens via taxes. Some of them didn't pass, but many of them did I noticed. I always wondered whether the votes fell down the line of those who had kids and those that had none. I think there would have to be more than those who had kids to pass a referendum. For those that didn't have kids or planned on having kids, why agree to pay for something that doesn't now concern you? Why choose to garnish your check in this economy? (*It is a rhetorical question by the way; I will get to the answer in a minute.*) I don't recall seeing those same types of referendums in Milwaukee County on Election Day, but perhaps I just wasn't aware of them. Maybe larger counties have different regulations when it comes to passing such referendums, I don't know. On the surface, it seemed to me that the smaller counties cared more as a whole about bettering their schools, about bettering the education system. They seemed more willing to sacrifice a mighty dollar to build a better classroom. I wonder if it is a coincidence that there isn't as violent of a gang problem in these same smaller communities, yet.

For years I have spoken with juveniles who are brought into the prison. They come from many different schools, but are all in either seventh or eighth grade. I've noticed something very interesting. For this particular program, approximately twenty-five kids come in at a time, with about 95% being Caucasian. As I began speaking to the kids, I assumed that they were all from the city or school district this particular prison is located in. I soon noticed however, that some of the classes acted completely different than the others. For the most part, the kids that come receive good grades, think school is important, and don't get into much trouble. In this particular area, it is part of the school curriculum to come and spend a few hours inside of a prison to discuss choices. (*An interesting philosophy, wouldn't you say?*) As I was saying, some of the classes acted completely different, as if they came from a different part of the country. It is difficult to put into words how differently they act, but essentially they talked with less respect, didn't care as much about education, and also had run ins with law enforcement. It blew my mind and I couldn't understand, so I spoke with one of the staff facilitators about my observations. He informed me that one of the classes I spoke about came from a school district that was within a "less than affluent" community. Now let me be clear, the rest of the classes that come to the prison are not from well to do rich school districts, rather just your average middle income communities. The other kids simply came from a more poverty ridden community. One question that I ask every student is whether or not they know if any gang members go to their school. Most simply say no or just a couple, but they don't really know what gang they belong to. As for the kids that come from the lesser funded school district, the answer is completely different, from yes to lots, to I am one. While it is true that most of these gang members would be considered by those in major cities as wannabees, that point is not the issue here. I was amazed because all of the kids that come here come from surrounding areas. You wouldn't think that there would be that much of a difference. It isn't as if the lesser funded school is any closer to a major city and is just the overflow. The only real difference is the poverty rate of the community. This helped me understand that while money may not be the cure-all, funding surely plays a far bigger role than most would care to admit. Beyond that, far less gang activity occurred in the better funded schools than the underfunded schools.

Even as I write this, I am seeing in my mind the difference in behavior from the students that come here. Had I not witnessed it personally, I probably wouldn't have believed that there could be such a drastic difference. I guess a huge part that strikes me is the fact that while there is a financial gap, it isn't that large. At least not as large as one would think after interacting with both groups of students. I've been speaking about money as it relates to funding for the school system and the affects it has on increasing a gang presence. I believe so many aspects of the gang presence in America are related and intertwined. This is why solving the gang problem seems so unbelievably difficult. I was constantly surprised at how many seemingly unrelated issues were connected to the gang problem. I liken the situation to trying to clean up a corrupt third world government that has been corrupt since its formation. When you start to clean house, you soon realize that the corruption is rampant everywhere. In those situations there is usually a coup d'état that wipes out the entire government. Unfortunately for us, we cannot be successful with a coup d'état because so many American institutions are contributing to the gang problem. (*In this chapter, the education system.*) I asked the question whether or not school is part of the problem. In many instances I would say that yes it is. I know there are many that don't want to hear this, but it is the truth.

Schools are in some ways, like breeding grounds for assembling new gang members. Location is a huge part of it. I know of certain schools that are in a particular gang's neighborhood. You cannot tell me that it is purely coincidental that most of the gang members that go to those particular schools all claim allegiance to the gang their school resides in. It is not a coincidence and I almost feel stupid for having to point out something that should be so obvious, but there is a reason why I am pointing this out. From a recruiting standpoint, it is akin to shooting fish in a barrel with a shotgun. You can't miss. Seriously, think about it. Let's say that you have a major organization in a large city. In the heart of their neighborhood is a middle school with a couple thousand youths in their most vulnerable of ages. Kids usually go to school relatively close to where they live. There are exceptions, but for the most part this reasoning holds true. To whoever is reading this book, I don't know from what background you come, so I don't know if you have ever been to any inner-city schools before and after the school day. Woe to any gang member that is affiliated with anything other than whom resides in that particular neighborhood. Many older brothers and sisters pick up their siblings, some of them gang members with flashy cars, pretty females, and instantly transforming the one being picked up as part of the "in-crowd." This creates a pedestal like existence for gang members on a subconscious level. Teenagers see everything, whether they are conscious of what they see or not. Few *don't* want to be part of the "in-crowd", whether they admit to it or not. No one *wants* to be "un-cool" as it were. No one wants to be ostracized from their peers because let's face it; humans rarely want to be alone. Humans are by nature, social. This is why kids who are too young to even talk, gravitate towards one another at the sand box or playgroup.

If I had to make a case for why this is at such a young age, I would chalk it up to curiosity. If infants could have a train of thought, I believe it would be, "What is that?" The desire to figure that out, to figure out what "that" is, leads to interaction. That desire for interaction is ingrained from then on I believe. Of course you have your recluses and introverts, but they are far less common than the opposite. Out of that desire to interact, comes the need for acceptance. I believe that it is acceptance that leads so many kids to do such wrong and bad things. Acceptance is a disease, a cancer. It can grip the most aspiring teenager and bring them into a world wrought with crime. Unfortunately I speak from experience.

Looking back, I can do nothing but shake my head in disgust. Personally, I could never understand the emotional enormity of acceptance because I was always popular. I was so entrenched in the things that made me "popular", that I couldn't see that I too had a desire to be accepted. I was never picked on, always had a pretty girlfriend, and never felt the need to pick on others to feel good about myself. I *thought* I was confident in who I was, but I think it was acceptance's greatest illusion; making me *think* I was confident in who I was. With all of that said, in hindsight I had a huge need to be accepted by everyone. It didn't matter who you were, or of what age. If I even thought someone did not like me, it would drive me crazy. Yes, the desire of acceptance was the beginning of my eventual demise. Stupid acceptance!

There is I'm sure, a science behind why acceptance is so important for some and not to others. I wonder if under a brain scan, whether a certain area of the brain would "light up" more for those who need to be accepted as opposed to those who couldn't care less. While acceptance may be worth sacrificing everything for to some, but only worth some to others, I do believe that everyone on some level wishes to be accepted. This desire to be accepted may wane as we age and mature, but in the early stages of adolescence I believe acceptance by our peers is at the forefront of our necessities. Writing this made me think of something. There was another individual that used to speak to juveniles brought into the prison. He used to ask the kids how many times they have seen a good kid begin hanging out with a group of bad kids and start doing bad things. Many have seen this happen, to which he replied, "How many good kids have you seen that start hanging out with the bad crowd and turn that entire bad crowd *good?*" Thus far, none have witnessed that happening. Why? I would say that it is a numbers game if I had to explain it. It's the pack mentality. If you have a circle of students all homogenous in how they think, that is a powerful force. This force is so strong, way too strong to be changed by the likes of a single do-gooder, if they are the "bad crowd." It's different in different schools, but to be honest, I don't know that it is all that different. For instance, in one school, the "in-crowd" could be the athletes and cheerleaders whom both get very good grades and don't get into trouble. In another school, those same athletes and cheerleaders could be on the bottom of the social circle, with the trouble makers and gang bangers residing near the top. The interesting thing is that these two schools with such different social standards can be within the same state and even the same city. There would probably be one glaring difference between the two schools however, and that would be income level. It's interesting I've noticed, that many schools that are considered to have a high poverty rate, tend to have social classes that contain more of the rebellious types near the top. These rebellious groups may be drug dealers, gang bangers, taggers, or other such groups.

As I was stating before, while money isn't the cure all, there obviously has to be more to it than what meets the eye. I'm betting that if you took the worst school from the poorest community and piped millions of dollars into the infrastructure of that school, i.e. the best teachers, the newest curriculum, and the best up to date equipment, I know that there would be a rise in the success of their students. I don't believe however that the school would be cured of their gang problem. So by default, I am saying that part of the problem within the school system has to do with funding, but I don't believe the schools individual infrastructure is the main culprit. I believe poverty has a virus like impact on the psyche of one's community. It starts at home, transcending through the community, eventually finding its way into each individual school; not just the brick and mortar elements of a school, but the human element as well. I mean think about it, why do most schools in highly-funded school districts have a smaller gang presence, but a school a few miles away on the "other side of the tracks" so to speak, is besieged with violence committed by gang members? There isn't something in the water, though it seems like some would like to think so. I will speak more on neighborhoods and their impact on the gang problem in an upcoming chapter, but I do need to speak on how parenting is one of the places that virus like effect begins to shape and mold the mentality of a failing school system. Very early on in this book I spoke on the widely used saying of "actions speak louder than words." I believe this is once again an apt way of explaining how parents are crippling their child's chances of success.

It's a widely known fact that most kids do not in the slightest bit, enjoy doing homework. *HOME* work. Personally I could not stand it, and yet I was still constantly on the Honor Roll. I did everything in my power to make sure I got as much work done in school so that I didn't have any homework to worry about. I knew my father would be asking what homework I had as soon as he got off of work. I wanted to hang out with friends or go do this and that. There were times that I remember consciously thinking, "My grades are good enough to withstand the hit of missing this particular assignment." I wouldn't necessarily skip an assignment, but I would sometimes rush it. As long as I kept my grades high, my father was none the wiser. Some of my friends' parents on the other hand, did not care if their child's homework was done, nor did their actions show that they cared if their grades were up to par. *Verbally* they said, "Get good grades and do your homework." There was not however, any bark behind the bite because their grades were not good, and when they did not do their homework, there were not any serious consequences. In their "defense", many of them were single-parents and worked all day, so there wasn't much they could do had they wanted to enforce punishments or sanctions. Obviously the right thing would have been to instill certain values from an early age. I'm not speaking about a Gestapo type regime where the kid ends up hating their parent. Rather, I'm speaking about creating an environment of respect from a very early age. Respect is born out of the loins of discipline I believe. There has to be some sort of discipline for there to be any sort of respect. I think respect can in some instances be learned later in life with age and wisdom, but I feel "life learned" respect is different than a respect learned from infancy. I want to also emphasize that when I use the word "respect", I am referring to more than just the respect one human gives to another with how they treat them. I am referring to that as well, but more importantly I am speaking on respect for life, and how our actions reflect on society as a whole.

Generally speaking, to have respect for life, I believe man should treat others how he wants to be treated, always strive to make this world a better place, learn, and simply be grateful for the gift of life. I believe many of these traits are instilled in us at an early age. Perhaps you can classify these as values or even attitudes. If a child doesn't have respect for life, they aren't going to want to learn, want to "do good", or want to work hard to get ahead in life. When this attitude is carried into adolescence, it is there that the conditions are at their ripest for possible gang membership and other criminal endeavors. It is greatly unfair in my opinion that so many kids are cursed with parents that either can't or don't instill these positive life attitudes. As I've liked to say throughout this book, if a child is born into a seemingly hopeless situation, isn't it *more likely* that they *will* fail? So often we look at people and judge them without even knowing it. We scoff to ourselves, "how could they do that, why would they drop out of school, how could they be stupid enough to join a gang?" People think this way without the "luxury" of knowing what they would or wouldn't have done had they not had positive values instilled in them. The sad reality I'm afraid, is that so many young people are becoming parents and they have no business becoming parents. Right now, the "entitlement generation" is having kids at an alarming rate and it is going to get worse before there is any chance of getting better. I hate to say it but it's true. Right now we are in one vicious cycle where one set of unqualified parents have had kids that will become even less qualified to procreate themselves. What do you think is going to happen? Are you naïve enough to believe that magically, subsequent generations will have positive values instilled in them by parents that lacked them? The only question in my mind is; how many generations will it take to "fix itself"?

Many communities are comprised of parents that don't really care, at least from anything more than a verbal standpoint. This creates a community culture, one that has a lack of respect for life. These communities are sometimes massive in scale, encompassing multiple schools, neighborhoods, recreation centers, etc. Unfortunately this culture becomes the norm. They become victims of their self-created plight. What plight am I referring to? In short, these communities have created a culture that by their *actions* imply that it is OK to be disrespectful to one another, to not help each other, that good grades aren't important, that it is alright to sell drugs on the street corner, and that it is no big deal to join a gang. Etc., etc., etc., etc. Now obviously if you ask anyone in that community whether these things are alright with them they will say no, but their actions say something far different. I feel as though I am beating a dead horse, but actions speak louder than words. There is a lack of responsibility. As this lack of responsibility translates into the school system, schools become a place where kids "hang out." It's almost like a night club but without the legal selling of alcohol. Teenagers are not coming to learn fundamental skills that can help them achieve a job that will pay their bills. They are coming to "kick it" with others of similar mindset. The boys are coming to have sex with the girls, and the girls....well, who knows what they are thinking. My father told me, "Never presume to understand what a woman is thinking." I'll heed that advice here. Needless to say however, the fault between boy and girl nears 50/50. This mentality in and of itself becomes a culture, one of which becomes normal or acceptable.

Teenagers aren't stupid; they realize they will be unable to support themselves when they "grow up." They know without an education they will not be able to get a good job, so they do what they feel they need to do in order to possibly support themselves.

Crime is one way, with selling drugs the easiest way to do so. As I was writing this, a bizarre experiment came to mind. This will never happen, but I would be curious to see the outcome if the following were ever to happen. Say the government passed legislation to legalize every single drug known to man. The reasons are really not important for the sake of this scenario. Ten years from now, do you think that there would be more or less gang members as a result of the legalization of drugs? Obviously there would be a plethora of other negative side effects from this taking place, but solely for the sake of this experiment, put them aside. And for the record, I am in no way shape or form insisting that drugs should be legalized, I am merely letting my mind wonder.

My belief is that the amount of gang members would decrease. So much of the drug trade within the United States is controlled by gangs. Yes there are other rackets that would most likely try an replace the drug trade; like gambling, prostitution, extortion, etc. I don't however, feel any of these "rackets" would have anywhere near the financial upside as does the sale of narcotics. If you could buy any type of drug you wanted from the local corner store as you can with alcohol, what would gang members who have dedicated their lives to selling drugs do? The more I ponder this scenario, the more interesting it becomes to me. I have absolutely no idea how the gang culture would change with the legalization of narcotics. I wonder if teenagers would take school more seriously knowing they did not have drug dealing as a backup plan. On the flip side, I wonder if more teens would drop out of school because they became addicted to the drugs that would be so readily available. You would have to believe the latter to be true. In countries where drugs are legal however, there are not bodies strewn everywhere via drug overdoses. Now as I said earlier, were the U.S. to legalize drugs, a whole plethora of other problems would I'm sure materialize, some so bad that who knows, perhaps we would have preferred the gang problem over this new problem. Again, I am not in any way in favor of legalizing narcotics. I don't want to be quoted as having that desire. I have seen first-hand the devastating impact drugs have on families, communities, and schools. My only reason in raising this scenario is because sometimes to solve problems you have to for a moment; eliminate certain variables to understand the impact of said variable on said problem. Yes, sometimes my scenarios seem odd at times, but so do most new or unorthodox ways of problem solving. To solve the gang problem in America, we are going to have to learn to think in new ways because clearly the way we think now is not eliminating the gang problem.

Many schools have taken the stance of creating zero tolerance policies for everything, from bullying to bringing weapons to school, to drugs etc. On the surface this seems like a good idea. I agree that schools should have a zero tolerance policy to ensure the safety of their students. The unfortunate aspect concerns what happens to the kids that have the zero tolerance policy enforced upon them. They are expelled and while some of them attend alternative schools, many take expulsion as a cue to be done with school altogether. Alternative schools, at least the ones in Milwaukee, were a joke. Class lasted for an hour and a half, with class work consisting of multiple choice type assignments. Granted, it was very easy to obtain your GED, but it kind of reminded me once again of placing a Band-Aid over a bullet wound. It might be aesthetically pleasing for a few seconds, but then unfortunately you bleed out. There is no easy or cheap solution to this problem. There is no way around this. On the one hand we need to keep our schools safe, but expelling kids to sub-par alternative schools isn't doing much to help the situation. Why do you think so few people that graduate from alternative schools attend college? There are many reasons, but one is because they are nowhere near academically ready to enter college, even though they have the paperwork saying they are. I suppose funding comes into play here too. Understandably, the majority of funding for public schools goes to the normal 7:00 am to 3:00 pm facilities. There isn't even enough money to fully fund them, much less the alternative schools.

It's interesting, I remember when I was in eighth grade and many students wanted to get expelled and go to an alternative school. In their minds, in *my* mind, I thought to myself, "Why would I want to go to school for seven hours a day when I could go for an hour and a half and still graduate?" It was like the ultimate school loophole. Even at fourteen I remember thinking to myself how absurd it was that I could be "rewarded" with six less hours of school if I got expelled. I couldn't believe it, so what did I do? Why I got expelled of course. I was sent to an alternative school for an hour and a half each day. I still remember getting off of the bus after my "school day", shaking my head at how insane this whole alternative school situation was. I most certainly was not complaining because I had an entire day to do whatever I wanted, to go "kick it" with my friends who were not in school at all. If I got stopped by the police that looked for students skipping school, I needed only to say that I went to an alternative school and am done for the day. It was diplomatic immunity for teenagers.

In hindsight, I obviously was a complete moron for having this mindset. I couldn't have made a more foolish decision than to get expelled. I had the power to "play the system" so to speak. Yes I know, I only played myself, but the point I am trying to make is that I shouldn't have had the power to play myself. I don't know how it is in other cities or states, but Milwaukee can't be that far off from other large cities, so I can only imagine what other school systems are like. If a child gets into trouble within the public school system, the "punishment" should not be to send them to a school that lasts only an hour and a half. Many kids don't have the capacity to rationalize why graduating from high school is so much better than receiving a GED. It's odd, this whole subject of alternative schools seems almost unbelievable to me and I experienced it first-hand.

Had I not went to an alternative school for an hour and a half, I don't think I would have believed that the school system could be that----- what adjective do I use here? Foolish, stupid, irresponsible? I'll use irresponsible. Granted, I understand that something is better than nothing; in that if a student is expelled from the public school system, better to send him to an alternative school for an hour and a half verses nothing at all. I get this, and in a way can even agree with the logic of the lesser of two evils. It's difficult for me though, because I experienced first-hand what alternative schools entail. I will never forget when I walked into my first class at the alternative school; almost the entire class was comprised of gang members. Even worse, they were not of the friendly variety. I remember thinking that I was clearly going to get shot after class. It would have been ironically funny if it were not such a serious situation. I felt like a bird walking into a cat store. Needless to say that it was somewhat difficult to take my new teacher seriously as he gave me my first assignment when all I cared about was how I would make it home after school. How about that for an alternative disaster? I can hear my teacher asking why I was not focusing in class, with me wanting to respond; "Well you see, it's hard to care about algebra when all I care about is not getting shot after class. Beyond that, though, no reason."

At the very least, more time should be added to the alternative school day. I know this will cost more in the short run, but if the alternative ten years down the road consists of society paying with gang violence, isn't it worth the sacrifice now? It is inevitable that society will have to pay. We can choose to pay now with money, or choose to pay with lost innocent lives and *more* money to incarcerate these juveniles after they victimize someone. How much longer can we satisfy the short term at the expense of the long? This is backwards logic. Society has focused so long on a quick fix that now the consequences are a complete mess that seems to enormous to rectify.

Some communities are expelling juveniles from schools for their first offense and then giving them the poorest alternative education possible. Society then scratches their heads in wonder when none of them go to college and eventually lead a life of crime. These kids need the most help, the most supervision, the most classroom time because somewhere along the way of life, they became unable to succeed on their own. Their cries for help are muffled by the drone of politics and the screeching tires of a quick fix. Again let me be clear before I am misquoted, I am in no way saying that a kid who brought a gun into school shouldn't be expelled and or arrested. There absolutely has to be law and order, there is no way around this fact. When a juvenile is expelled however, do not wash your hands of them, rather we need to do everything we possibly can to help them. We are a smart and innovative country with no rival, there are many options. Unfortunately everyone is so quick to react overzealously. Perhaps this happens out of the fear of not knowing what else to do. I guess history would reflect Society's stance of; "If all else fails, punish, punish, punish." I am not saying that there is an easy solution. If there were, I most likely would not be writing about this now. However, if we as a society keep sending our children to schools with overworked teachers, overcrowded classrooms, and underfunded budgets, why would the situation ever get better? I don't know that I would go so far as to say that some of today's schools are the enemy, but the reality is that they are close.

It is no secret how an American education now compares to countries like China and Japan. It seems that every year the United States falls a little more on the comparable education list. Is this acceptable? Our actions would have to say that yes, yes it is. When are we going to wake up and rectify *this* reality; America is in a financial crisis, we cannot magically "make it better" overnight. Cuts must be made in many areas by each and every one of us. With that said, the one place that should never be cut is education. We should be cutting more in other areas to pay teachers higher wages and creating newer and better curriculum. It's so frustrating to me that politicians can even consider cutting our educational system. It should be renamed our *future* system instead. This doesn't even take into account those who have yet to be born. This problem will avalanche until it is so impossibly big that we will have no options. Why do you think third world countries stay third world countries for such long periods of time? They don't have education systems that are worth anything. They have nothing to teach the future. I know it seems impossible now, but what of the United States in 200 years if nothing is done to rectify the problem? Could we become Third World-esque? I am also not giving those in charge of the education system a pass. Much of what has occurred is a result of poor management and improper allocation of existing funds. So much money is wasted and can be better spent in other areas. What do we think is going to happen if we cannot or do not give our next generation a fighting chance? Many people spend almost a quarter of their life pursuing an education; shouldn't we at least make that quarter of a life worth it?

Chapter Six

Race: the affect it has on the gang culture

Depending on the state and particular city, you will find that most gang members in rural and suburban America are Caucasian. The inner-cities are populated with more minority gang members, whether they be African American, Latino, Asian, or Native American. Poverty stricken Caucasian communities, some call them "trailer trash communities", also have a higher Caucasian gang population. This is simply due to location, location, location. Many in society think that the "gang problem" is really only a minority problem though they probably won't come right out and say so. This may be true within the inner-city, but not so for the suburbs or other "white" populated areas.

Gang membership isn't the result of some genetic defect in minorities alone. When you look at the totality of circumstances such as parental involvement, educational funding, and community resources, you will start to see a pattern between white and minority gang members. In this chapter you will hear detailed accounts from a few different gang members of different ethnic backgrounds as to how they were raised, what led them to become a gang member, and what led them to eventually commit a crime at the behest of a criminal gang. You will hear from gang members that were raised within the inner-city, and from those who were raised in the suburbs. Again, you will see a distinct pattern between these individuals. The similarities between white and minority gang members are easy to see once you know what to look for.

Topics and questions elaborated on in this chapter will include:

- o Why the unbalanced race ratio?
- o Family un-ties, is there a racial disconnect?
- o Are minorities doomed to fail via location of birth?
- o Is there an expectation of failure for those born into poverty?

12345 6 78910

*   *   *

I'm wondering if you will do me a favor. After you read this next sentence, please close your eyes and picture what a gang member looks like to you; really examine everything about the person you picture. Go ahead.

Did you picture a younger person or older person? Did you picture a man or a woman? What type of clothes were they wearing? Were they wearing a suit and tie, baggy clothes, or something else entirely? What color did you picture their clothes to be? Did you picture someone with tattoos? Was their hair long or short, clean cut or unkempt and dirty? Finally, of what ethnic background did you picture the gang member to be? Were they White, Black, Asian, Latino, Native American, or did you not picture any particular race? I highly doubt this is possible, but who knows.

Are the gang members featured in movies and television an accurate reflection of the gang member *you* pictured? If Hollywood is a reflection of the masses, then clearly you pictured a gang member to be a minority. Let's forget what the *true* reality is for a moment; whether there are more minority or white gang members. I've always felt that the most important "entity" (*For lack of a better word*) in existence is perception. Perception in my opinion is everything. As unorthodox as it may sound, I believe that in many instances perception in fact supersedes reality. What *is* "reality" compared to perceived reality? There are obvious situations where there is no such distinction. For instance, if I am walking down the street and I am suddenly hit by a car, my reality is that I just got hit by a car. No amount of perceived mental semantics will change that reality. (*Though I'm sure there are ways of distorting reality if one tries hard enough*)

A little more on the difficult to prove scale, would be proving or disproving the following statement: John F. Kennedy and Ronald Regan were great presidents. I think there would be many people who believe this to be true unless you are extremely fanatical in your political beliefs. For the sake of argument, let's say that most people agreed that they both were great presidents. The perceived reality for them then, is that they were in fact great presidents. As would be expected however, there will always be those who do not feel the same way. For instance, let's say John Doe was laid off because of legislation J.F.K. pushed through the House and Senate. It could have been an agricultural bill of some kind that made it illegal to sell certain pesticides. This pesticide just happened to be manufactured by John Doe's company. He is laid off and cannot find a new job. He cannot support his family, his wife leaves him because he can't take of her and their kids, and he commits suicide. His individual reality is that because of the legislation pushed by J.F.K., he lost his job, family, and eventual life. (*I am not saying his suicide is J.F.K.'s fault either.*) As would be expected, his perception of J.F.K. would not be that he was a great president.

I believe our perception is in large part created by the circumstances of our life. That same agricultural bill that took John Doe's job also applied to all those who perceived J.F.K. to be a great president. The only difference is that the bill didn't *adversely* affect them. Nothing else in *reality* is different. That bill didn't just apply to John Doe, though it may have affected him more. So which is real, perceived reality or the real reality? Which one is right? Can I even preface the word reality with perceived, or are they one and the same? Which is more important? Do we as a society exist in our own individual perceived realities with the majority's perceived reality becoming the true reality by default? I think so. To this point then, does what "really is", *really* matter if the majority believes "what isn't", *really* is? I will get back to this point in a moment.

Carrying the question of reality vs. perceived reality in an even more difficult direction, let's say you see on the news a story that simply says, "Two people found dead in suburban home, both were fatally shot. Your first perceived thought was/is that they were probably murdered and so for you, this is *your* perception of *their* reality without hearing anything else. The next day more information is offered. You learn that there was no sign of forced entry, and the victims are believed to be husband and wife. Now what is your perception? Do you still believe both were murdered, that both are equal victims, or does your mind start to wonder about the circumstances?

The next day even more information is offered: two guns were found at the scene, one next to each victim. The husband was shot once, and the wife was shot nine times. Sources say that the couple was in the midst of a divorce. What is your perception now? Are both still equally victims in your mind, or has one (*The husband*) graduated from victim to murderer? If so, why? Is it because the wife was shot nine times and the husband was shot only once? Is it because generally society's perception is one of that the male is usually the victimizer in domestic violence? Is this *your* perception? If I am to be honest, without consciously thinking about it, my perception is that I probably do view the male as being the one more likely to victimize. I don't why it is that I think that, I just do.

Sometime later, more information is released: allegedly the wife had an affair, which was the basis for the divorce. The wife had since moved out, but is believed to have come back for some of her possessions. The situation became violent, with both eventually shooting one another. This is the last information you hear about the story, so your overall final perception of the situation is what? Is it one of that the husband in a jealous rage, shot his wife nine times, and the wife while trying to defend herself shot her soon to be ex-husband? This is probably what I would have thought transpired if I had only a cursory interest in wondering what occurred. For the sake of this scenario, this is also what the authorities found. With the cause of death being murder, the insurance policy was voided for the kids. Everyone involved was as sure as they could be of the events that transpired. There was no other evidence to contradict said evidence, so it essentially became the "reality" of what happened. Let me tell you what really happened however, though no one will ever know it because both victims are deceased. The affair and impending divorce were in fact true and one night the wife came over but not to get her possessions. She had the hopes of reconciling with her husband. *Both* wanted to get back together. While they were sleeping, the husband thinks that he hears someone in the house downstairs. They are both members of the NRA and were avid gun aficionados. They enjoyed going to gun ranges and were excellent marksmen. It was dark and he went downstairs with his gun. He tripped over one of the kitchen chairs making a loud noise. His wife awoke in a startled state. She saw that her husband was not there and that his gun case was open and empty on the bed. She was terrified so she went and retrieved her gun for protection. She went in search of her husband. She got downstairs but was afraid to call out in fear she might give her location away to any possible intruder. As she got to the bottom of the stairs a figure suddenly came around the corner and out of fear she shot at the shadow. The husband also out of fear fired as many shots as he could at the shadowy figure that just shot *him*. He hit the shadow nine times. As the shadow fell to the floor, so did he. They both soon passed away.

I'm sure a similar situation has played out over the years. I don't think it is that unlikely. This is the true reality of what happened, but as I said no one will ever know it because the only two people who knew are now dead. I've gone through all of this to ask: is perceived reality more important than true reality? Obviously true reality will matter in the next life when we meet whoever our maker is; if that is the philosophy you live by. In this life and in this instance however, it is my opinion that true reality doesn't really mean a thing if peoples' perception of reality is different than the actual reality.

I've gone on and on about perception because I think it is society's perception that most gang members are minorities, so whether this is actually true is of no importance. I'm sure some people in society when they think of a gang member might picture a white male in a biker gang or maybe even some sort of white supremacy group, but I think they are in the minority. I wonder what I as a white male would have pictured a gang member to look like had I never been one myself. I suppose I would have to revert back to an earlier age before I became a gang member. As I think back to the first movie I saw that dealt with gangs, I think it was "Boyz in The Hood." It was a very popular movie; at least I thought it was. The actors in this movie were black for those of you who have never seen this movie. The next two movies I remember seeing were "American Me" and "Blood In Blood Out." The gang members in these movies were Latinos with the main character in the latter being white. As one of my favorite sayings goes, you cannot un-ring a bell, so as hard as I think about what I would have pictured; I just can't do it without being prejudiced by my memory. There is a high probability that I would have pictured a minority, probably in either blue or red clothes because it was the Bloods and the Crips who were prevalent out West where I grew up. For the rebellious 1980's teenager, it was the "gang life" that offered a path to "cool" under-culture status.

I suppose every generation had a version of the rebellious teenager. The 50's and 60's had the 'greasers', the 70's had the stoners and anarchists, and the 80's, 90's and 2000's have had the gang banger. As I think about it however, the day of the gang banger has been quite long. I don't think any other generation's version of the rebellious teenager has lasted as long as the gang banger. Why do you think this is? Perhaps some feel it is because there are so many more minorities in this country today than when other generations of rebellious teens existed. In fact, I'm sure that there is a large sect of this country that blames minorities for the gang problem. That is simply reality, whether they are vocal about it or not. Are they racist for that belief? Let's say a majority of white people's perception of reality is one of believing the gang problem is a minority problem. Does the majorities perceived reality in fact become de facto reality? (*Similar to the scenario involving the husband shooting his wife*) If the majority of the people in this country believe the gang problem to be a minority problem whether consciously or subconsciously, doesn't it in an unfair way become a minority problem by default?

I do think most Americans think this way. I could be wrong, but that's what books are written for anyway right, to offer an opinion? To this point then, is the gang problem a minority problem? I guess there is no real way of determining this for sure, short of statistical analysis. There are some statistics out there but I don't know how accurate they are or can be. It makes me think of the political poles you see that give a 5% +/- margin of error. I suppose much smarter people than I have come up with equation upon equation legitimizing those numbers. I believe it would be almost impossible to accurately identify how many gang members there are in the United States. Trying to determine their ethnic make-up would be even more difficult. The first step would be to identify who is a gang member. In an earlier chapter I broke down just a few of the various groups that all seemed to be lumped into the category of gang member. I spoke on cliques, sets, blocks, crews, street gangs, organizations, crime families, etc. Do all of them get counted and identified as "gang members"? I think that they would have to simply because most of America views them all in the same light. There's that perceived reality again. As long as the majority believes something to be true, it in a sense becomes so. Do we count all of the wannabee gang members who technically are not officially "on count"? I would say so because their mindset is one that almost mirrors those that society deems as gang members. I believe adding these wannabee gang members certainly increases the Caucasian statistics. I'll speak on this later, but in short I think that there are more white wannabee gang members than any other race.

Let's say that all of the gang members are identified and to make up a number, we'll say there are one million gang members. It's interesting the way the numbers are gathered now. If someone is arrested or detained, they are asked whether or not they belong to a "gang." They are also checked for tattoos. The first problem is that many gang members never get arrested or get tattoos. Beyond that, many gang members do not volunteer to the police that they are gang members. On the other end of the spectrum, I know that there are many who are in fact not gang members but are labeled as such for general stereotypical reasons. Other identifying tactics are used as well, such as information gained from informants and witnesses to crimes. I can't imagine though, what the +/- margin of error on these numbers would be. I wouldn't even know whether to think that they are too high or too low. I would think too low, but I could be completely wrong. For the sake of this argument however, let's just say that the million identified gang members is accurate. How would we determine the ethnicity of each? Would we go by what the gang member identifies their self as? Would we go by appearance? That has discrimination and ignorance written all over it. Talk about perception problems. DNA technology is far too expensive. There are numerous problems with asking each gang member what they are. The first obvious problem comes to mind is dishonesty. The second problem is that many people don't know all of the races that make up their racial background. Even if one did, what would you consider a gang member that was half Asian and half white? Would you consider them a minority? What if the racial makeup was 60/40, 70/30, 90/10? If an individual is ten percent Latino, and ninety percent Caucasian, but when asked simply states "Latino", which box do you check? Do you check both the white *and* non-Caucasian box? I guess multi-racial would be the most logical box, but what does that mean in the context of determining whether there are more or less minority than white gang members?

It's interesting also to take a perspective from prison. Prison is somewhat like a "bizarro world", with many things within the walls being the opposite of the outside world. For instance, in the free world there are minorities with fair complexions whom acknowledge more of their "white" side because they feel it is advantageous to be white in America. In the penitentiary it is the complete opposite, at least in the Wisconsin prison system. The Wisconsin prison system is predominantly comprised of minorities so as would be expected; there is a disadvantage in being white in this world at least from an inmate to inmate perspective. This probably isn't so from a guard to inmate relationship. I will simply be blunt; white people are often looked down upon in this system. Of the fair-skinned minorities in prison, when asked what they are, they usually say black, or black and latino, or black and native. Very few want to acknowledge their "white" side in prison. If they have even a drop of nonwhite blood in them, they will claim to be a minority.

I remember being sixteen years old in this state's most violent adult prison. The prison was essentially broken down into two separate cell halls and two dorms. The cell halls were four stories high with cells on the front and back of the cell hall. Each tier had seventy-four cells, with two inmates to a cell. One day I was coming back from the dining hall and I was looking around and realized that I was the only white inmate on my tier. It was one of those surreal moments and I remember thinking to myself, "Man, I couldn't be more screwed if a race war were to manifest itself." I will be honest; there were a few times that I felt fear being so young in an adult prison, but that occasion was near the top. There I was, a 5' 3" 120-pound young white kid all by himself in the state's roughest adult prison. There were no special units for juveniles simply because I was the youngest inmate in the entire prison so they did not know what to do with me other than place me in the general prison population. Of all the places one never wants to find themselves in life, this is certainly near the top. It's odd, as I'm thinking back to that day as I write this; I can only shake my head. That was definitely not a fun situation.

Anyway, I have raised some of the difficulties that arise when trying to identify the number of gang members in existence. With that being said, I just thought of something out of curiosity. As soon as I finish this paragraph, I am going to walk onto the prison yard with a pencil and paper. I am going to walk onto the track that inmates walk around and identify the race of the first twenty five gang members that I see. I'm curious as to the number of minority gang members compared to non-minority. I shall return in a moment.

Alright, I ended up counting twenty six because when I got to twenty four, I next saw two gang members walking with one another and don't know who I actually saw first, I sort of just saw them both at the same time. This is obviously not a scientific pole by any means; all I did was walk outside and count the first twenty five gang members that crossed my line of sight. Here are the results: (*I ended up doing this five different days and times to eliminate work from skewing the results. The season is also summer, so there are a lot more people out on the yard in the summer compared with winter.)*

Tuesday	Wednesday	Thursday	Friday	Saturday
10:40 am	9:00 am	2:50 pm	6:38 pm	8:40 pm
Asian 2	Asian 3	Asian 1	Asian 0	Asian 3
White 3	White 2	White 5	White 5	White 4
Latino 9	Latino 6	Latino 4	Latino 10	Latino 9
Black 12	Black 11	Black 14	Black 10	Black 8
Native 0	Native 3	Native 1	Native 0	Native 1

I suppose the results don't make me feel one way or another. I didn't know exactly what the numbers would be, but I guess they are close to what I thought they would be. I did think that I would see a couple of more white inmates. As I think back to my years in the prison system, these numbers seem pretty reflective to what I remember. These numbers would be completely different in other prison systems and perhaps even in other prisons within this state.

At the end of the day, I really don't think it matters how many gang members of each race there are. For one, society is going to believe that there are more minority gang members than non-minority, and why wouldn't they? If you look at the mainstream media, whether that media be TV, movies, music, or the news; you will see an abundance of minorities reflected rather than non-minority. You will see a Latino with a plethora of tattoos, a black guy with his hat tilted one way or another and occasionally you will see the wannabee tough white guy that seems to be suffering from an image crisis. Seriously, just pay attention to the next movie or TV show that portrays a gang member. I will almost guarantee that the actor will be a minority. Go watch any music video concerning any type of gang life and you will see very few white individuals. You will see a few, but not many. I cannot speak upon what is on the internet because I have never been on it so I don't know what if anything is being portrayed there. Can you honestly tell me that society's witnessing of mainly minorities being portrayed as gang members has not had a subconscious effect on what the average citizen thinks a gang member looks like? The same applies to the 'mafia'. As soon as many hear the word mafia, they picture what? An Asian female? No, they picture an Italian male. There are plenty of "mafia's" in existence, but why do most mentally picture an Italian male? There are Russian mobsters, and you also have the Jamaican Posse that are just as ruthless and organized but no one pictures them. Mass media portrays Mafioso's to be Italian. "The Sopranos" and "The Godfather" gave credence to this stereotype. I too would most likely picture an Italian male if I were asked to think of what a Mafioso looks like, and I am aware of stereotypes. When "The Sopranos" came out, there were groups that protested its portrayal of Italians in a negative way, but that didn't stop them for airing the show. What's even more interesting is that some of the

"*Italian*" mobsters portrayed in that show are not even Italian. Think about that for a minute. They are cast in these roles because directors feel that they *look like* what Americans *perceive* an Italian mobster to look like even though they may be Latino for example. What does this say? Even race doesn't matter, but rather the perception of what the majority thinks. Reality again plays second fiddle to perceived reality. It's like when Jennifer Lopez played Selena and many Mexican advocacy groups complained that it was not right for a Puerto Rican to play a Mexican singer. It does seem like a pretty big slap in the face if you think about it but again, producers felt that Jennifer Lopez "looked the part."

There is another issue with labeling the gang problem simply a minority problem. Let's say that of the one million gang members identified, 750,000 of them are white, while only 250,000 are minority. This would lead one to believe that the gang problem is a white problem, correct? What if however, that 750,000 was only .5 of 1% of the white population, while the 250,000 was ten percent of the minority population? Would this change your mind? Again, I am not using actual racial percentages or numbers; these numbers are completely fictional. Would you now using the same exact numbers feel that the problem is a minority problem? How can one's perception change when nothing but the percentage of *non* gang members is added to the equation? What if the numbers were reversed with 750,000 gang members being minority and only 250,000 being white? The percentages are still the same. Would you then view this as proof that the gang problem is in fact a minority problem? If it is proof, that then means what to you?

I have spoken on this for quite some time in this chapter to point out this: if there *are* more minority gang members and you are not a minority, does this mean that you will not care as much? Does this mean that you will say to yourselves, "Let them kill themselves off"? If this is not what you think, then who cares what race has more gang members?

There is something to be said about this though, and that is the perceptions that minorities have about themselves. The term self-fulfilling prophecy comes to mind. We are in large part what we think we are. Perception of oneself is so unbelievably important. I'm sure we have all either told someone or been told that we have to first respect ourselves before we can respect others. Race is one of the most hot button issues in existence today. I feel race, religion, and politics all battle for supremacy when it comes to topics people cannot discuss without getting angry. I refuse to speak about politics, race or religion with other inmates because I have seen so many "debates" turn quickly into battle royals. Prison magnifies everything. People are not in prison for having good communication skills. In fact, many people's communication skills in here are no better than a wet rag's. Prison has a way of highlighting one's flaws in a way never before seen. I guess in large part, you cannot run from who you are in here. In society there is so much distraction; many people are never really forced to look in the mirror. Nor are they free enough from distraction to really take a look at someone else's flaws. In prison everything is stripped away. Every word in every sentence, every expression and tone in one's voice is analyzed a thousand times over simply because we have nothing else to do.

It's interesting; I've always overanalyzed things in life, even as a kid. When I came to prison I was obviously too small to really defend myself physically against many of the adults I was surrounded by, so I had two options; **1.** I could try and fight my way out of the various problems I would find myself in, but those results could be less than desirable to my face. **2.** I could take every second to study every nuance of every interaction that I had with people. I could learn to read people, understand what people were really saying though their lips were saying something else. I chose option number two. I analyzed everything. I rarely listened to the words that came out of someone's mouth other than to understand what they *wanted* me to hear. So much of communication in my opinion is nonverbal. This is when I learned perception was everything and reality was merely interpretational. Along this line of thought, I heard a great quote some time ago that went something like this; "people say that they want to know the truth but this is a lie, people only want to see what they feel they are capable of handling." That is so true in my opinion.

Getting back to race, prison is a racist place. Speaking about race with someone in prison of a different race will often lead to an argument. On both sides, each often wants to put the other down to feel better about their own race. I've often wondered what I would be like if I were raised by a racist family. I spent the majority of my life being raised by my father, and he was pretty liberal in his philosophy. He had the mindset of live and let live so I picked up those same values from him. I refuse to talk about race with other inmates mainly because I couldn't care less, but also because I have seen where those arguments can lead. Had I been raised by a racist father, I too however would probably feel the need to argue and put another's race down. I am a realist as well though; we all have some prejudice within us. I think much of it comes from how we are raised, or rather with what values we are raised with. When we meet someone with completely different views on life, we may not always get along. Oftentimes people of different races are raised with different cultural values, so when two individuals with opposing beliefs meet and/or interact, there is a strong possibility that there might be conflict. Does this mean that they are racist? I don't think so, but I could be wrong.

From a gang aspect, I feel some of what I believe might anger both white and nonwhite alike. It is time that some things need to be said. Political correctness has made this problem worse because politicians are afraid to offend certain sects in society.

Because of this inability to put the true problems out there in the public eye, the problem has gotten worse. Life is rarely fair and sometimes hearing the truth is hard, but that is also life. It's as though we have tried to shelter the past two generations with mirages of everything is fine and OK. I guess this could even be an exception to the rule of perceived reality supersedes true reality. Many try so hard to believe the world is such a kind and gentle place, but this perception hasn't the power to supersede reality.

I believe people run from the truth if they see a possible path of less resistance. They/we think somehow that whatever situation in question will just have to magically better itself because surely the world is comprised of only kittens and gumdrops. This coddling of our youth has made them weak in my opinion. They are often unable to find the strength to handle tough situations. Now it is up to many of these weak people to deal with problems caused by the last generation and they simply don't have the strength to do it. Everyone is entitled to their opinion; it's one of the few things no one can take away from you, whether right or wrong. So, I'll upset white America first.

In my opinion, I think each race tries to blame the other for the origins of the modern day gang problem. While I don't think it matters in this day and age who was to blame, I think it is important to understand why gangs came to be in the first place. Unfortunately someone has to be at fault, right? I think if I absolutely had to point a finger, it would be at the white segregationists and lawmakers of the early to mid-part of last century. At least this is who I originally thought was to blame until I put some more thought into it. I think it was actually the "white Americans" that self-segregated after segregation was illegalized who are to blame for the original problem being created. I think segregation became worse after it was outlawed because in reality it was in name only for a while. I will give an odd example of what I mean.

Up until the year 2000 when someone was sentenced to prison, they were eligible for parole after serving twenty-five percent of their time, at least in the state of Wisconsin. In the eighteen years that I have been incarcerated, I have never once seen or heard of someone getting paroled at their first parole hearing. For this topic, I am not debating whether this is right or wrong. I'm stating that legally, an inmate *can* be released from prison at their first parole hearing. Parole was created to offer inmates incentive to rehabilitate themselves with good behavior and completion of programming. It's a classic carrot on a stick scenario and is actually in my opinion a logical tactic. However, this has in a sense had an adverse impact because no inmates are getting out when they first see parole. They know that no matter how good they do, how many programs that they complete, the parole board will not let them out at their first hearing. Politics has come into play with certain politicians stating that they should not let any inmates out of prison until they do all of their time and so "Truth in Sentencing" was born. Again, I am not debating whether these new prison policies are good for society or not. That is for someone else to decide.

What has materialized out of them, however, is a mindset by many inmates that is detrimental to society in the long run. Inmates now feel that there is no point in taking any of the offered programs because it won't help them get out of prison any earlier. Yes I understand the argument that inmates should take their programs to better themselves and not to "get out early." In theory yes, that should be the way it works. Unfortunately, most inmates are in prison because they were incapable of doing the right thing so what makes you think that just because they are in prison that they will simply start doing the right thing now? Why would you expect this? It is not reality. Beyond this, a mindset of rebellion is formed because many times inmates are forced into their programs. This is done by firing them from their jobs if they do not participate. Obviously it is the inmates fault but they don't see it that way. They see it as though the institution is "messing with them", or playing games with their future. You don't know how many times I have heard an inmate say, "Man, fuck their programs, they aren't going to let me out anyway, so hell with 'em." Then they go and smoke a joint or cigarette, gamble or participate in other destructive behaviors. Now let me be clear, I personally believe that change comes from within regardless of the outside influence to do so. I think it is a horrible mindset that most inmates have, to not want to embark on positive endeavors simply because said endeavors won't help them get released from prison sooner. I will be the first to admit that people who commit crimes should come to prison, myself included. Parole was invented to offer incentive to better oneself, but now that inmates see they will not be let out on their first, second, third, or fourth time at parole, they choose to become bitter. Out of bitterness often comes other self-destructive behavior.

Segregation has had a similar impact because *desegregation* was a mirage just like incentive for parole is a mirage. Whites were still segregating minorities but in ways that either didn't violate the law, or in ways that flirted with that edge. The most glaring method of un-segregated segregation was economical. Yes, slavery the way most people understand it was atrocious. The economical slavery post segregation seems to have been overlooked by so many however. It is this economic segregation, the "whispered" segregation that eventually led to the creation of so many gangs. Gangs are a negative "side effect" of economical segregation years later. Let me be crystal clear, this is absolutely no excuse and I don't offer this as such. Just like if someone comes up to me and punches me in the face for no reason, this does not give me an excuse to go and shoot someone else because I was wronged. I offer it only to show how the gang problem originally came to be.

Just because something isn't right however, or is not an excuse doesn't mean certain things were not inevitable outcomes due to certain circumstances. As I have spoken on in this book, *we* don't always know what we would do in certain situations. Here is a scenario: let's say that you are a husband and father of four; ages two, four, six, and eight. Your wife is a homemaker and neither one of you has any other family that you interact with. The economy is horrible and you lose your job. You try everything you possibly can to find a job but there is simply no one hiring. The bank forecloses on your home, your car is repossessed and you now have no more money to buy food for your family. What do you do? This isn't like other "unlikely to happen" scenarios that I have raised, this happens every day. You explore your options, correct? Are all options on the table? Are you wondering if I am speaking upon whether you would commit a crime? Perhaps I am, but not necessarily. Your kids are starving, you are now homeless because the shelter is full, so what do you do? I think some people would in fact turn to crime. How many I don't know, I guess it would depend on the specific circumstances of each person. If you did turn to crime, I don't believe *your* circumstance is an excuse to commit a crime. I feel this way because I don't feel that there is such a thing as victimless crimes. When one robs huge stores of even a penny, we as a society pay for it in some way, even if only in loss of security. Many I'm sure would feel justified in robbing or committing a crime to put food in their child's stomach if they felt that they had no other alternative. I'm sure that there are many who also think that they would never resort to such behavior. To you I say perhaps not, but perhaps seeing your little five-year-old girl cry because she is starving and cold might make you do something you never dreamed of doing.

After desegregation, white America did not suddenly hire minorities to fill jobs. White bankers didn't just start giving them loans or treat them equally just because it was now illegal to segregate. In fact, this behind the scenes racism or "racism with a smile" was almost as bad as legal racism of the early part of the last century. Whites searched for legal ways of hiring only whites, not offering certain loans, or being late to a scene when a crime was called into 911.

This led to poverty on a grand scale. Community upon community became ravaged by poverty. I've always felt that poverty was the devils womb for so many of man's ills. Throughout history, just look at what was born out of poverty. The "have-nots" have always suffered in crime and I am not speaking solely upon minority America, but poor white America as well. How sad it really is if you think about it. I wonder if ever there will come a day without any "have-nots." This would be the ultimate utopia would it not? I don't know, perhaps everyone being equal is an impossibility because there will always be those who desire fortune and the only way to acquire fortune is by lessening someone else of theirs in some way. Sometimes life seems so cruel and without point doesn't it?

Some days while I am thinking about the issues I speak upon in this book, it feels so hopeless. Mankind seems so unworthy of existence to me at times, and of course I include myself in this sect. I am just as guilty.

When poverty- ridden communities are created, the *have nots* desire to have. A psychological culture is created within the community. Bitterness is spawned and acts like an incubator for lessened morals. I feel bitterness is a disease, acting like a cancer. Bitterness deafens that voice within us that exclaims "this isn't right." Bitterness allows man to do what he could not otherwise do having clear convictions of right and wrong. Again, this is no excuse, merely reality. (*Perceived or otherwise.*) This culture of bitterness affects many in so many different ways. Resentment is always on the forefront of bitterness's creation because humans as I said earlier need someone or something to blame. No one can ever take responsibility for their own wrongs. "It is *his* fault, or *their* fault! Perception is key here as well. For minorities, they perceive (*perhaps deservedly so*) that the "white man is to blame" for their current plight, their title of have not. Out of this a culture of resentment is born and unfortunately instilled into younger generations. Of course this is not an excuse but again, merely the way it is.

This bitterness, this resentment didn't in and of itself create gangs and the eventual gang problem per se, but it laid the ground work. It is the overall culture that bitterness bred and still breeds today that created the conditions for many gangs to assemble "out of a believed necessity." When we resent something, whether it is a race, an establishment, an institution etc., it becomes "easier" to not care if your actions directly or indirectly negatively affect that in which you resent. We without even thinking about it, feel a lessened degree of guilt when doing "wrong" in general because there is a sense of, "Well I was wronged, so I now have a right to wrong someone else, or take what I want." Hence my coining of the phrase "entitlement generation" in an earlier chapter. Maybe in a "just" world, entitlement would apply but the world is not fair or just, so with that said, entitlement does not qualify as an excuse for an individual to go and get what they feel they have coming by any means necessary. Unfortunately sound reasoning does not prevail in most instances. Yes, resentment also has the power to smother "sound reasoning."

When a child is raised in this type of environment, how can we expect them not to soak up their surroundings? How can we expect the cycle not to perpetuate? It does not make sense. A lifetime of resentment whether perceived or not, whether justified or not makes little difference. The fact of the matter is that many in poverty whether white or otherwise, all grow up resenting the "haves." In some instances it is true, there are those who are born into the world of the have-nots and resent it so much that they vow never to be held down. Rather than getting out via the criminal route, they immerse themselves in sports, school, and other positive extracurricular activities. They earn scholarships and attend prestigious universities, often being the first to ever attend college. They succeed. Their desire comes from the same destitute "have-not" birth place that so many others use as an excuse to cry woe is me and take the route of victimization. I have seen brothers go in two separate directions, with one going into the life of crime and death, the other receiving straight A's and becoming ultra-successful. This is the ultimate perplexing scenario to me. You have two brothers living in the same home with the same family, same school, and same initial friends, and yet they go in two completely different directions. I don't understand it at all. I know it really makes me wonder if some people are simply "born bad." I would hate to believe this to be true and I don't, but it does make me think. How could this not make one wonder?

It is because I don't believe some people are born "bad" that leads into why the gang problem does not affect minorities alone. Humans are humans; though it seems so many don't buy into this philosophy. When you start to get down into the trenches of the "lower class" psyche, you will start to see glaring similarities between white and minority gang members. For the record, when I say "lower class", I speak in terms of tax bracket, not human status. Out of poverty, this culture of bitterness and resentment that I have spoken upon, do you think it only occurs in minority neighborhoods? Absolutely not. Thirty-three percent of food stamp recipients are white. That is a higher ratio when you compare it to minorities individually. When poor neighborhoods are inhabited by minorities, people call these neighborhoods the "Ghetto." Do you think there is not a white equivalent? The "upper-class" refers to these as "trailer-trash", "hicks", or "rednecks." One's own people are often their own worst critic. Do you think that gangs are not rampant in the thousands of trailer parks across this country? Do you think that there is no poverty, no drugs or violence born out of that same sense of resentment that mirror minorities'? There is absolutely no difference, except maybe in the color of skin, name of gang, and drug of choice. Today's children are being born into this culture of resentment, and whether these kids are Black, White, or Latino makes no difference. In these communities there is a plethora of drugs, violence, prostitution, and just an overall sense of rebellion towards the "establishment" if you will. The "establishment" being the upper class and possibly some upper middle-class people, for that matter. Poverty is almost like a living entity, almost despotic in reign. It discriminates not by race or religion.

When children are born into poverty I think there is almost more of a sense of wanting to be close to those around you. Perhaps it comes from not wanting to face those miserable surroundings alone. With this line of thought comes the most prevalent answer to the most asked question of why kids join gangs. So many think it is because they are searching for a family and while this may at times be true, the real answer is much different. Juveniles join gangs these days because so many of the other juveniles in their community are also in gangs. I know that there will be those that think the answer cannot possibly be that simple, but it is. Note however, that the key words were "these days." This is important because juveniles didn't join gangs for the same reason years ago. There is another chicken and egg question that arises here as well. How could a juvenile become a gang member if his friend was a gang member if there were not previously any gang members? There is an important distinction to be made as to why juveniles join gangs now in relation to why they joined gangs thirty and forty years ago.

You may question why I raise this topic in a chapter concerning race. Race is an important factor in why gangs are in existence. You need only look at the names of some of these mega organizations: *Latin* Kings, *Spanish* Cobras, Maniac *Latin* Disciples, *Black* Gangsters, *Black* Stones, Dirty *White* Boys, *Spanish* Lords, Crazy *Hmong* Boys, *Mexican* Posse, etc., etc., etc. Are you starting to see a pattern here? I'm sure it is not very hard to see one.

Though much of society will never believe it, the ***foundation*** of these mega organizations were not intended to be criminal in nature. The younger generation especially is unaware of why their particular organization was ever created. Many of these organizations have laws that prohibit most if not all of the criminal behavior most now participate in. By laws, I mean that every organization has founding member(s) who originally created a set of bylaws that every member is to follow. This was done to give the organization structure. For instance, almost every single organization requires its members to obtain an education; whether while free or incarcerated. Many of these bylaws were formulated in the hopes of bettering those in their community. These organizations were originally created to uplift their race from a "perceived" oppression. I use perceived here not to say that there oppression was a figment of their imagination, but rather to say it doesn't matter if it was real or not, so long as they believed that oppression to exist. I think it is worth noting that I don't believe much of the oppression was in their minds, but in fact did exist. This is what I was referring to earlier when I spoke on what happens after desegregation. Many minorities were treated bad, were being oppressed by white America, so they felt as though they had to come together in order to have the strength to make a difference. Now let me also note that there were many of these groups that created an organization with the intentions of inflicting harm on the public via radicalism. The Black Panther Party comes to mind, or at least some arms of that party.

In the whole grand scheme of things I suppose it really does not matter "why" most gangs were originally created because at the end of the day, today's gangs are nothing like what they were intended to be. Let me also be clear as to the fact that most of the newly created gangs today, were and are not created to uplift their community/race. Most if not all of today's gangs are being created for no other purpose than to "get money" by any means necessary. In my estimation, the last of the "social changing" gangs were created well over thirty years ago. Beyond that, all of the older mega-organizations that were created to uplift their race/community are now just as bad as the newly created ones. There is really no difference between them other than their numbers.

People in society just assume that all gangs were created equal, but the truth is that they were not. It is odd however because even as I am writing what I know to be true, a huge part of me is saying "what's the point"? In that, who cares that many of these organizations were originally created with positive intentions when they now wreak so much havoc upon this country? The more I think about it, the more I feel there is no point in pursuing this subject any further.

I interviewed many, many gang members over the years as I wrote this book. I wanted to know why different gang members of different races joined gangs. There were some that I asked to write for me, the how's and why's they became gang members. Some were willing to do so without any hesitation, some did not feel comfortable at all writing down anything because they felt it would somehow be used against them if the wrong people were to read their story down the line. I suppose there is some possible truth to this, because many of those that I interviewed are still affiliated. It is interesting, so many of the active gang members that I interviewed truly want to prevent their younger brothers and sisters from joining a gang, yet they themselves will not renounce their own affiliation. I will speak more on this topic in a later chapter but in short, there are many that don't want to be in a gang anymore but are afraid to take that final step of renouncing their affiliation, ensuring their actions supersede their "want."

In speaking with all of those that I have for this book, there was very little in the way of surprises from what I heard with the exception of one thing. Something really stuck out to me when I was speaking to a member of the organization that I once belonged to. He was someone that could have had anything done to anyone simply because of who he was. He told me that there was nothing he wouldn't do to keep his younger family members from joining any organization, and furthermore he hated that he himself was still affiliated. I looked at him for moment, evaluating whether or not I believed him. I did. Most I'm sure would say, "Well, just get out if you no longer want to be in a gang." If it were only that simple.

I have interviewed White, Black, Mexican, Puerto Rican, Native American, and Hmong gang members. I have spoken with those from the "hood", the suburbs, and those from the middle class. I have interviewed those with the highest rank and who run the show, down to the wannabee rich white boy that seems to be more confused than anything. I have spoken with them all for years. I have lived with them all for well over half my life in prison. As you read their short stories, know that I asked them to write what they wanted. I had no prerequisites of any kind, other than asking them this question: Why did you as a (*Racial background*) join a gang? I have not edited a single word. I have enclosed a few stories from a few different races just to give you somewhat of an idea why particular individuals from different races join gangs. Perhaps one day I will publish all of the stories I have gathered over the years.

I want to be clear however, that in no way am I saying that every person of each of the following races joined a gang for the same reason(s) as those in the stories you are about to read. I hope if nothing else you've learned that I am a firm believer in not generalizing. Every single person in existence is an individual. There may be patterns but I believe in the world of prevention, we must treat everyone as an individual. Too often society becomes lazy if they feel they can solve a problem via mass marketing prevention. As I stated many times before and will continue to say, more will continue to die if we continue with this old approach.

I have taken only a few stories from a few different races to show that yes, there is a commonality when it comes to "why" juveniles of all races join gangs, but as I will get into later, the solution is somewhat different for different races. Some have included their name, particular affiliation, and whether they are currently still affiliated with said gang. I know there are those that feel active gang members can offer nothing good in the realm of prevention, but I am not one of those people. I am of the mindset that some people regardless of lifestyle choice possess valuable information and insight that can benefit many in many different situations. Far be it from me not to take full advantage of any offered information I can acquire if it can help in the task of preventing future juvenile gang violence.

The first story is from Derrick Sanders.

"I would first like to debunk the misconception of why people (Teens especially) join gangs. Many people think joining a gang is crazy, or that people join gangs solely for illegal purposes. In reality, joining a gang is a normal act when looked at from the proper perspective. –I'll explain.

In society, as humans we all have social needs. These needs involve being accepted by one's peers, interaction with others, loving and being loved. Therefore when a person decides to join a gang, he/she is actually trying to fill a social need.

If you look at society, all humans form a sort of "group network" among themselves. These networks usually consist of people that share the same interests and values. For example— athletes have certain bonds, policeman have certain bonds, and even neighbors have certain bonds.

Within these bonds, outsiders are typically left out, and within the "circle" members tend to gravitate toward one another and share a certain comradeship. Therefore in a gang members eyes, the gang is no different than a fraternity, union, or social club. In fact, the gang can sometimes replace the family unit within a person's life.

I'm explaining one of the many reasons why people join gangs, I am in no way attempting to justify joining a gang nor am I attempting to minimize the destructive behavior that gangs exhibit. My goal is simply to give you a reason why a person may join a gang, in hopes of showing an outsider a view from inside a gang members mind.

The following narrative I will share with you is true and accurate as I recall from my two decades of not only being in a gang, but also being a high ranking member of one of the largest and most violent gangs in America—(Vice Lords).

My goal is to give parents, teachers, and all those concerned, a realistic view of the inner workings of a gang, in hopes of preventing teens from joining a gang as well as help current gang members leave the gang.

My experience is very unique—I joined a gang when I was (13) thirteen years old. I rose through the ranks and achieved the highest rank possible- 5 Star Universal Elite. I then denounced my membership and walked away from the gang after over (20) twenty years, here is my story:

I was raised in Gary, Indiana, a small industrial city 30-45 minutes south of Chicago. Gary is predominately black (85%) and since 1967, has ranked no lower than 5th in its murder per capita rate. In 1995, Gary was the 1st American city in the post-World War II era to utilize the national guards as a policing method. In short, Gary was labeled "America's Most Dangerous City." This is where my journey begins.

Growing up I always had friends. We did everything together-played sports, spent the night over each other's houses, and shared secrets with each other. In reality, my friends were a part of my extended family.

I was always a good student in school and I participated in extra curriculum activities such as band, sports, and after-school programs. So at an early age, social networking was always important to me.

As expected, my childhood friends were a very important part of my life. I cherished the bond that we shared. When I was 13 years old and attending junior high school, I experienced interactions with other teens outside of my neighborhood for the first time in my young life.

This was the first time I was able to see how different groups interact with or against each other. An incident that I would like to call- "my 1st step" stands out the most.

After a school football game, a group of boys from another neighborhood was walking home. As young boys naturally do, we started throwing rocks and just having adolescent fun. The group approached us and words were passed. Before long, a fight broke out.

I joined in because to see my friends fight, I felt obligated to help. From that day forward, we would fight this group of boys from "across the tracks."

I didn't realize it then, but this was my initiation to gang life. The neighborhood I grew up in was known as a Vice Lord neighborhood. Although I was to young to know it back then, the older boys were all Vice Lords. I simply admired how they talked, walked, and dressed, and just waited my time to be just like them.

In my eyes, Michael Shorter, Big Brian, and "Flea boy", were just older dudes I looked up to. Everyone in our neighborhood "respected" these men and I admired them.

It was after the few fights that me and my friends had when these older boys approached us. Here is what they said; "I heard y'all been having problems with the G.D.'s?" "Remember, you have to stick together because we all family. If y'all need us, we'll be there."

To me, I was happy to be accepted by not only my peers, but also from the older dudes that everyone respected. I also remember how Steve didn't help us fight and how he was ostracized for it. I never wanted to be treated as such.

Without knowing it, that day in the park, I was initiated into the Vice Lords. We all hung out and spoke about what we will do tomorrow at school to the G.D.'s.

As I recall, my early years as a member of the Vice Lords was natural to me. Natural because my only job, my only motive was to help the boys that I had grew up with all of my life. It never appeared wrong to me to assist my friends when they needed me. In fact, all of my life I was told to help those in need—so quite naturally when someone would fight or attempt to fight one of my friends, I helped.

As the years passed by, we went from fighting to carrying guns. Also my group of friends or gang members began to widen. So I started to get deeper into illegal activities. As I said, I've always valued friendship, so my dedication to the gang was unquestionable! If you needed me I was there! I would never turn my back on you no matter what the situation.

This loyalty enabled me to become trusted and loved within the gang. Members knew I could be counted on and they would listen to what I had to say. I lead by example.

I must be honest, although I knew that selling drugs and shooting people were inherently wrong, I rationalized my acts as simply—a product of my environment.

I never viewed being in a gang wrong or bad. I viewed the Vice Lords the same way as I viewed a fraternity or the Republicans, a close knit group of friends looking out for one another. It wasn't until I became one of the highest ranking members and was able to interact with other leaders that I was able to see just how wrong I was.

It's amazing, in becoming a leader, I was able to see how the gang operates. What I saw disgusted me. The leaders don't care, they simply use members or exploit them for their own gain!

My decision to walk away from the gang was more based on why I joined—I realized there was no love, respect, or unity. Simply exploitation! The more I observed, the more I realized—a gang was not what I wanted and being in a gang ruined my life, my family's lives, as well as friends and society.

So at the age of 35 years old, at the highest ranking one can obtain, I contacted the leader and denounced my affiliation. Today, I speak against gangs, especially Vice Lords, every chance I get. Today when asked why did I join a gang? My reply is simple—I joined because I valued friends and I wanted to be accepted amongst my peers. Had those same peers and friends joined the military, a fraternity, or went to law school, I would have done the same.

I always laugh at people when they say, "What type of person joins a gang?" Because I think to myself—the same type of person seeking acceptance, friendship, or family bonding. Parents need to know that teens joining gangs do so for many reasons, with acceptance being high on the list.

Until people look at gangs as a social ill instead of simply teens committing crime, the problem will continue to grow.

As I read Derrick's words, I thought it interesting that he used some of the same reasoning that I have throughout this book, at least as far as why teenagers join gangs. I was conversing with him after I had a chance to read what he wrote, and I kind of joked that I should go back and change some of the things I had written earlier in this book because they sounded so similar. He had not been given an opportunity to read what I have written prior to giving his story. I wanted him to write without any biases from me. He and I share many of the same beliefs when it comes to why juveniles join gangs. In fact, of all the people I have met, he is near the top of those whom I feel honestly care about preventing juveniles from joining gangs. His brother is another individual that I would place on this list of mine, he is also one of the few individuals I would consider to be my friend.

Derrick and I met in a super-maximum prison where we were both isolated in our cells twenty-four hours a day. In my early years of incarceration, the organization he was affiliated with (*The Vice Lords*) warred constantly with the one I belonged to. I was a Spanish Cobra. The entire prison was locked down because our organizations went to war with one another. (*"Going to war" means that when you see a member from an opposing group, there will be an exchange of violence. In free society, going to war isn't the same because there are many places one group might not see the other. In prison however, there is nowhere to "hide" so it is a certainty that you will see members of an opposing organization the next time one comes out of their cell.)*

In "Supermax", since there was no physical interaction with other inmates, we were only able to speak to other inmates via the ventilation system. It was like an intercom. I cannot recall the first words exchanged between Derrick and I, but we eventually became friends with one another. Its "funny", for years we did not know what each other looked like because we knew one another only from how the other sounded through the ventilation system. He could have walked right up to me and I wouldn't have had a clue who he was. As I think about how he and I began our friendship, there is an interesting social experiment to the whole situation. Think about it; take two individuals from different backgrounds of different races from two warring gangs, and try calculating the odds of them befriending one another within the walls of a normal penitentiary. However, putting those two types of individuals in conditions where there is no physical or visual contact with other inmates and giving them nothing else to do but talk, and imagine what can happen. It almost sounds like one of my odd, unlikely "what if" scenarios that I have raised throughout this book. It might have read like this: Let's say you take a white teenager with a life sentence for a gang-related homicide and place him within the walls of a super-maximum prison for three years. Next door to him, you place a black rival gang member serving a life sentence for a gang-related homicide. They will never see or interact with one another for at least the next three years. They have only a vent in which they can communicate to one another through should they ever get bored enough to want to talk. To put this in perspective, the last time I was housed in segregation I was there for almost four years straight. I was there for the equivalent of almost 12,000 NFL football games if you were to watch that many straight through. On average, an NFL game takes about three hours to air. Imagine watching 12,000 football games in one sitting, except during the time it took to watch those games you were left in solitary confinement with no books, magazines, TV etc. Boredom is not even the word.

At the end of giving that scenario, I would have asked what you thought transpired. I would love to have known. Had I been given that scenario prior to living it, I would have guessed that the two opposing gang members would have disrespected each other through the ventilation system and tried to kill one another whenever/if ever they got a chance to meet. As they say however, fact is often stranger than fiction. If you would have told me that thirteen years after the black and white rival gang members met that not only were they no longer gang members, but would be working together to keep kids from joining gangs, I would have thought you to be delusional. That is exactly what transpired though. I have often wondered why and how this happened. The phrase "The Perfect Storm" comes to my mind for some reason. It's like it could happen only under the perfect conditions because the entire penitentiary system was/is so unbelievably violently volatile. I will never be able to put into words how on edge everyone in prison was back in the eighties and nineties.

For example, there would be race and gang wars that would erupt out of nothing more than a wayward glance. I know it must sound unbelievable, but let me share my very first day in the adult prison system. As I said, I was the youngest inmate in the entire maximum security prison and as I awaited the bars to open for my first breakfast, I had a million things racing through my mind. I am not ashamed to admit that I was scared to death. All of the images I had seen in movies and TV shows about prison were playing over and over within my mind. I was determined above all, to not be raped. Prior to being sent to prison, I was sent to the County jail as I went through my jury trial. I was also the youngest inmate at the county jail, so the sheriffs thought it would be amusing I guess to "tell me about prison life." They told me "what to expect." It was them that told me I was surely going to get raped and bullied because I was so young. I don't know if they thought this was amusing or if that is what they thought went on in the adult prison system. Either way, I had no reason to believe they were not telling me the truth.

The cell doors were opened for breakfast and as I walked into the chow hall, I could feel electricity in the air, almost like pulling a rubber band to the point you know it is going to snap and hurt you. The tension was almost physical in feeling. Sure enough, a rival gang member pulled out a shank (*Penitentiary knife made out of any number of items*) on three tables of rival gang members. Guards were able to apprehend him before he could stab anyone however. That was my first *breakfast*. At lunchtime, another rival gang member ran from one dining hall to the other and attacked a member of the organization that I belonged to who was sitting at the table with me. We had our backs turned and the other members sitting at our table didn't see the rival gang member coming. Guards tackled us all immediately because they were only a few feet away from our table. (*In this particular prison there were two dining halls separated by only a couple of feet. There were two gates that separated the chow halls but they were often kept open so as not to trap officers inside.*) That was my first *lunch*. At dinnertime, two gang members jumped one of their rival gang members a few feet away as I entered the chow hall.

That was my very first day within the walls of the adult prison system. I honestly thought I would not live to see the end of the week. Sleep did not come at all that night. Thankfully day two was less eventful.

I raise this because that first day's violence I later found out was caused by a single look someone felt was disrespectful. That is insanity! This is how prison was and still is in some states. This is the reason that it is so hard to let one's guard down to get to know someone you are taught to hate, taught to view as the enemy; much like how Derrick and I were taught to feel about one another. Often it is difficult for me when I think of things like this because I feel so unbelievably stupid. How could I have thought that way, participated in those acts? How could I have rationally convinced myself that "that person" was the enemy simply because he belonged to a rival gang? I can at times do nothing but shake my head in disgust because I can find no answers that quell the questions I have for myself. There is absolutely no excuse for some of my actions, none!

Moving on, I was speaking of the "perfect storm" as it relates to conditions within the prison system. The conditions make it nearly impossible for members of two rival gangs to become "cool" with one another. One of the only ways this used to be possible was via sensory deprivation. That is essentially what segregation is. For many, segregation compounds their social ills or problems by placing them in an environment that breeds insanity. Fortunately for me it did the opposite, though as I will detail later on it almost made me feel as though I was losing my mind by spending so many years in solitary confinement. I am one of those individuals who tend to overanalyze everything, often much to my own detriment. There were times during those years of solitary where I did think I was losing my sanity and who knows, maybe I was at times. Who is to say what sanity really is for that matter? *Is* there an arbitrary line between sane and insane even if we cannot quantify that line physically? Sometimes I think one cannot be sane to cope with some of the aspects of the adult prison system.

While in Supermax, it was almost as though some of my humanity was stripped away because at times we literally had nothing in our cells and knew our conditions would not change, sometimes for years. It is an odd phenomenon, I have always felt that many high ranking gang members have a certain cockiness about them; perhaps it is machismo at its best. For many, the first few months spent in solitary confinement are spent acting out, trying to compensate I believe for being stripped of any reason to be cocky. I always felt that "the hole" was humbling if nothing else. It put "life" back into reality by giving you nothing but time to relive your life, your mistakes. Some cannot handle this "awakening" or time to oneself, and so they act out in the hopes of not going "crazy." After months go by, reality starts to set in for many; the realization of the situation, that there is nothing to feel cocky about. This often gives the Hatfields time to get to know the McCoys as it were, at least for a while. It's interesting; I have seen some of the strongest bonds formed between two individuals that were enemies prior to spending years "together" in solitary confinement. (*Together being able to speak through the ventilation system*) When you strip everything from man as solitary confinement often does, and allow them to only interact verbally with one another, amazing bonds can be formed. Does it happen all of the time? In short, no. Do some become "cool" with one another during segregation and then once again become enemies when they are sent back to the general population? Absolutely, more times than not.

I can remember this other individual whom also was a Vice Lord that coincidently was always in segregation at the same times I was. For years we never met in general population but had an opportunity to converse through the cell bars in a different segregation unit. As I said earlier, the Vice Lords and the Spanish Cobras were always going to war with one another and we would joke about what we would do if we ever saw each other in general population and we *had* to go to war. We were "cool" with one another, and as I think back to some of our conversations, it was interesting how we wanted to tell each other that if a war broke out we would look for another member to fight but neither one of us wanted to be the first to admit this. No one wants to appear weak in prison. I can't remember how it worked itself out, but eventually we agreed that should the situation arise, we would fight someone else first unless we could not avoid the situation. I remember meeting him in the general population for the first time and as penitentiary paranoia would dictate, there was a little part of me that wondered if he was sincere and I'm sure the same thought crossed his mind.

After all, you can never be too sure in these situations. As it was however, we were both sincere.

Getting back to Derrick Sanders' story, the number one thing that he said that just jumped out at me was this: "Had those same peers and friends joined the military, a fraternity, or went to law school, I would have done the same." Friends do what other friends do, for the most part anyway. There are always exceptions. I have spoken with at-risk youth for many years and will never forget what one twelve-year-old said to me. It was one of the wisest things I have ever heard. He said, "If you can see your friends, you can see your future." Every elementary school in the United States should teach a class that focuses on the meaning behind that very quote. There should be one period, just like math or reading that teaches kids the importance of making "good" friends. There should be a textbook that caters to each grade just like in math, science, history, etc. I remember being taught about peer pressure in the D.A.R.E. Program, but it only lasted an hour or two. It was nothing more than a presentation given to me at a time when I was to young to care about drugs. Now that I put more thought into it, having an entire class based upon the aspect of friendship is a great idea. If you really think about it, what would be more important if you had to choose; history or a class that asks a child to focus on what a friend should be, and the consequences of choosing the wrong friends. I use history not to imply that it is not important, it is, but rather because kids often dread it the most. Most probably use it the least as they age.

Juveniles if you think about it are usually committing crimes with "their friends." I believe that it is rare for a young juvenile to go out and commit random crimes by themselves. I am not speaking about stealing a pack of gum when I say crime by the way. The idea of the class would be to get juveniles to really take a look at who they are considering to be a friend, why they are labeling them as a friend, and what positive or negative consequences these particular friendships can have. One of the questions that I ask the kids I speak with is whether or not they have friends their parents don't want them hanging around. On average, I would say that eighty percent of these kids raise their hands. Eighty percent! For those that don't raise their hands, I ask if they are great judges of character, or whether they have listened to their parents and no longer hang out with said friends, or whether it's possible that they are the "friend" that other kids' parents don't want their child hanging around. If there were a class on friendship, imagine asking those last set of questions to the class but also asking them to point at any of their "friends" their parents do not want them hanging around. This will obviously embarrass them which is exactly the point. Out of embarrassment often comes change. I will speak more on this subject later when I discuss what needs to be done differently. The more I think about it though, the more I think schools need a class on social relationships and how they can affect the rest of one's life.

Back on topic, I agree whole heartedly with the reasons Derrick Sanders gave for joining a gang. At its core, it is/was his need for social acceptance that led him as a black male to affiliate himself with a gang. What is important to note is who he looked up to prior to him officially joining a gang. More importantly even, is why. The "who" is easy, it was Michael Shorter, Big Brian, and "Flea boy." They were older gang members. They were in a way, his community's version of the "haves." They had money, nice clothes, and beautiful women. They had status; what more could an adolescent male want? Before juveniles are old enough to truly understand why they have those nice things, they become envious of their status. Envy is another one of those societal ills that allows man to quiet one's conscience in order to achieve whatever it is that they are envious of. In the case of Derrick, there was a moment he became envious of *something*. There is another point in time when a child realizes they can obtain whatever is desired by a single decision. (*Often the choice is to do something illegal.*) This is such a critical point in the life of any juvenile. This is the time when a child determines whether or not something they want is *worth* doing the wrong thing for. This is not always a cut and dry situation however, because right and wrong in the eyes of a child can be interpretational depending upon the values that they were instilled with by their parents/guardian. Beyond that, another factor would be the community they grew up in and what was acceptable behavior within their particular community. The latter might in fact be more important than the former depending how much time the parent spends with the child. If the parent lets the neighborhood essentially raise their child, then there is a good chance the child will become a reflection of said neighborhood. Also, when I speak of environment, I am referring to everything within their environment; media, music, movies, internet, etc. They are all sources of input, often on a subconscious level.

Here is one example: take a child and give them parents that swear like sailors. Every other word is a swear word. That child goes to school and of course uses swear words as well. Why would they not? The teacher says to the child that those words are not appropriate and they are not to use those particular words again. The child is confused because their parent's use those words all of the time and have never told them that they are bad words. Many kids envy their parents, or rather try and emulate them. This is one of those points in time I spoke of earlier when a child must decide whether acquiring something they are envious of is worth doing something they have been told is wrong. It may seem like such a trivial issue here, but I assure you it is not. Do you remember that old adage about how smoking a cigarette for the first time often leads one to cough but the second and third time become easier and easier? Well that same philosophy holds true here. When one does something wrong to get what they want, it becomes easier and easier to do "what is necessary" the next time they wish to get what they want. Every time you do this, you push further and further away that little voice inside our heads that says, "This is wrong."

Now take that same scenario but replace the child's parents with those who never swear but the child hears another kid swear and then swears himself in front of the teacher. The teacher tells the child that they cannot use that word. When that invisible point in time comes to decide whether using that particular word is worth doing something wrong for, what do you think the child will think? (*In this case, getting what they want is approval from the friend they heard the word from by mimicking them*) I guarantee if nothing else, uttering that swear word will seem *less worth it* than the child in the first scenario. Whether the second child feels it is worth it or not, really isn't even important for the point I am trying to make. However, for the sake of the argument, let us say that the kid does swear again. We have two kids that were raised in two different ways. One who had parents that felt it was alright to swear, the other had parents that felt it was wrong to swear. Each child swears, do you consider them to be equally wrong? Perhaps, after all they both swore in school at the end of the day right? Are both kids equally *to blame* at least from a responsibility standpoint? Are those two separate questions? I do not think that both children are equally responsible. I want to be clear once again however, that both are equally wrong, but how can you blame both equally from a responsibility standpoint? The first child's parents essentially taught him to swear as if there was nothing wrong with it. Is it possible that the first child doesn't believe that swearing is wrong because his parents did not teach him to believe so? On the other hand, the second child knew that swearing was wrong and in knowing that, still chose to swear again. To me this is where life gets difficult to sort out.

On one side you have an act committed that was wrong so there has to be some sort of repercussion in the realm of punishment so that a lesson is learned. Of the parents that "taught" their child to swear, do they not shoulder some blame? Is it not partially their fault for instilling something in their child that goes against what is acceptable within the society they live in? Forget for a moment whether or not the child should be punished less because his parents were sub-par in the values instilling department. How can anyone say that the parents do not deserve some blame? Whether this means their child deserves to be punished less for the same act than the other child, I don't know. It is definitely a possible slippery slope situation. Just because it may be however, does not in my opinion mean that we should not examine the situation. I spoke on this issue in a previous chapter when I gave the scenario about a child who is raised by two gang members. I raise it again in a different way under the chapter of race because I feel race is a factor as it relates to the overall environment many minorities grow up in. I don't particularly care if I offend anyone at this point, but it is just a fact that many inner-city communities are more violent than other communities.

There is no way around this fact and I am not going to hide behind political correctness. It is because many people are afraid to say the truth out of fear of being labeled racist that has led to many aspects of gang culture becoming worse. White America has their heads in the sand in believing the gang problem is solely a minority problem, while minority America has their heads in the sand as well in trying to convince themselves that they are not to blame for why the gang problem *still* is as much of a problem as it is. At some point minorities within the inner-city are going to have to say to themselves that enough is enough. The gang problem within the inner-city will never end until the communities themselves say enough. The same applies to white America. At some point they are going to have to admit that the gang problem is not solely a minority problem but rather an "everyone" problem. Beyond that, everyone has to admit that the gang problem is a culmination or end result of "bad neighborhoods", failing schools, bad parenting, and poverty.

Getting back to Derrick, he essentially became as he said, a product of his environment. Whether that diminishes his culpability in any way for what he has done, I don't know and am not debating. I think so many people try and jump right to the statement of "His childhood was/is not a justifiable reason to punish him less." That is another issue altogether. Why do people have such a hard time separating these two questions: **1.** Is an individual more likely to commit a violent crime if they were raised in a violent community

(*Becoming a product of their environment*). **2.** If so, should this become a mitigating factor in terms of punishment? Society has this problem with only addressing the second question, often with the answer being no. We do not put enough thought into the first question. This is the most important one because without the first question, there can be no second question. The reason behind this is because when someone like Derrick commits a serious crime, society only cares about punishment. Should we not try and find out "why" Derrick committed this act so that "john doe" from the same community does not commit the same act one year from now?

It is my opinion that yes, I believe people often times are products of their environment. Not all of the time as I discussed earlier, but I think it is somewhat natural to become a product of one's own environment. This can go either way, whether it's a child growing up in the "best" neighborhood who becomes president, or relating to a child who grew up in the murder capital of the United States and ends up murdering someone. Yes, I know life is unfair but this reality seems especially so, and while I won't go into detail about how I feel about the second question, my opinion is one of we cannot pretend many children are not products of their environment. How can we treat people the same in regards to punishment when it is very possible that one child never received a fair chance. (*Growing up in a negative environment*) Are we that short sided as a society in that we are unable to understand this concept? Or do we simply not care so long as a criminal is punished? One problem is often that a minimum sentence is applied to a specific crime. In Wisconsin for instance, the charge of 1st degree murder carries a mandatory life sentence. If a ten-year-old is found guilty of this offense, they are given a mandatory life sentence irrespective of their age. Some states mandate that even a five-year-old will receive a life sentence for this offense. Beyond that, many juveniles are convicted as "party" to a crime, meaning that they didn't kill anyone but were at the scene of the crime and or participated in it in some way but did not take the life of another human being. Many juveniles are serving mandatory life without parole sentences for being party to the crime of murder committed by an adult. A judge has absolutely no power to apply mitigating circumstances because they must sentence them to the mandatory life sentence. If you think the law does not work in this way, simply look up a case entitled Graham v. Florida on the internet.

Getting back to question number one, are we a product of our environment? If so, does it translate to race in some way? In Milwaukee County for example, it is quite clear that from a community standpoint, the crime rate is much higher in neighborhoods populated by minorities. Some might try and say this is a racist statement, but that's nonsense. The facts at least with respect to what neighborhoods have higher crime rates are clear. Granted, there are times when certain neighborhoods have "sweeps." (*Profiling*) This is where police blanket certain neighborhoods and "arrest" everyone that might look like a gang member regardless of whether they are doing anything wrong or if they are even gang members. Does this skew the numbers? Probably, but by how much I do not know. We also have to be realistic. In a neighborhood where the median income is well into to the six figure range, there is going to be a very low arrest rate because I'm positive very little manpower is sent to these communities to "police" from a verbal standpoint. Does this mean that crime does not occur in these communities as well? Absolutely not, but the reality of the matter is that there are not drive-by shootings every night nor people selling drugs on the street corner.

It is ironic, even though I am trying to speak in realities, trying not to be worried about being politically correct; I can see why many are worried about it. The brutal truth is this; white America is afraid to make a statement like "there is more crime in minority populated communities", out of fear of being labeled as a racist. This is not in my opinion a racist statement. "*Why*" there is more crime today in minority populated communities however, does result from our countries past racism as I discussed earlier with desegregation and the effects it had on many minority communities. I don't know, perhaps white America cannot raise this issue without being bristled at by those who by default become the accused. Maybe it is like finding God or religion; one has to find it on their own. A person cannot be forced to have faith in God, rather can only have it of their own free will.

So is Derrick in your mind, a product of his environment? Gary, Indiana had one of the highest murder rates in the United States. Derrick was exposed to this environment his entire childhood. Do you think he became desensitized to the wrongfulness of murder from a moral standpoint because he grew up witnessing so much murder? Do others become less and less affected by "murder" and similar crimes if they grow up in an environment where such things occur daily? I suppose we cannot say for sure, but it is a "no brainer" for me. I could be wrong I don't know, but it seems to me that one would have to be less affected by violence the more they are exposed to it as they age.

I remember the first time I was shot at by rival gang members. I was fourteen years old and remember ducking for cover. I compare that feeling I had with another time I was shot at a couple months later. I was with an older gang member when his girlfriend came to talk with him with one of her friends. It was late and we were standing near the front porch of some house. He and his girlfriend started to walk down the block when a black car with tinted windows turned the corner. It was such a surreal moment. I should have run and I don't know why I didn't, but I remember feeling a sense of calm as crazy as it sounds. I wasn't frozen. The car approached and the back window went down. I remember just looking at the car right before the shooting started. I was talking to the girl that came with her friend, waiting for her to come back when we heard the gun shots. I remember putting my hand on her head and pushing her to the ground. She really didn't need my assistance because she dropped to the ground so quickly. Time somewhat slowed down for me. I could see that I was not being targeted, so I did not feel the need to run. I was standing there with my hand still extended from where I had placed it upon her head to push her down. I was kind of just looking at her with I'm sure quite the quizzical look upon my face. The shooting lasted maybe three seconds. I consciously remember noticing how differently the female and I reacted when the shooting started. She looked terrified, probably how I looked the first time I was shot at. She was looking at me as though I was crazy for still standing up. I helped her up and her friend returned along with the older gang member. She asked if I would walk her home because the boyfriend and girlfriend wanted to go somewhere else. I walked her home, unaffected by what had just happened. She was clearly still moved by the shooting but was not crying or anything like that. I was still fourteen years old, but was clearly affected less that time compared to when I was shot at for the first time. There were a few other times I was shot at in between those two book ending shootings. I wasn't exposed to shootings at a very young age as Derrick was however. My first was at age fourteen which is still young but I cannot imagine the impact "murder" would have had on me if was I exposed to it from birth. If I was desensitized after only a few months and shootings, I can only imagine that a lifetime of such exposure severely desensitizes some people.

When one is desensitized by violence, I believe they are either more apt to commit violence or go in the opposite direction and are unable to hurt a fly because they do not want to ever become a product of their environment. Did Derrick and others like him get a fair chance at life? This is a little off the path, but I am sure many of you have seen documentaries on the violence ravaged wars in Cape Town and other such areas. There are pictures of kids shooting AK-47's. They are killing people and being killed as well. Were they given a fair chance at life? They did not ask to be born into such violence. They did not choose to be born in a country that happened to be going through one of the worst cases of genocide in recent history. The violence they experience dwarfs that of anything in the United States. Would you sentence a nine-year-old Cape Town boy to life in prison for killing someone when he has experienced nothing but violence from birth? And we have the nerve to complain in this country.

These children are *born* into death. You can see it in their eyes; it is etched upon their face. Yes it is "wrong" that they take the life of another human being, but how can their life not be a mitigating factor? How can they not be expected to commit egregious acts of violence when they literally know nothing else?

This is all they have been taught. Again, I am not saying that severe punishment does not need to be handed down when crimes are committed, but I really don't know what the punishment should be for some of these children.

Getting back to America, as I said, though the children in the United States are not subjected to the same degree of violence as those in some third world countries, there are some communities that are extremely violent; like Gary, Indiana for example. If you can understand how and why children in Cape Town are more likely to commit murder due to their violent surroundings, then why would that same logic not apply to certain youth raised in the most violent of U.S. cities? Do you think the violence level in some of these communities is not high enough to have an impact on a human being? If so, where do you draw that arbitrary line? You would have to draw the line somewhere would you not? Would you base it on the number of homicides or other violent crime? Would it be based solely upon your perception? I don't know that we can draw a line which makes this even more difficult.

Regardless of the reasons "why", it is clear that young minorities that grow up within many inner-cities are subjected to a higher level of violent crime within their communities. It is not their fault they are born in what society calls bad neighborhoods. Do you honestly think that the violence they witness or see on the news or hear about from friends does not desensitize them? I'm sorry, but you are delusional if you think it does not. To me there is a clear desensitization on some level to violence. Because of this, there is a higher propensity to enter into a lifestyle that is in fact violent, i.e. the gang lifestyle.

Here is a scenario: take a child who grew up in the most affluent neighborhood in this country. It does not matter what race they are. In this community there has never once been a shooting or any homicide for that matter. Every home is a million dollar home with the average income being even higher. The child is raised in this community until the age of sixteen when he meets someone from the worst neighborhood, at least from a crime rate perspective. The "poor" kid takes the "rich" kid to meet some of his other friends that happen to be gang members. They are on the porch when rival gang members come and do a drive-by, killing one of the gang members the rich kid had just met. What do you think the rich kid does? How does he react? This is his first brush with violence. He has never even been in a fight before. What are the odds do you think, that the rich kid will soon join a gang after what he just experienced? Would you give him a five percent chance of later joining a gang? One percent? Why? I personally think that his odds would be next to zero.

On the other end of the spectrum, I have known countless individuals that grew up within the inner-city and experienced

firsthand, that same type of "event" (*The drive-by shooting murder*)
before they chose to become a gang member. Why do you think this
is? Why is there a difference? I don't believe that humans are meant
to witness or experience violence. If they are, I don't think they are
left unaffected. Violence equals pain; there is no way around it. I am
not so much even speaking of the physical pain, but rather of the
emotional   burden   pain   leaves   one   to   carry   via   the
witnessing/experiencing of violence.   As I think back through
history, the past was filled with so much war, so much violence. I
ask myself why? Three stupid little letters, W-H-Y. I have heard that
peace is born from war, that war is a necessary evil. Really, a
necessary evil? Can there truly be such a thing? I understand the
reasoning behind these statements, I understand why these great
philosophers make them, but I don't know that I can agree. But who
am I, right? Merely a former gang banger and what candle could I
possibly hold to Plato, to Sun Tzu?

I have always wondered to myself, whether "good" can only
exist if "evil" does as well. Does there by default, have to be a yin
for there to be a yang? Can there be love without hate? I look at
gang war and compare it to some of the infamous wars throughout
histories past. The only real difference I see, sadly, is the scale of
them. Was WWII really that different from the "war of insanity" in
Chicago between two organizations? What about some of the mafia
wars in the early part of the 1900's? "Real" war is either born out of
a frustrated oppression, or the desire to acquire what another has by

any means necessary. Gang war is no different, just fought on smaller scales.

At birth, what would you say Derrick Sanders' odds were of becoming a gang member, knowing that he would grow up in Gary, Indiana? Compare his odds with those of some rich kid born in Pleasantville, USA. If you believe that Derrick's odds of becoming a gang member are even a fraction of one percent higher than the rich kids, then by your own admission Derrick was *not* given a fair chance to not become a gang member as a black male. To me, this is unacceptable as it should be to everyone else. I again feel the need to say that I make no excuses for what Derrick has done with his gift of life, and knowing him personally he himself does not blame anyone but himself. Is it fair do you think that society turns its nose up at Derrick and others like him for joining a gang when society increases his odds of joining a gang simply due to where he was born? Think about that for a moment.

I always try and play the devil's advocate with my own thoughts. I feel one should always do this to better understand that in which they are trying to understand. Along these lines, the phrase "free will" comes back into my mind once again. Can it be said that we are all born with free will? I'm sure many would say that we are. At one time I might have believed that as well. I cannot remember believing that way for sure, but I am sure I did at some point or another. I guess it would depend on one's own definition of free will. What is yours? As I ask you this, I realized that I never really tried to define it for myself. I guess it was always one of those things I thought I just knew. It's kind of like when you think you know what a word means until someone asks you to define it out loud. I wonder why that is; why I can know exactly what you mean when someone uses a word in a sentence, but might have a hard time defining it on paper. Perhaps it is the other words that are used that surround the word in question that lends a hand in understanding what is being said. So, free will....... This is a hard one for me because it has to be looked at or defined without being prejudiced by everything that has been instilled in me up to this point in life. Right off the bat I would discredit what most people's generic definition would be, that free will is the choice to do what one wants with their life. I suppose there is truth somewhere in that statement, but I don't give it much weight. To me, that definition is more geared to the physical body and what is done with it.

I feel free will in its narrowest of definitions, has nothing to do with the physical world. I'll explain. Let's take two individuals at birth. One is born into your average middle income family; mom, dad, sister, brother, dog and white picket fence. Well it should come as no surprise that this next part is going to sound weird and crazy, but sometimes certain elements can only be explained in this way, so please just humor me. The other individual is born into a room where he is handcuffed to a wall. He is kept there for thirty years.

The room is windowless, and he has no contact with another human being for those thirty years. Food is shoved through a small trap in the door and he is sedated any time he needs to have human contact, whether it be for medical reasons or sanitizing his room. Compare the "free will" of the two after thirty years of life. The physical aspect is non-existent because the one handcuffed to the wall hasn't the free will to physically go anywhere. This scenario is clearly unlikely to ever happen, but it is *possible* for it to happen and as such, instantly proves that everyone is not born with physical free will, other than to possibly move certain body parts.

As to free will from a mental and spiritual standpoint, some would argue that they are one and the same but I don't know. Perhaps. One of the aspects of free will to me is whether one has the actual conscious choice to choose whether or not to be "good" or "evil" irrespective of external influence. In this realm of thought, I don't see how one cannot bring fate and destiny into the equation. If fate/destiny truly exist, wouldn't they by definition deem free will as non-existent? I think so. Wouldn't you have to look at it this way? Preordination by definition relieves us of our will of freedom does it not? Even if the paths allotted to us at birth are in the trillions, that still means ultimate free will does not exist. The paths would have to be infinite to coexist with "free will." Now that I think about it, I don't think one can believe in both free will and the existence of fate/destiny. Wouldn't destiny in a sense be the ultimate enemy of free will? I ask you; do you believe in free will or fate?

It's odd; it has taken me awhile to write this last page because I have been lost in thought asking myself which one I believe in; fate or free will? Up until now, I kind of haphazardly believed one has free will to choose whether their heart is good or evil, but also thought we all had a destiny. As I examine it now however, I don't know that those two philosophies can coexist. I cannot help but be amused at something. From a marketing standpoint, one of the quickest ways to get a person interested in a product is by using the word "free." When the word "free" is used, the product really doesn't even matter; all we know is that we can get something for free, so we are naturally interested. Even if we absolutely do not need the product being offered, there is that little voice in our heads that says, *"But it's free."* As I'm sure most know by now, the so called "free" campaign is one of the biggest marketing scams to ever have existed because nothing is free. The crazy part is that even though we KNOW nothing is free, we still are intrigued by this marketing practice. "Free" is the ultimate salesman gimmick is it not? Wouldn't it be something if God were the ultimate salesman? I have this image of God standing at some podium yelling, *"Step right up ladies and gentleman, get your free will here, it's free. Free will here, get it while it lasts!"* Think about it for a moment, wouldn't God *have* to sell "will" as "free"? Otherwise, what would be the point of life? We would simply be along for the ride. We would be nothing more than a character in a video game, being controlled by something other than our own free will. Life would be nothing more than putting up with non-pleasurable experiences while we search for the pleasurable. In that regard, shouldn't it be "fee will" rather than "free will"? I think that non-pleasure is the method of payment because if our lives are preordained, the only question is determining how much non pleasure we are willing to endure to experience the amount of allotted pleasure our particular path grants us. I say "pleasure" because I believe pleasure is the only universal need experienced by the human being, and anything other than pleasure is non-pleasure.

We all seek pleasure, as I am in complete agreement with Sigmund on. Whether that pleasure is the love given by a soul mate, the perverse pleasure of killing to a serial killer, or the pious pleasure of truly giving oneself to God, it is all pleasure. If fate exists, we just have to hope our "life path" gives us the amount of pleasure we feel is worth experiencing the non-pleasurable moments for. Nothing else would really matter would it? If you were to feel it is not worth it, you just "end it." Another aspect of free will I've often wondered about is suicide. Do you believe we are able to at any time, kill ourselves? On the surface, you would think sure. If one had a gun, you could put it to your head and pull the trigger at any time right? I don't know that this is true however, but there is no way of ever knowing whether this is true or not. If you think it is true, then tell me this; if someone asked a suicidal person to hold their breath until they passed out and died, could they? If they could only use their "will" power and use no ropes, guns, buildings, etc., to help aid in the act, could they do it? Can one use their free will to hold their breath until they die of suffocation? I don't think so, but why is that? I know the medical reasons about certain involuntary responses via the autonomic nervous system, but I don't know if I am satisfied· with them being the only answer. I have read about certain Buddhist Monks that can slow down their heart rate and breath, but I have never heard of anyone being able to hold their breath until they die. What of mind over matter?

Does the fact that we as humans cannot take our own lives without the aid of some "device" prove that we don't have the free will to kill ourselves at any time? No, but I think this line of thought leads to some interesting scenarios. I'm sure that everyone has at one time tried to see how long they can hold their breath. At the point just prior to going unconscious, there seems to be some sort of safety mechanism if you will that prevents us from proceeding any further. This safety mechanism tells our mind that it is time to take a breath right now. I ask you this however, how is that same safety mechanism "disabled" when someone puts a gun to their head and pulls the trigger? I don't understand. I'm sure that some would say that the difference is that the person with the gun to their head is truly suicidal, truly feels that they have nothing else to live for. To those I again say, ask that same suicidal person ten seconds before they pull the trigger to hold their breath until they die. Will they be able to? If there is truly a lack of will to live and one has the free will to end one's life, why then do they need an instrument of some sort to end their life? Is it because suicide is unnatural? Unnatural in the sense that in order to commit suicide one needs something other than what God gave them to complete it. I have also thought of breaking one's own neck by grabbing the head and twisting it. This would be a way of committing suicide without any instrument other than what God gave you. I don't know that this is possible either though. I would think that same safety mechanism that kicks in when you need air would prevent you from twisting your own neck hard enough to bring on death.

I have raised the suicide aspect under free will because what if that safety mechanism that kicks in when you try and hold your breath isn't really a safety mechanism but is instead fate/destiny forbidding you to expire at time other than when you are destined to? If you believe in fate, then you have to believe the time of your death is already known to "someone" or something, right? To this point, if one is scheduled by fate to die at a predetermined point in time, then just like you couldn't hold your breath or break your own neck, isn't it possible that you couldn't "pull the trigger" or "jump off a building" until that preordained time came? Fate would intervene would it not? Wouldn't it have to lest it lose all sense of its worth? What use is fate if we have the power via free will to supersede it? I don't think we can kill ourselves whenever we want, but that is just my opinion.

I think many who are serving life sentences contemplate suicide at some point or another. I have. There were times during my sentence where I had lost what I felt was all hope for wanting to exist. I wondered how I would "do it", or if I could do it. I remember lying in my cell and in the deepest recesses of my mind would visualize the different possible ways I could end it, but they all seemed like they would hurt quite a bit. How trivial of a thought, that killing myself might "hurt." I have always had a high pain threshold so it was this that made me think that I really did not want to kill myself. Perhaps this was my particular safety mechanism offered to me by fate, letting me know that it was not my time. I don't know what I would have done had I been able to acquire a gun. I do know that there were times when I really wanted to not be alive, and I cannot imagine that the feeling could have gotten much stronger. It's amusing to me that people say that suicide is the coward's way out. I understand *why* they say it, implying they are a coward to not face whatever they would be facing had they not taken their own life, or of facing the pain that their suicide would cause others. I get it, but I don't think the physical act of suicide is cowardly. To the contrary, I feel that I didn't commit suicide because I was a coward. I was afraid of the act itself. I see it in reverse. I don't think that I am afraid of death per se, at least my own anyway, but the act of taking my *own* life does scare me.

I remember trying to "cheat" those fears. Yes I know how odd that must sound. Something happened in my life that left me no desire to live. For me, no one else existed that was worth living for in my mind. I honestly did not want to live any longer. I am religious, I do pray, but it got so hard for me mentally that I begged God every single night to not wake me the next day. I begged to die in my sleep. Even as I look back, I really did not want to wake up the next morning. The pain I was experiencing at that time was not worth what possible pleasure I might experience later in life. I tried to circumvent the act of suicide with prayer. I'm sure that I will pay for that in some way when I "meet my maker."

You would think that based upon this line of thought that I believe in the existence of fate, i.e. if I believed that I couldn't kill myself because it was not my time, this proves that I believe there is a set time I am determined to die. I don't want to believe this to be true. I want there to be free will. I want to believe that we all have a choice in life, to be good or evil. It would be unfair if some people are simply born evil, born to be gang members that victimize. What would be the point? If science can eventually prove the existence of an "evil" gene prior to birth, what would we do with these people? Incarcerate them from birth? Put them under a form of house arrest? Scientists are already looking for areas within the brains of criminals that can possibly lead to a "criminal" gene. They are trying to determine whether there is something physical that can be seen or found in humans that will prove they are more likely to commit crimes. If people are destined to be gang members, then I guess there is no need for this book, right? We don't need any gang prevention programs because kids will either become gang members or they won't right? They are doomed to fulfill their gangland destiny.

I think about myself concerning this line of thought. I was such a good student and child as I grew up. I then joined a gang for a few months when I was fourteen and was involved in a gang-related homicide. I was sentenced to life in prison where I renounced my gang affiliation and then dedicated my life to preventing juvenile gang violence. I look at this a few different ways. Was it my fate to become a gang member but not die as one? Was I born evil, and only led a good childhood until the true me came out when I was involved in a homicide? Was it *me* who changed for the better of my own free will, or was it my destiny? Was I meant to be sent to prison so that I could find my purpose, find the desire to dedicate my life to prevent that in which I was once a part of? Essentially losing myself so that I could find myself?

I do not know the answers to these questions, nor does anyone else have them. At the end of the day, there is no proof of destiny, of fate, or of free will. One can have their theories, their opinions but nothing more. With that being said, because there is no conclusive proof either way, I believe that we must error if we have to error, on the side of hoping that there is free will. We have to assume that people are not simply born evil, that it is not one's destiny to become a gang member. If we are wrong, no harm done. This is so because if we believe that people are not born evil, by default we believe in change.

On the flipside, if we feel people are born evil, born to become gang members and we choose then not to help them change and we are wrong? Then we have not only wasted their lives, but have also let them victimize countless others because we didn't try and "get through" to them. Maybe they needed that one person in their life to lead them in the right direction, to give them that positive push. Wouldn't it be the ultimate Karma when it's all said and done that the person you chose not to help because you thought they were born evil would one day kill you? I personally refuse to take that chance, but I am merely one human being. My debt is with God and my victims. I owe it to them to spend the rest of my days preventing what I once was a part of. If I am wrong for trying to help others change, then at worst all I will have done is led a productive life in which I tried and failed to get through to today's youth. I can live with that.

Derrick Sanders is a black male and due to his place of birth, was surrounded by circumstances that raised his odds of becoming a gang member. I don't believe that there is a way to logically argue against this. He was surrounded by crime, violence, failing schools, and a culture that those circumstances create---a self-defeating culture. Some could argue that he was dammed from the start and might sound convincing in fact. I know him today, as well as other members of his family and I do not think that they are evil, or were born evil. In fact as I said earlier, he and his brother have worked with me for years in trying to prevent juvenile gang violence. Just imagine who they could have been were they given the same chance as others born into the best of communities. We cannot help but be affected by our circumstances. We are often a product of them but I believe that God has given us free will to overcome our circumstances should we want to badly enough. Sometimes we cannot do it alone and I don't know why the path for some is easier than for others. I do know that we are born young and naïve, not old and wise. We can never truly know if a decision we made yesterday was a mistake because we do not know God's plan. To that end, we should live giving help as well as knowing when to accept it from others.

Moving on from a black male's perspective; I enclose the following words from a Latino male. As I said before, I have left his words unedited. He wishes to remain nameless.

"I am a young Mexican and Puerto Rican who is involved with a gang. I am 22 years old am currently doing a 10 year prison sentence for a gang-related shooting of two people. I was 16 years

old when I did it, but my downhill slope started way before then. It probably started when I was about 5 years old when I held my first gun. It was a .357 snub nose put into my hands by my grandfather. He was involved in an organization and so was his son which was my uncle. My uncle was the guy I looked up to. He was a gang member and one of the most gangsta' people I have ever met in my life and I loved him for it and wanted to be just like him or so I thought.

I grew up on the south side of Milwaukee and if you know anything about Milwaukee that is pretty much gang bangin central. Now as I was growing up from 5 years old I used to run around and see a lot. I seen all the money, guns, and shootings from the gang lifestyle and knew that was what I was going to do. So at about age 12 is when it all started. I technically wasn't official but was running around saying I was a gang member and thinking I was tough shit, thought I couldn't be touched but boy was I wrong. I finally got myself into a situation where I got into it with another organization (Which I won't say who) where I was almost killed and I called some family up and nobody wanted to help so I figured I would have to start taking things into my own hands and that didn't really end up in a good situation. Between the ages of 12-14 was bad. I was fighting and got stabbed but nothing compared to what came later.

I actually became official when I was about 15 when my uncle got out of prison. The crazy part was the same uncle that I

*looked up to was the same one that tried to stop it at first but after a
while he already knew it was too late and I wasn't stopping.*

*So eventually it went from me fighting to me carrying around
a gun. Now let me tell you about one thing before I continue at this
point in time. The south side was pretty much in chaos—there wasn't
any allies and everybody hated everybody so when you are young
you are pretty much the person on the frontlines at all times and the
older guys are behind you in your head and having friends outside
of your organization was pretty much out of the question. So it was
pretty much us against everybody else on the south side which was
probably about 8 other organizations and all of the fun I was having
became me constantly being paranoid and having to worry about
being killed and constantly watching out for the police trying to lock
us up.*

*So back to me having to carry a gun mainly because there
really wasn't much fighting going on anymore so my mentality was
shit, it was pretty much kill or be killed and I definitely didn't want
to be the one with a chalk outline around him so I figured I'd have to
put somebody down. Now as I was trying to do that I ended up
getting caught with a gun while I was 15 years old. I went to juvenile
detention for about 2 weeks and swore I would never do it again if I
got a second chance but I pretty much flat out lied to myself. I went
back to school because I probably went 1-2 weeks out of 6 months
but forgot that's where all of my problems were and I was on
probation so I couldn't carry a gun and they had metal detectors.
But none of that mattered because there was too many oppositions at*

my school and I wasn't about to get punked out so I came in swinging. I was kicked out of all MPS schools and didn't really care. I was living my life how I seen fit. Now as you are in an organization, I was constantly gang banging, fighting in school, tagging up garages, school walls, lockers, houses it really didn't matter as long as I was known. Plus with my father not being an avid supporter of me, I looked for guidance and ran deeper into my organization so at this point they tell me to jump and I pretty much say how high. I loved everybody around me from my hood and I thought I was loved back.

So I was out there in the morning posted in the hood on point not letting anybody in. There is this older guy that is guiding me like I'm a puppet and he is a puppeteer. So in the midst of all of this in comes my uncle which is one of the oldest around trying to talk to me again. He was telling me if I kept going the way I am I was going to go to jail for a long time and I pretty much said they gotta catch me first because I love the hood and it's all I know. Didn't really think about what it was doing to my family because I was caring only about one thing, earning respect and boy did I earn it. I was 16 years old and have been around for a minute. Now I received a phone call telling me I was needed to do something and I said come on lets go. So off I went to go and shoot 2 people in broad daylight with everybody outside but I didn't care. I thought here is my chance and I did it like it was nothing. Cold blood, no conscious no anything. But in that 1 minute of my life was one of the worst and best mistakes of my life.

Well after this incident I was arrested and my whole world was flipped upside down. I was in jail facing 2 attempted homicide charges and a 120 year sentence. Now in the streets there is a code or at least supposed to be what happens in them stays on the streets but both of the people I shot gave statements and turned states evidence on me. So I am 16 years old facing 120 years of time and still don't care and still thinking that everybody from my hood is stand up. So eventually through me going through my court hearings the person I was with (Who was from my hood) came to court willing to testify against me. And that was pretty much it. I was done. So I talked to the defense attorney and told her I was willing to plead guilty for less time. I ended up getting 10 years but that was when my eyes finally started to open up when one of my own was "snitching" on me.

So now I am sent to a maximum facility prison feeling like shit because I have all this time but little did I know that what I had was a blessing. I ran into somebody I hadn't seen since I was about 10 years old and he had 4 life sentences and he was doing the same thing I was but worse. But as my time went on, I finally started realizing this was my second chance and that nobody from my organization really did care about me and the ones who really did were the people who were there all along. My mother and brothers and sisters and friends I grew up with. I could call them cause they will put money on the phone, come see me, write me and actually are here for me. The people I thought had my back I haven't received a dollar from and if I need underwear socks or hygiene, I could never count on them. When I see them in prison they try to lead me astray but I stay focused now and finally understand what I never would have if I wouldn't have come to prison. I could have had life in prison for killing somebody so I got lucky. I know people who weren't so lucky."

What are your first impressions after reading this story compared with Derrick Sanders? They are both minorities, one Black the other Mexican and Puerto Rican. They grew up in two different states however. Did you notice any similarities or glaring differences? I'm sure right away you can see the age difference and how they speak. I have purposely tried to find individuals from opposite ends of the spectrum. I could have talked to just one type of individual but what then does that do to offer insight? As I said before, I do not in any way imply that all Black and Mexican/Puerto Rican kids grow up like this. I will constantly preach that everyone has their own identity, but that certain circumstances are similar.

Just like Mr. Sanders, the Latino male's first impressions as to what a gang member is, was seeing one through envious eyes. For Mr. Sanders it was the older kids in his neighborhood, for the Latino male it was his uncle. He looked up to him and wanted to be just like him. Unfortunately that entailed him eventually becoming a gang member. It was that first envious thought that started the proverbial psychologically destructive avalanche. What concerns me is how powerful envy can become. Remember, it was the Latino male's uncle whom he wanted to emulate. The uncle however tried to tell him to essentially not be like him. The gang lifestyle is so alluring to today's youth that they are willing to disregard the wishes of those they first wanted to be like in order to be a gang member. It is disheartening to hear that the one person he looked up to the most couldn't even get through to him. I'm sure many think then, what chance does anyone else have of getting through to him? This is the sad reality of the situation. This is one of the reasons why the problem is so hard to fix. As much as I hate to admit it, once a juvenile reaches that envious stage it is impossibly hard to reverse that envy without some sort of huge traumatic experience.

What this means is, that more has to be done prior to a juvenile reaching the envious stage—at least becoming envious of a lifestyle wrought with pain and violence. This doesn't mean that we just abandon those that have reached that point; however there are things we have to be careful about because when a teenager is at this stage, their blinders are on. They have a one-track mind to attain that lifestyle by any and all means necessary. The problem that arises is that there are probably people in the child's life who are trying to steer them in the right direction, but are being met with resistance. As I discussed in an earlier chapter, people tend to overreact in these situations. This is as I said, one of the worst things that can be done.

Not only is overreaction the worst thing to do, the worst time for it is when the juvenile has just reached the envious stage and has their blinders on.

Another issue the Latino male had was the fact that he felt his father was not supportive of him in a positive way. This was /is a huge factor as I have stated in earlier chapters as well. The lack of a father in the latest generation has done so much damage to the teenage male of today. What makes it so much worse is that the damage is perpetual in nature. It becomes a learned behavior, worsening each generation. Again, it is no excuse. Having no father gives a teenager no right to become a gang member. On a side note, I hope it has become clear by now that I did not write this book to make excuses for gang members. I hate that I always feel the need to say "It is no excuse for this or that" but I don't want anyone to disregard what I have said if it doesn't agree with what they already believe. I admit that some of the things I say do sound like an excuse if you take them out of context, but in reality they are not.

I have a father who in my opinion has no rival, so I definitely cannot use the "I didn't have a father excuse." My father was involved in almost every aspect of my life, and from the standpoint of gang membership, if anything he kept me out of that lifestyle. I will point out however, that I did not join a gang until after I moved out of his home to another state. For my particular circumstance however, I chalk this up to coincidence because I moved in with family that had the same values my father had.

It is interesting to note that one of the most shameful moments of my life came when my father came to visit me for the first time after being arrested. He obviously knew that I was in jail for a gang-related homicide so he could only assume that I was a gang member myself. I was out of his home for about four months before I became a gang member, and was only a gang member for a few more prior to committing my crime so I hadn't gotten a chance to interact with him as a "free" gang member due to him living in another state. As I walked into the visiting room, I tried to hide my tattoo from him. I was allowed to sit next to him and all I could think about was him not seeing my tattoo on my left hand. It was a gang tattoo but I wasn't afraid that if he saw it he would hit me or anything like that. I wasn't afraid that he would get up and leave if he saw it. I had this feeling of shame because for my entire life, my father had instilled in me the best of values. He had spoken with me about gangs and their destructive nature. My father was the one I looked up to most in the entire world, and essentially I let him down. That little tattoo was like a beacon of my failure. It was not long before he saw it. He questioned me about it in his gentle way; not angry or hostile which made me feel even worse. That was one of the worst moments in my entire life. Perhaps this does not make sense, I don't know. It was/is just how I felt at the time.

For me, it is clear that having a father involved in my life was not enough to deter me from joining a gang. As I say, there are always exceptions to the rule. While not having a positive male role model in one's life is not the sole element as to why juveniles join gangs, it certainly in my opinion is one of the most influential reasons. If I am to be honest, saying what needs to be said regardless of whether or not it offends anyone, then it has been my experience growing up in the prison system that there is a huge lack of positive role models within the minority community. It obviously transcends race, but within these walls there is a clear attitude of resentment towards fathers in general. That is just the truth. If you wish to be offended by this then by all means be so offended. You can continue to be a part of the problem if that is the case. I make no apologies for stating the truth as I have witnessed it in here.

The Latino male also spoke on the violence that he was surrounded by all through his childhood. Do you believe that he was desensitized in some way by this violence as he grew up? Did it make it easier for him to enter into a lifestyle of violence? I think so. He had that, "I have to get them before they get me" attitude that I spoke on in an earlier chapter. This *paranoia* in a sense, allows them free reign emotionally to commit acts of violence without the feelings of guilt. It is almost like a predetermined sense of justification, a misleading if you will of one's moral compass. I also italicize "paranoia" because while it is paranoia to believe they will get you if you don't get them first, this is the reality for many gang members. This doesn't justify their behavior, but rather explains sometimes why they do what they do. If you are a member of a gang and are caught by rivals, there is a good chance you will not be given the chance to make that same mistake again. Gang members know this, and many of them live with this understanding. The south side of Milwaukee is as the Latino male stated, known for nothing but gang banging. In Milwaukee, the south side is known for gang banging while the north side is known for "making money" by selling drugs. The reverse is true on smaller scales. There is definitely gang banging on the north side and drug dealing on the south, but there is a clear difference. Why is that do you suppose? A couple of factors come into play. The racial makeup of the south side was nearly all White and Latino in the eighties and nineties. (*This is when I came to prison*) The north side was comprised predominately of Blacks. I imply nothing; I am merely stating the racial makeup.

From an income standpoint, the poverty level was higher on the north side, which is *one* reason there could have been more of an emphasis on making money via drug dealing rather than gang banging simply for the sake of gang banging. Another interesting aspect that was quite obvious to me when I first entered the prison system was that while there was no longer any north or south side, the same mentality existed. Latinos and Whites took gang banging much more serious than Blacks did. You would often see two rival

Black gang members speaking with one another while you rarely if ever saw this from White and Latino gang members. Don't get me wrong, you definitely had certain sects of Black gangs that were just as serious when it came to gang banging, but they were in the minority. The structure of Latino and White gangs compared to that of Black gangs was very different as well. I chalk this up to the numbers ratio. There were/are far more Black gang members in this particular prison system than any other race. At least on a surface level. In a previous chapter, I spoke on those who claimed to be members of an organization and those who actually were sanctioned members. In prison, White and Latino Gangs strictly enforce the rule that you are not to claim membership unless you are "on count." There is a zero tolerance policy for those found to be claiming something they are not sanctioned to claim. For many Black gangs however, this same policy was/is not as strictly enforced. Certain Black organizations had "counts", and were as structured as Latino organizations, but the majority of them were not. I think this was because their numbers were too large to keep track of everyone. A consensus leader was rarely approved by all.

Also, I say Latino and White gangs but in this state there is really only one "White" gang. There are really no other recognized "White" gangs in this state like there are in the federal system and in other states. Most White gang members belong to Latino gangs within this state. I will say that one of the issues that Black gangs enforced in here was that no white people were allowed to be members. Let me be clear, when I say Black gangs, I am not speaking of racist gangs, but rather of gangs that are comprised almost entirely of Black individuals. There are a few Asian and Latino gang members that are allowed to claim their allegiance, but rarely are any whites allowed this opportunity. On the street in these smaller communities where gangs are just starting to make a presence, there is a lot of whites that claim to be Gangster Disciples or Vice Lords but they are in my opinion, unsanctioned. They are wannabees.

Earlier in this chapter I asked you to close your eyes and picture what a gang member looks like in your mind. Now I will ask specifically what race you pictured. Did you picture a White, Latino, Asian, Native American, or Black gang member? I would say that mass media these days would portray most gang members as Latino. I have noticed that over the years, there is a clear Latino portrayal in TV shows, videos, and movies. I really notice this about female gang members. They are almost always portrayed by Latinas wearing heavy makeup. Why is this? Does society via Hollywood feel that the majority of gang members are Latino? I think so or Hollywood's portrayal of the average gang member would be a little more racially balanced. Hollywood is financially motivated. They put much time and effort into creating a product that will be viewed by the public as "real." They wish to make their *fiction* as believable as possible, so for reasons only they know, think the most believable looking gang member has a Latino look to them.

I have lived more years in the penitentiary than I have lived free. As a result, I have essentially been surrounded by the states most violent gang members for the majority of my life. It has been impossible for me not to understand the gang lifestyle because I have been surrounded by it for so long. I have talked to, been celled up with, and observed every race of gang member you can think of. It has been clear to me that Latinos by far, take gang membership more seriously than those of any other race. Asians and Native Americans would be second and third. I would say that this holds true in and outside the walls of the prison system. By serious, I mean that they will gladly die for their organization in a heartbeat. Obviously all gangs have these members that take it seriously, that will die for their colors, but the ratio is highly skewed in favor of Latinos. I have often asked myself why this is. Is it an issue of honor? Loyalty? Stupidity? Why is there such a clear difference? As I said, I would rate Asians as number two and one of the commonalities between the two is that they often both come from strict families. Especially Asians. I have witnessed how White and Black kids act in front of their parents compared to that of Latinos and Asians. Night and day from a respect standpoint. One of my best friends when I was young was a Korean female. We used to speak for hours on the phone when we were kids but I was terrified to ever go to her house based upon what I heard in the background. I can only imagine how she felt.

One of my best male friends who was murdered when I was younger was Mexican. His parents were so unbelievably strict. There was no back talking and everything had a "yes, sir" behind it. Of course all Latino and Asian families are not as strict but this is one commonality that I have noticed between the two. I think this is important though because this strict upbringing creates a culture as well. What's weird however, is how it works because it really does not make any sense.

One element that arises from a strict family is a heavy emphasis on respect. This respect is somewhat selective however, because obviously the law isn't respected in many cases or they wouldn't break it. I think the respect issue morphs into one of pride. There is a belief that one's masculinity is being challenged if some sort of disrespect is given. In prison, many fights are born out of a single disrespectful act that an individual cannot let go. The situation is often magnified when witnessed by others. If someone is disrespected by another, everyone looks to see if the disrespect will be "let go." Obviously one should not let small situations explode into something bigger, but in prison if you are viewed as weak, blood will be smelled within the water so to speak. When others see that you are not willing to rectify the disrespectful act in kind, they will feel they too can disrespect you. Here is something that many in society would not expect as a probable outcome based upon a given scenario. Two individuals are playing cards and one gets caught cheating. The cheated individual gets up and punches the cheater, but quickly is beaten up very badly. Officers witness them fighting and they arc sent to segregation. Both are let out in a couple of months after they complete their solitary confinement time.

That same individual who got beat up is now playing basketball when he gets fouled very hard. It is clear that the foul was meant to hurt the one who got fouled. So the individual who got beat up the first time throws a punch at the individual who fouled him, but misses and gets beat up again. They also get caught fighting and are sent to segregation for a few months. It goes without saying that the individual who got beat up both times will most likely be the butt of some ridicule from those he is "cool" with. After all, he did just get beat up twice in a row. However, I guarantee that he will be given some respect because regardless of the fact that he cannot fight very well, he has also demonstrated that he will not allow you to disrespect him. The next time he is in a situation when someone is contemplating doing something disrespectful, I can promise if nothing else that they will put some thought into whether it is worth it or not because he will fight you. They still might choose to test him, but at least they know he isn't a "punk." Everyone has a different tolerance level for respect. In the prison system at least within this state, there is a clear difference depending on race, as to how much disrespect will be tolerated before it escalates to a physical level. As an example, let's say that one inmate calls another a "bitch." In prison, this is about as disrespectful as one can get, or at least it used to be. Times are changing though. From least to most likely to respond with violence at being called a "bitch" would be the Whites, Blacks, Asians, Latinos and Natives. I think it also depends on the race of the individual who is doing the disrespecting. For Whites, they are more likely to fight another White individual who calls them a "bitch." They are less likely to fight a minority perhaps out of fear, I don't know. Blacks and Latinos are more likely to fight someone of another race quicker than that of their own because it is in a sense more disrespectful to be called a "bitch" by a member of another race but they do fight one another a lot as well.

As far as strict households concerning Latinos and Asians and how they produce individuals that take gang banging much more serious, I believe the respect factor morphs into one of honor. Honor then morphs into pride, and with that pride comes a much lower tolerance level *for* disrespect. From a gang banger standpoint, simply being in an opposing gang is in a way disrespectful. This is due in large part from past events; like shootings, stabbings, and or murders. Look at it this way; if I am a gang member and am shot by a rival gang member, all who belong to that gang are now my enemy. You are so because obviously being shot is very disrespectful. I know that "disrespectful" is an odd word to use for being shot, but it is definitely a form of disrespect. So, one day I see a member of that same gang that shot me, the same gang that "disrespected" me and by proxy, they are disrespectful for the actions of their fellow member who shot me. As such, it is now my duty to "disrespect" you. I understand that this may be hard for some to understand but this is just how things work. Of course it is insanity, but if "gang bangers" used rational reasoning skills; they wouldn't be a gang member in the first place. To this point, you cannot look at these situations with thoughts of how you would act if in a similar situation. It will never work that way. There are many gangs of different races that share this very serious philosophy, but more so in Latino and Asian gangs.

When I first got to the maximum security prison after being sentenced to life in prison, I remember hearing two black gang members asking why Spanish Cobras and Latin Kings were always fighting one another for "no apparent reason." The Latin Kings and Spanish Cobras are the two largest Latino organizations in this state and happen to be bitter rivals. They are very similar if you want to look at it this way, rivals like the Bloods and Crips are rivals. They hate each other. These two groups will fight for reasons you would not believe because there is still so much hatred for one another from when they were on "the streets" together. It gets interesting though, because on the street if a Cobra and King see one another, there will not be any talking. One will try and either hurt or kill the other simply because they are rivals.

When these two groups meet in prison however, the philosophy changes somewhat. This gets difficult to explain because the philosophy has also changed over the years during my incarceration. When I was first sent to prison, Kings and Cobras did not speak to one another at all. Each looked for reasons to start something with the other. Security staff tried to separate as best they could, members from each group but this was not always possible. There was not a "fight on sight" philosophy but it was very close to this. Other states do have this philosophy, and as I explained in an earlier chapter, are forced to be kept separate by security staff. In fact, there is a "kill on sight" philosophy for some organizations in some states. Within this state, if something happens on the "street", it can quickly start a war within the walls of the penitentiary however. I don't know why Wisconsin is different than many other states. I am sure that there is some valuable information in determining why though.

Over the years, there has been a developing philosophy of "what happens on the streets stays on the streets." This is often hard for some to buy into, mainly for Latinos and Asians. It is difficult to now tolerate the same rival gang member that has previously shot at you. Some look for the slightest acts of disrespect so that they can fight. This may be something as simple as a look that lasted a fraction of a second to long. I'm reminiscent of the famous "looks"

Clint Eastwood used to give in his movies. He would have surely gotten into many fights with a "stare" such as he had.

When I first came to prison, one of the most "disrespectful" acts that led to the most fights came from sitting at a table in a rival gang's area of the chow hall. I am sure this will sound so very stupid, but the chow hall was/is the closest semblance of a neighborhood one can have within the walls of a penitentiary. We were able to choose what tables we sat at. Of course inmates took this opportunity to territorialize an area, a "hood." In the prison I was sent to, the back row belonged to the Spanish Cobras and other affiliated groups. There were times when a member of the Latin Kings or other opposing gangs would sit in the back row. This was sometimes done because they were new and did not know where to sit, or as an act of aggression. I cannot tell you how many fights I witnessed over those tables. You would think that they are just stupid tables, but they/we took them so seriously. This is a good example of what is tolerated by certain races of gangs. White and Black gangs also had their own area in the chow hall but were very rarely likely to fight over someone sitting at their table on a single occasion. I would not suggest that you push your luck however, I am merely stating that they are more tolerant than the Latinos, some not by much however.

As I stated earlier, in the federal system and other states where the racial numbers are a little more even, I can promise you that the Blacks and Whites will not tolerate any other race sitting at their tables or anything of that nature. I am only speaking about this state. In the federal system, race is everything. In that system, whites will not tolerate any other race disrespecting them as they are more likely to do in this state. The Aryan Brotherhood and Dirty White Boys are ruthless in that system and do not tolerate any sort of disrespect because it would show weakness. Their numbers are virtually nonexistent in the Wisconsin system.

As far as Latinos within this state taking gang banging so much more seriously, I think it stems from that pride to be respected as a man. This may be somewhat difficult to understand, but when an individual joins a gang, their particular organization essentially becomes a part of their manhood. They personalize it within themselves. If you disrespect the organization, by default you disrespect the individual behind the organization as a man because the organization is now an extension of his manhood, his masculinity. At this point, certain primal traits begin to make an appearance. The battle for Alpha supremacy begins. There is a need to show dominance towards other rival gang members.

I am sure you have heard some of the stereotypical remarks about the Irish and Latinos having the shortest fuses/tempers. I don't know if this is true, but stereotypes usually come from certain truths.

I know that the IRA and Mexican Mafia are some of the most ruthless organizations this world has seen in recent history.

Many things in life, no matter how crazy or shocking can be broken down to a level that one can see how and why it got to that point. It doesn't make these things right or just, simply because we can understand them, but rather gives us the chance to decide what to do if we hope to prevent these things from happening again. Think about it; Latinos and Asians are raised in stricter homes that tolerate disrespect less than others. For those that eventually become gang members, why would you/we not expect that same philosophy to translate into other areas of their life? If certain individuals place more emphasis on respect as a result from how they were raised, why would you expect there to be a lesser showing of violence when they are disrespected by rival gang members? As I said, it justifies nothing nor is it rational in the sense of what is right and wrong, but can you not see why certain individuals would take gang banging much more seriously than others? Growing up in a stricter household does not by itself create gang members either. You have to once again take a look at the totality of circumstances. If you take these same "strict" households and place them in "poor" neighborhoods with failing school systems, you have the perfect environment for creating gang members that have a much lower tolerance for disrespect.

Moving on to another sect of society that also join gangs, though mainstream America often does not want to admit this, are Whites. As I've stated, I have spoken with many different gang members of all races and income levels. For this book, I have tried to get a few words from a few different races of gang members. The next individual you will hear from can be classified by those in high society as "privileged", or by minorities as "rich white boys." Yes, Caucasians to be more precise. Earlier I spoke on whether the gang problem was solely a minority problem. I am of the opinion that it is not. For many white males, I believe that poverty also plays a major role in deciding whether or not to join a gang. Most of the white individuals that I have met who are gang members were/are definitely not rich. They share almost all of the same traits as minority gang members possess. To be completely blunt, the major difference that I see between white and minority gang members is the desire of whites to want to "fit in". I am sure that there are some white people that are offended by this remark, but it is the truth. I will say that this is more so true for whites that join non-white gangs. (*Gangs that are not comprised solely of white people.*) For organizations like the Aryan Brotherhood however, there is no desire to "fit in" with other races. They do not allow members of other races to join. There are predominantly white gangs however that do allow members of other races to join. All white gangs are not race or hate based as many think. You can look at it this way. In the Midwest, certain Latino organizations like the Latin Kings and Spanish Cobras have Latino, Asian, White and Black members.

Certain "white" gangs are the same way. They are predominately white, but also allow other races to become members.

In the federal system however, things change a bit. It would be very hard for a white male that belonged to a Latino organization on the "street" to survive in prison. His biggest enemies would become other white organizations like the Aryan Brotherhood. They would seek him out and make him regret his decision to join a Latino organization. The Latino organization does not want to have to deal with that situation either so essentially he becomes a very lonely forsaken individual.

I think many in society would be shocked if they truly understood white gangs as well as white gang members. To that point, I'm positive that the *un*-incarcerated "gang world" would be shocked to learn how the white gang world operates within the federal prison system. I think many don't have a clue. One aspect of this book is about reality vs. perceived reality, and the power/ability of perceived reality to become de-facto reality. To be blunt once again I think that the overall perception in "gangland" is that white gang members are "soft", "scary", and are not really much to worry about. Is this true? As I said earlier, stereotypes are often born from some sort of truth. As I said before, it really does not matter if this is actually true so long as the perception is there. For the whites that are none of those stereotypical things, then woe to those who make the mistake of believing them to be. There is also a perception that many white gang members are wannabees. I was speaking of these individuals earlier concerning those who want so desperately to fit in. I think this perception comes from both white and minority America. There is another perception that the wannabees are not, or cannot be that big of a problem. This is important. I believe that there are two groups of people that from a gang violence standpoint should be worried about the most from society. The first group would be the individuals that are considered by those in their respective gangs to be the truest of the true. It does not matter what race they are, every gang has those few members that are viewed as "crazy." Crazy in the sense that they often are known to commit heinous acts of violence with the smallest of provocations.

These are the individuals that will die for in a second, their colors. Most gangs have members that will die for their colors if the circumstances are right or will kill if they are provoked, but I am not speaking of them at this point in time. I am speaking of those that need no provocation but rather only need to *see* a rival gang member before they try and kill them. They do not do it for the accolades but rather because they are pure killers. Their numbers are small I believe, though I am sure most in society would not agree with me on this. Of course all gang members can inflict great harm upon this country, but the reality is that some are more dangerous than others.

The second most dangerous group, and this may come as a surprise, are certain white wannabees that have the desire to fit in on a disease like level. These are the individuals who will do anything to fit in. I would love to see the statistics if there were any, concerning the murder rate for whites trying to fit in with a minority gang. I guarantee that these numbers would shock everyone, most of all, the entire gang world I think. The lengths people will go to fit in are nothing short of extreme.

I am sure regardless of race, that most everyone has on some level done things to be accepted by a friend or peer group. You may not even know that you are doing something to be accepted, but this is the way of the world. Humans wish to be accepted by other humans. What have you done to be accepted by a friend or group? Stole? Made fun of someone? Drank one too many beers? This doesn't only apply with negative things either. You might have gotten really good grades to fit in with your "smart" friends. There are countless scenarios this applies to. Some people have a larger desire to fit in than others. Some have a need on an addictive level. I think back to the hundreds of teenager cast movies set in school that details the power of the "in crowd." There are those who want so desperately to be a part of the in crowd and will do outrageously cruel things to "fit in" with them. There is a reason so many movies are based on this premise; because it is reality.

Concerning whites who want to join a minority gang, think about it in this way; there is a perception that whites are weak, and whites know this as well. The gang culture is rampant with machismo. There is this need to prove how tough you are. There are a few ways to accomplish this, but the "easiest" and quickest way to show how tough one might be is by a showing of violence. Violence reigns supreme bar none. Whites know this as well. There is another term known to those in the criminal world, and that term is a "send-off." For those of you who do not know what this means, I will define it as simply as I can. Let's say you have a group of six teenage boys. They are all pretty good friends. It does not matter what race any of them are because all races have send offs. There is one teenager that is kind of like a tag along. He is not that bad, but he is certainly not looked at like the other six teenagers. He is usually the brunt of many jokes but he laughs because he wants to fit in with them. They are all hanging out one night but do not have any money to buy any alcohol. They are not of legal age but have in the past gotten an adult to purchase the alcohol so long as they have the money. They cannot find an adult however so they come up with an alternative plan. The liquor store has an older cashier and there is beer very close to the exit. The group of six does not want to take the chance of getting caught stealing the beer so they ask the "tag-a-long" to go and steal it. He does and the rest of them give him the accolades he so readily was willing to break the law for. In some instances, the "tag-a-long" will eventually become a part of the crew, sometimes not. Up until that point however, he will get "sent off" to do things no one else is willing to do.

This same philosophy applies to many young gang members of all races. I am not trying to imply that all white gang members are send offs either, but rather that I have witnessed more white send offs than that of any other race. This is what makes them so dangerous however, because as I said, they know that the quickest way to get respect is with a showing of violence on a large scale. There is some irony to this whole situation. Many minorities feel that they have to work twice as hard in the work place to receive the same respect and pay as the white male. In gangland, the very opposite is true. The white male has to be twice as violent to earn the same respect as minorities, at least in gangs that are comprised predominantly with minorities. The universe has odd ways of trying to balance itself out. I just wish it were done in more positive ways.

Alright, let's say that a gang gets shot at by a rival gang. The worse the injury, the harsher the retaliation. When this happens, the air is often dripping with testosterone and the desire for some to earn their stripes so to speak is clearly apparent. A few things can take place depending on the psyche of the organization/gang that was shot at. If they are particularly ruthless, then very little "chest pounding" and/or "talking" will take place. They did not become ruthless for simply being all bark with no bite. People will take it upon themselves to retaliate. Repercussions or consequences make little difference to them. For other gangs whom are a little less impulsively retaliatory in nature, there might be a pause before someone steps up and offers to "take care of business." This is where the white wannabee will often step up and posture aggressively. He won't necessarily do so out of bravery, loyalty, or "trueness", but rather because he knows that he needs to wield twice as much violence to be given the same amount of respect. He understands that this is an opportunity to reap the rewards of what he thinks he wants; acceptance/respect. Unfortunately it often comes at the expense of life, the birth of a victim. Yes indeed, these wannabees are fathers many times over in the context of creating victims to fit in.

It amazes me that no one really notices this. White America doesn't really want to admit/believe that they are contributing to so much serious gang violence. Minorities in gangland do not want to acknowledge that a huge number of "rival" gang members are killed at the hands of these so called wannabee white boys. It's interesting; in gangland there is also a hierarchy as in almost all walks of life. At the very top are the heads of each mega organization. Below them come those who have sacrificed their "free" lives for the benefit of the organization, usually via murder. If you are white however, there is almost an asterisk next to one's name. It comes as just a little reminder, the smallest of slights. One last implication that the white person who committed murder did so only out of fear or the desire to fit in. Let's say that this *is* true. The sad and forgotten part is that via whatever means the white victimizer took a life, their victim doesn't become any less of a victim because of motive.

Do you think it makes one bit of difference to he who lies in a pool of blood, what race the individual that pulled the trigger was? Are they any less dead because the bullets came from the gun held by the hands of a white wannabee gang banger? Do their bullets somehow make smaller holes when they enter the body because they were fired only with the desire to "fit in"? It baffles me that white males are essentially given a pass by society and are not held as accountable as minorities are for the violence that they wreak upon society. This sect of white males contributes hugely to the amount of victims that die as a result of gang violence. Very little is offered in the way of prevention to these white males who so desperately need to fit in because no one thinks that they are that much of a problem. Society feels that funds can better be allocated elsewhere perhaps.

The next words I would like you to read come from a white male that I met shortly before I was transferred from a maximum security prison to a medium security prison. As I have stated before, I wanted to show perspectives from different backgrounds. He would be considered by many as being one of those "rich white boys" you see represented in movies as having a huge desire to be accepted by others.

"My name is Timothy but everyone calls me "Tim-Tim." I am 28 years old. I was talking with Adam (me) one day about some past war stories. This particular story was about a time when I pistol whipped a dope fiend. Out of the blue, Adam asked me if telling him this story made me feel as though I was "cool." I asked him what did he mean, and I will be honest, I could feel myself getting a little pissed off. He bluntly said did pistol whipping a dope fiend make you feel cool? I didn't really know what to think. I kind of felt like he was disrespecting me. I was asked to be honest in writing this for Adam. I wanted to punch him for asking me that! Before I could tell him what I felt, he said just think about it and come holler at him later. He walked away. A couple days went by and I saw Adam in the gym. He didn't say anything to me and I didn't say anything to him. It got me thinking, what the hell did he ask me that question for? Finally I couldn't take it anymore, so I asked him why he asked me that question. He said he noticed that I always had new shoes, new clothes, plenty of commissary, so he assumed that I had money. He said he knew I was in a gang and wondered why someone who had money joined a gang.

I guess I had never thought about it before. I kinda just lived life to the fullest and did what I wanted. Adam asked if I would think about why I joined a gang and put pencil to paper. At first I was like what's he on? Is he the police? He told me I was free to think whatever I wanted about him, but all he was trying to do was keep kids out of gangs.

You know, I am what I am and I can't imagine not being what I am. Maybe one day I'll leave this life alone but I still don't want my younger brother to be like me. So I told Adam I would give him a short version of my life. I hope it helps.

Like I said, I'm 28 years old and I have been a gang member for 12 years. I grew up down south in the suburbs as you would call it. I was a spoiled kid when I was little. I mean we were not millionaires but we were close. I lived with my mom, dad, little brother and older sister. My pops worked for an oil company. He was gone for months at a time doing I don't know. All he cared about was work. When he would come home for a week or two here and there, it was like he didn't belong there. At first it really didn't bother me, but my sister hated him or so she said. She sure acted like it. I could tell my moms wasn't happy. I feel bad for this, but I started actin out getting into trouble at school. I got caught stealing like 5 or 6 times. But we always had a good lawyer and so nothing really happened to me. I could tell my moms was hurting and it wasn't like I was trying to hurt her but I just didn't care about anything at the time.

My grades were so so, not good or bad. If I didn't skip school so much I probably would have gotten pretty good grades, I wasn't stupid. I hated school but the ladies were nice. I was kinda like the bad boy of the school. It was a really good school. My friends looked up to me because I was always fighting everyone. I wasn't afraid of no one. I got suspended 5 times for fighting.

All the ladies wanted to party with me and my boys. I started messin with pills at around 14. Sometimes I didn't even know what they were. I had a lot of pills, but I wanted more so I started selling them to buy more. I was 16 now and it was just pills at first then weed then X. I got robbed a few months into it, but like I said, I had money so it was no big deal to me. My moms and pops got divorced around this time. I was never home anymore so I didn't care. I still had little run-ins with the police but only did a day or two here and there. It's crazy how the ladies wanted me even more because I was going to jail and shit.

My mom said she was moving up north and we were going with her cause pops was never there. I didn't want to move especially to Wisconsin where I didn't know anyone. If it wasn't for my sister I would have ran away. She was always a goody goody. Still is today. She told me that her and moms needed me so I said the hell with it. We moved to Oak Creek Wisconsin. It was a nice neighborhood. Pops was paying lots in child support. I turned 17 and was going to high school it was different down south. Everything was different. The school wasn't as good. I liked it better because I got away with more shit. I wasn't the bad kid anymore. I was like everyone else as far as getting into drama. I was still sellin X but I started to have to carry a gun. When I went to school I just left it in my whip. (Car) I started kickin it with a few O.A.'s. There were some gangs I had heard of that were the same down south, but a lot were different that I never heard of.

It was pretty soon before I was doing everything they were. The only real difference was that that I didn't have any tattoos and I wasn't true yet. My car got shot up one day by some Kings when we went to Milwaukee. I figured what the hell, everyone thinks I was an O.A. anyway, I may as well join. That's just what I did.

I never really thought about my life and how I ended up a gang member. This is just a real short story about a few things that I thought were important. I read it back to myself and I felt like I should definitely have made some better choices in my life. I think about what Adam asked me, if I felt cool. I guess I did feel pretty cool. I don't know what that says about me or how this helps, but I really did feel cool.

This was just one example from a white male that was raised in a better than average home from an income standpoint. Again, no two people are the same; however I do think that there are some things that "Tim Tim" said that stood out to me. The first thing that I noticed was the relationship he had with his father. He technically had a father in his life growing up, unlike so many other gang members that I have interviewed. I say technically however because while his father *lived* at home, Tim Tim said that he was rarely *at* home. This appeared to create some resentment towards his father though he didn't come right out and say so. I won't go so far as to say that Tim Tim's rebellion was directly related to this because I don't have enough information about him, but I do think it was possible. It very well could have played some sort of role, but I don't know how much because I am sure there are things that transpired that Tim Tim didn't speak of. Another thing that Tim Tim spoke on that stood out to me was how his "bad boy" image in his first school sort of almost justified his acting out, at least in his mind. Most notably he was "rewarded" by the females in his school that thought he was more attractive because of his rebellious nature. I include myself in this next sentence. Boys are really stupid are they/we not? When it comes to impressing females, there are really no lengths that won't be explored to be successful.

Along these lines, I've wondered what role females have had on males joining gangs and committing gang violence. I am positive that there is a larger correlation than people think. I will be completely blunt. Many of the females that I knew who associated with gang members or were gang members were extremely beautiful. I wonder what would happen if all of the females in society made a point to never date a gang member again. Obviously it would never happen, but it is an interesting concept is it not? What *would* happen do you think? Would gang members lose their "mystique", their allure of leading a rebellious life that attracts so many beautiful women? It would be an interesting embargo. I believe as crazy as it sounds, it could have a huge impact on future men who are contemplating gang membership. After all, if females no longer dated gang members, who would gang members have to impress with masculine bravado?

I would say that Tim Tim's words definitely give credence to the philosophy of wanting to fit in. Only he knows if he did what he did to fit in, but it seems to me that he wanted to fit in with the O.A.'s in his new school. I suppose no one wants to admit that they are a follower, and most would equate wanting to fit in with following. Maybe they are one and the same, I don't know. I think there are similarities as well as differences. I believe we as human beings subconsciously desire to be liked by our fellow man. No one *wants* to be disliked, correct? Out of this will to be liked, this desire to feel as though we have the ability to impress another by our own actions comes the opportunity to do so. These opportunities can be via appearing smart with winning the Nobel Peace Prize, or by getting a couple of laughs at the expense of a bullying some poor kid who will probably be the one receiving that Nobel Peace Prize one day.

We all have the desire to "fit in." Our morals and values will dictate to whom and by what lengths we are willing to go to fit in. Who we are and who we become in large part stems from our circumstances when we were young. Some circumstances create higher chances of becoming a gang member. Unfortunately we are not all created equal, at least as far as the circumstances we are born in to. It is the sad reality of life. Even more unfortunate is the fact that we as a country at one point self-segregated ourselves, creating the haves and have nots. Out of this; the gang problem was born. Race does in large part dictate the circumstances we are born into, and it is *those* circumstances that raise the likelihood of becoming a gang member, not the color of one's skin.

Chapter Seven

Poverty: the root of almost all evils

Many juveniles that join gangs have parents that are in lower tax brackets. A large percentage of these juveniles reside within the inner-city where there is an underfunded educational system and a high rate of poverty. The prospect of receiving a good education from many of these schools is not realistic, at least in the eyes of many who attend these schools. Juveniles are very materialistic in nature. Many only think about money and what money can buy them; jewelry, cars, clothes, etc. This is the case with both rich and poor, maybe even more so with the former.

Education is ruled out by many inner- city youths as a means to acquire what they want in life. This mindset comes from many different factors that I will elaborate later in this chapter, but essentially today's generation feels that they are entitled to certain things. Feeling entitled to something no matter what it may be, often creates an attitude of "We do not have to work for what we want." When I say "work", I mean school and other endeavors that require time and effort. Juveniles are not blind; they can see that there are those in one's neighborhood that have acquired money, fame, and females. They have not done so via an education and or a legitimate job either. They say to themselves, "I want what they have, how do I get what he has?"

I am positive that many people would not join a gang if it were "easy" to make money the legit way. This is absolutely not an excuse to join a gang, merely the reality of the situation. Within the inner city, drugs are often regulated by gang members, so for those that are searching for the easy way out, there is a clear path. A "way out" by the way, is also a very relative term.

Even if one has their own drugs, you now have to find a place to sell them in order to make a profit. Most areas that have an abundance of drug addicts also have a high gang presence. If you are not associated with the particular gang that resides in that particular area, you can believe that you will not be selling your drugs there. The dope game is a very dirty game, one with very little to no rules. Gangs take very seriously, their particular area of drug-related income. Without this income, many gangs would simply vanish.

This isn't the case with only drug dealing, the same philosophy applies if your crime of fancy is stolen cars, guns, etc. You have to have connections in order to sell your merchandise, whether these connections are via street gangs, biker gangs, or organized crime, it makes no difference. It is always safer to have a group behind you when you are selling in a world without any rules. It keeps backstabbing to a minimum.

Topics and questions elaborated on in this chapter will include:

- o Why such poor communities?
- o How to earn a quick buck.
- o One thing can quickly lead to another.
- o Here comes the dope man!
- o Just another day in the "hood."
- o Is this life expected of inner city youth?
- o Why do gangs control so much of the drug world?
- o Greedy, greedy, greedy!
- o Comparing risk to profit, pushing the limit.
- o Looking ahead, well sort of.
- o No other way.
- o One-upmanship; such a deadly disease.
- o Why are we never content?
- o Get in where you fit in.
- o Accepting one's fate.
- o Safety in numbers.
- o Why is everyone always picking on me?

123456 **7** *8910*

*   *   *

I spoke a little bit about poverty in the last chapter. In fact, a few of the chapters I wrote about are related to poverty. I believe that gang members are essentially products that come off of our societal assembly line, with components being failing school systems, single-parent homes, violence in the community, and similar situated juveniles. As I said before; babies do not come from the womb with tattoos, nor do they wear bandanas and identifying gang colors.

In the last chapter, I spoke on Derrick Sanders being born in Gary, Indiana, the murder capital of the United States. While I believe his place of birth raised his odds of becoming a gang member, it does not guarantee that he become one. He had a choice, albeit a slim choice given the other circumstances he found himself in, but a choice never the less to make something of himself. His place of birth was but a single "ingredient" in becoming a gang member. You can look at in this way; to bake a cake you need flour, salt, eggs, sugar, baking powder, vanilla, and buttermilk. Separately they are mere ingredients, but *together* they make a cake, a *product*.

Poverty is an ingredient, just as butter is, but the final product is a gang member rather than a buttermilk cake.

Of the many former and active gang members that I interviewed for this book, there was one overwhelming answer to the most frequently asked question, "Why did you join a gang?" The answer most commonly given by police officers, psychologists, and the like is that kids join gangs because they are searching for another family. This plays a role, but much less of a role than people think. The true answer is much "simpler." Almost every individual whom I asked that question to stated they joined because everybody else was doing the same thing in their neighborhood. Nothing more, nothing less. Many in society will say that all gang members have a choice as to whether or not they join a gang. The lay person living in an upper-class neighborhood has every right to say that because there are very few if any true gangs in their communities. A child in their community does in fact have an *easy* choice as to whether or not join a gang. Many kids living within the inner-city have a choice as well, but the choice is not as easy as one might think.

To understand, you have to once again look at the totality of circumstances in your average inner-city neighborhood. Some of the elements include a very high crime rate, high gang crime rate, lowest educational funding rate, and level of poverty. Now take a twelve-year-old for example. He has no criminal record but lives in a single family household with his mother. He is "poor" and goes to a very underfunded school. He has bars over his windows and he hears gun shots every night. He has to walk to school every day but one morning on the way, he gets jumped for his jacket. He still goes to school but on the way home he gets jumped for his shoes. They beat him up pretty good because he tried to resist giving his attackers what they wanted. What is this kid to do? Call the police? And say what, that he was robbed? The police will tell him that he is lucky to be alive. If the police do look into the incident and arrest his attackers, they will not be in jail for too long. When they get out, what do you think that they are going to do to the little twelve-year-old that put them in jail? Another option might be to move to a better neighborhood you say? If they could they would but this costs money.

So what choice does he have? Keep getting beat up for his things? Is his only choice to join a gang and ask for protection, then becoming "friends" with the boys that are taking his things? If so, it is probably not long before he is the one jumping some thirteen-year-old for their shoes. It becomes survival of the fittest in a way. When you have a "choice" to live for a while you take it, consequences be dammed sometimes. It doesn't make it "right", but this is the reality for many young teenagers that live within the inner-city.

It is absolutely no surprise that with poverty there is crime. It seems like such an obvious statement, but have you ever really put any thought into why this is? It is more than the have-nots wanting to have what the "haves" have so to speak. I believe it goes much deeper than that, down to the psyche of young people born into poverty. Earlier I called poverty a societal ill, a disease. Poverty is a disease that resides in the heart and soul rather than the flesh. I am sure at some point you have heard that in order to love someone else, you have to first love yourself. There is so much truth to this seemingly simple statement. It applies to so many different situations in life, but most choose to apply it solely to relationships we have with our mates. It applies to that as well, but more so I believe in how we interact with the world.

This is a really odd way of describing poverty, but I feel it is almost akin to being a cold sore on one's soul. When people get a cold sore, they are unbelievably self-conscious. Their self-esteem drops significantly and sometimes do not even want to have contact with anyone because of the shame they feel from being seen with a cold sore. For those born into poverty; I think a similar shame exists but upon the soul, the psyche. The unfortunate aspect is that many do not even realize they feel this shame, this lessening of human value in a way. When we are ill, we as humans often try and find a way to cope. I think this is normal behavior. One way to cope with poverty is to acquire what you think will remove you from the status of poverty. There are multiple ways of doing this; getting a good education and a career to remove oneself from poverty is one way. Another way is to take what you want. It is the entitlement mentality that allows people to take what they want with little regard as to who is hurt *by* their taking.

From very early on "it" starts. By it, I am referring to the symptoms of the poverty virus and the subsequent mentalities that it creates. Children can be so cute, so nice and innocent but so unbelievably cruel as well. At this stage I believe it has more to do with the parents than anything else with how they have raised their child thus far. As children age, one seemingly trivial aspect concerns what they wear to school. I say seemingly because it should not matter what a child wears to school but as we all know, it very much matters. The clothes and shoes a child wears to school should make no difference in how they are treated by classmates but the world does not work this way. For example, if you send a poor kid to a very posh school, it will likely be brutal for them because he/she will stick out like a sore thumb via their attire. They are likely to be ridiculed and bullied. What do you think will happen to their self-esteem, their self-worth? Will it increase or stay the same?

I wonder how many suicides have been attempted and carried out because of the constant ridiculing from other classmates. Think how bad some of these children must feel to contemplate suicide as a result of being bullied. This is how cruel children can be and so often it can begin because a classmate cannot afford a new pair of shoes or is forced to wear hand me down clothes. Who knew that cotton and denim could have such an impact on today's youth? Suicide is in fact, an extreme reaction to being bullied for the teasing one may get for wearing old clothes and shoes but I think it happens more than people care to admit. Beyond that, I think it starts from the clothes one wears and migrates to other areas. The clothes are essentially a gateway to other means of ridiculing. The clothes simply place a target on their back. They are an easy mark for other situations like if something gets stolen. Who will be the first person to be blamed do you think? If someone silently farts in class, surely the richer kids didn't do it, so it must be the poor kid because they have less sophisticated manners right? Again, these seem like such small and trivial matters to an adult, but I ask that you recall when you were back in school. How important was it to not be the lowest on the totem pole so to speak? Of course these issues seem petty and juvenile to us as adults, but to your average sixth grader just trying to fit in, is there anything more important?

I remember a kid when I was in fourth grade that had big glasses and didn't have the same clothes many of the other students had. Let me be clear, I definitely did not go to a posh school. It was a public school on a military base. Soldiers do not get paid that much in the Army. (*A disgraceful reality for the record.*) Very few kids wore Jordan's. (*Jordan's were the popular shoe of the day*) No one drove Mercedes or anything like that. I'm sure many of the parents were near or at the poverty level from a statistical standpoint. This one boy however, was worse off than most everyone else. He was picked on. I remember one day we were all at the bus stop and it had just snowed, so obviously we had to throw some snowballs at each other. The poorer kid wanted to fit in so he also threw a snowball and hit another student. He did not throw it hard or hurt her in any way, but her brother got mad and pushed him to the ground. I grabbed the guy and told him it looked like an accident, and it was as I think back. This did not matter though because of *who* threw the snowball. It surprised me that the brother got so upset because he was definitely not the bullying type. As I look back, it was solely due to the negative stigma that kid had because he came to school wearing really old clothes. He didn't deserve any of that ridicule, that psychological torture. I think it is torture by the way, I don't think you can call it anything other than that. How unbelievably horrible he and others like him must feel.

I raise this issue because I believe this takes a toll on the mentality of a child. Their self-esteem is not likely to be high. Their self-worth cannot be that much better. What do you think happens to them as they get older? On one extreme they will potentially become brilliant and be the CEO of a Fortune 500 company. On the other end of the spectrum they become like those in Columbine. The extremes in both are rare. What isn't rare however, are all of those kids that fall in the middle. It is them that so often turn to drugs, crime, and gangs. When children feel ostracized from the "in" crowd for whatever reason, what do they do? To whom do they gravitate towards? Others similarly situated? On many occasions yes, but of what character are those "others" similarly situated? I am again reminded of the words inscribed on the tablet in the hands of the statue of liberty that asks for the worlds huddled masses. Every school has that group of kids that are considered to be "bad" for all intents and purposes. These groups are different in different schools and areas of the country. In one school it may be the drug dealers who are considered to be the bad crowd, but in others areas it may be the "Gothic's" that are considered to be "bad" even though they don't break any laws. Didn't you always notice how the "bad" crowd was so willing to accept with open arms, our "huddled masses" from a social standpoint? I would assume that it must be difficult for an otherwise good kid who has been bullied all of their life to turn down the advancements of the bad crowd. I'm sure that in a way it might even come as a relief to know that "someone" will accept them *for* them.

With every group however, there is a psychological culture. Whether right or wrong, if you consider the contexts in which the societal outcasts were created, the culture will likely be one of negativity. Why would it not? Their culture was born out of ridicule, pain, violence, bullying etc. How can you expect them to suddenly erase all of those experiences? We take it for granted; the good times in school, the boyfriends and girlfriends, the parties and friendships.

Replace all of those memories with ones of loneliness, being bullied, hopelessness and despair. How would you turn out? Who would you be? This "culture" often turns into one anti-establishment in nature, with the establishment being the popular crowd. Now that they are more than just themselves, sometimes that same bullying is repaid in kind. Out of this rebellion is born, from other kids at first but then turning to parents and other authority type figures that end up punishing them for much of what they do.

There is a sense of comradeship, of bonding. There is no desire to bond over a board game or playing basketball in the park. They feel the need to push the envelope and out of this comes criminal behavior. It may start out "small" with graffiti or vandalism but can quickly escalate into something much worse. Drugs usually come into play because drugs have been taught to them to be as American as apple pie for the societal outcasts of the world. From drugs come more serious crimes out of addiction. If addiction isn't an issue there are still other problems that arise. Social skills will not be up to par for one. Work ethic will not be very good. All of these elements will take their toll mentally. Happiness will slowly become a mirage. A "wasted" life born out of the ridicule one got because they could not afford "cool" clothes and shoes. This is an example of poverty at its finest, so easily able to rape the future potential from our youth.

The prior few pages concerned what might happen if you take a child born into poverty and send them to an upper tax bracket school, a "better" school. Again, will all poor kids that are sent to a rich school end up like this? Of course not, but I just wanted to show how a simple pair of hand me down shoes can affect a poor kids life. I don't think that scenario was that far-fetched, either. Gang involvement can arise out of these situations as well; it all depends on the social status of gangs in that particular area. In some areas, gangs are not looked at by other kids as residing on the bottom of the social ladder. I wanted to show how poverty can affect the emotional aspect of one's self value.

Now I will turn to entire communities that live in poverty because that same sort of psychological self-devaluation takes place, often times with the children being none the wiser. You may think that in a school where everyone is considered to be living in poverty, that there wouldn't be the cliques of popular and unpopular from a designer clothing aspect. You would be wrong. There will always be some sort of hierarchy. It does not matter if one's parents make a million-plus or are way below the poverty level. Children will find a way to create status. I've often wondered why this is. Is this learned behavior or is it innate? From what I can remember, it really starts pretty early on. My first memories of being conscious of a social status came when I was in second grade. That seems insanely young to me as I write this, but it was the age I noticed that we as kids were not looked upon as equals. I also cannot help but remember the movie, "Lord of the Flies." This was a masterful movie, albeit in a horrific manner. As I remember more and more of it as I think back, it goes hand in hand with what I have been speaking about so far in this chapter. The premise is about as bizarre as many of my scenarios, but makes sense if you look at them from a different angle. They make you think if nothing else. I think that while the behavior in the Lord of the flies is extreme, I don't know that it is all that unbelievable. It goes to show that when we as humans have "nothing", we will always find a way to posture ourselves above or below someone else.

It's ironic, around the time I was writing this page; I was having a conversation with two individuals about softball. In this particular prison, softball is taken very seriously. When you don't have much, you tend to take very seriously the things you are allowed to do. There are over two-thousand inmates in this prison with three softball fields. Each summer there are about twenty teams created and a season is held with playoffs and a championship. This year I was fortunate enough to be on the preseason number one team along with one of the two individuals I was conversing with. The other guy admittedly said that he sucks at softball but enjoys it. He wanted to find other players that also weren't considered to be the "best" players but loved to play just like he did, and wanted simply to have fun. They knew they would get destroyed in every game but didn't mind so long as they were having fun playing. The other member of my team said that this was impossible because even if you have a team with players who start off saying they admittedly are not good, as the season progresses; there will be players who will think that they are better than others on the team. There will be those that say they can throw harder, run faster, and hit harder and turn their nose up at you if you mess up. He is absolutely right. I have seen it each of the years that I have played softball. There are always a couple of teams that everyone knows will be very bad. At the beginning of the season they seem to have fun even though they are getting destroyed on the scoreboard. Things change however as the season goes on and usually things come to a head when they find themselves in a close game. Someone will mess up and it will cost them the game. It is amazing to see them turn on one another. They know they had pretty much zero chance of winning the game, so why get mad when someone messes up when the game got closer than anyone thought? What does it matter? It baffled me but then I thought about it. It matters not that they didn't have a chance, but rather only made me understand that when you have nothing you are likely to grasp at straws so to speak.

If you are wondering why on earth am I speaking of softball, I'll explain. Poverty in most people's minds, relates to a lack of money and material things. Poverty is simply a lack of *something*, and while yes it is used primarily to define income levels, the word can also be applied to other situations. In the softball scenario, the "something lacking" was talent. There are some teams that will completely admit they are without enough talent to win a championship, but play anyway. Strictly from a talent standpoint, they are all similarly situated and it matters not whether they were born un-athletic, never practiced softball, or never even played softball until now. When that team sets foot on the field, they are all lacking talent. This is life and as life would have it, people begin to realize that they no longer want to live in poverty (*Lack talent*) with everyone else. The reasons for this desire will differ for different people. What happens when there is a desire to free oneself from *poverty*? A few things, with one of them being practice. I have seen individuals on horrible teams come out and practice hard every single day. They put in the work to become a better softball player, a *talented* player. They are akin to those born into poverty from a financial standpoint that go to school, skip parties, refuse drugs, and don't join gangs. They go to college and become successful, both financially and emotionally. They put in the work to pull themselves out of the grasp of poverties grip. It is not easy, but it is very possible. In fact, I think the strongest people on earth were those born into hardship but subsequently struggled to greatness.

Back to those in softball that no longer want to exist in "talent poverty" but are not willing to put in the work to practice; some will become vocally negative to their own teammates. They will put them down, not solely to make themselves feel better, but also to make themselves look better to the crowd. Sometimes I wonder for which reasons they do it more. I believe if they feel others "think" that they are better than other members of their team, it will somehow increase their own perceived self-worth, or talent. It is a false sense of talent however. The crazy aspect is that sometimes it works for a while. I have seen situations where an individual on a team who isn't that good keeps puffing his chest out, talking about how good he is, and who always lets his teammates know if they mess up. For a time, the perceived reality is that *"this guy can play."* What is even more interesting is when you add the social aspect into the equation. Just as in any walk of life, there is a hierarchy within the prison system. In fact, prison hierarchy is magnified to ridiculous levels. Essentially from a crime standpoint, child killers/molesters are at the bottom of the social scale. Non-sexual murderers rank the highest, in competition with certain gang leaders. Others near the top are those that act very aggressively towards other inmates and who can fight well. They simply *take* their respect or level of hierarchy. Here is a scenario; take a child molester and gang member and place them on the same bad softball team. Let's say that the child molester becomes a better softball player, but the gang member no longer wants to live in "talent poverty" but does not want to put in the work of practicing to get better. He chooses to verbally bash the child molester whenever he makes a mistake. The child molester really cannot say anything because social etiquette prevents him from doing so because he knows that he is in a no win situation based upon his crime. People on other teams and the crowd begin to "believe" that the gang member has more talent than the child molester but in reality it is nothing more than a mirage. This mirage manifests itself over the course of the season when the gang member clearly sucks and is clearly less talented than the child molester. The insanity of the situation comes from everyone knowing that the child molester is a far better player, but refuses to admit it simply because he is a child molester.

The gang member in this scenario is akin to someone being born into financial poverty who attempts to rise above poverty by less than productive means. I say attempt because while they may make money to nullify technically their financial status of poverty, the means are often criminal. Their status of no longer living in poverty is also a mirage, a perceived reality both physically and emotionally. Remember, my reasons for these scenarios in the beginning of this chapter were to show the emotional impact of poverty. Obviously the physical aspects of poverty are enormous as well, like being unable to pay rent, or purchase food and medicine. The physical has the ability to affect us emotionally. In many ways, what actually ends up hurting those affected the most are the consequences suffered from the lengths they will go to free themselves from poverty. It does not matter from what lengths are in question; they all have impacts in some way or another. Whether people sell drugs, prostitute themselves, rob or murder to "rise" above poverty, they never really raise above the feelings within that poverty leaves behind. These scars can never heal when one takes the negative route because while you may be able to "trick" society into believing that you are not living in poverty, eventually that perceived reality dissolves into the bitter clarity of true reality. All of this is important in regards to this book because often times drug dealers, robbers, murderers, and prostitutes all maneuver in the same world as gang members.

I have spoken many times about desensitization and it once again makes an appearance in this chapter as well. In the poorest communities there is often a high rate of drug use, robbery, murder, prostitution, and other violent crime. Why is this do you think? It does not matter what the particular race of people are whom live in these communities. It may be a trailer park consisting primarily of white people, or the inner city where there are many minorities that comprise the population. It really does not make any difference.

We cannot change the past, and I spoke upon why certain communities became poverty ridden in the earlier stages of their development. As harsh as it sounds, "how" they became impoverished really does not matter any longer. It will matter in terms of ensuring that it does not happen again. The sad reality is that many communities are living in poverty. When a child is born into one of these communities, they see with their own eyes what poverty creates. This can come out of being hungry because there isn't enough money to buy food, or via seeing a woman dressed like a prostitute standing on their street corner. These feelings and observations begin to become the "norm" unfortunately. This does not mean that they are "alright" with what they see and feel, but just as I gave the example of smoking a cigarette for the first time, the more you do it the easier it becomes. The more one witnesses certain things, the less affect they will have on you.

As I have stated, a culture is born out of this. There is always a culture, no matter the people, the race, or income level of residents living within a community. For instance, in privileged communities where children grow up with nannies, chauffeurs, butlers etc., do you think these children are unaffected by what they witness? Personally I think that the culture formed from super privileged communities is almost as destructive as some of the cultures created by poor communities. Just as I said that many people who live in poverty have that entitlement mentality because they were born in a poor community, many rich people have an even greater sense of entitlement for what they were born into. It is interesting to me how both rich and poor can believe that they are entitled to something. The world is an odd place. Sometimes I think we pretty much suck in regards to being the so called "superior intelligence." I wonder if animals laugh at us when we deem ourselves this. I always try and keep in mind that the world is exactly as it should be considering how we have evolved. There really is no "rule book" in how we should go through life. We are kind of just winging it are we not? We exist on a rock of a planet that has provided us with enough resources to exist, and the mind/intelligence to know what to do with those resources. That's really it if you think about it. Some believe that the Bible and or other religious texts are the roadmaps to become who we were intended to become, but if everyone is using a slightly different instruction manual, the "instruction" manual becomes somewhat counterproductive does it not? It would be like getting your first computer but the instruction manual is in a different language. The computer can make your life so much easier, but if the instructions are in a foreign tongue, what are you to do? Trial and error I suppose.

I don't know, sometimes I get so bogged down in wondering why things are the way that they are, that it seems hopelessly impossible to make things better. Certain problems are on such massive scales that sometimes it seems far easier to just start from scratch. The collapse of civilization seems inevitable at times to me. I think of what I learned in school about various empires throughout history; they seemed so massive and powerful yet eventually crumbled due to their own enormity. Why could that not happen again? What have we really learned since then? Everything is on a larger scale. I think back to all of those doomsday movies I have seen and cannot convince myself that they aren't in some ways, prophetic. I am not speaking of asteroids or other natural disasters, but rather about world war being the vehicle of destruction. I think people forget that the last world war was only seventy years ago. It makes no difference whether the next war is over race, income, religion etc. It seems inevitable because it appears that we have never really learned the very first thing taught to us by our parents; *how to play nice with others*. Such a seemingly trivial lesson first given to us in the sandbox or on a swing set. Maybe that first lesson was the most important lesson of all. Perhaps that was the foundation to learning everything else. You can look at it like your first day in math class, you have to learn how to count before you can add or subtract. Learning to count seems so trivial, yet you are unable to do so much more without first learning to do so. Playing nice with others seems so trite and trivial as well, and perhaps it works the same way. Because we never really learned how to do so, perhaps we are doomed from being able to do anything else.

I believe that parenting plays the ultimate role in this and from a poverty standpoint; there is almost an immediate disadvantage due to the number of single-parent households in this country. It is tough to ultimately instill great values in a child when there are two parents, a decent income, a great school system, and good community. Magnify that toughness by a factor of who knows how much when you take away one parent, drop the income level below poverty, add a failing school system, and live in the most violent communities within this country. The disadvantages for these children are instantaneous upon birth. I know numerous strong single mothers, but know even more people that come from very bad single-parent households. It is not so much that these households consist of bad parents, but rather that they are unable to parent due to a lack of time. Common sense would dictate that if there is but one parent, they will have to work sometimes two and three jobs to pay the bills. When they are constantly working, do they have the time to parent in the verbal sense? It is a horrible situation. I suppose in that regard, a parent who brings a child into that situation knowing that they cannot support them could be considered a bad parent by default. I'm sure that may anger some parents, but is this not the truth? If one cannot even support themselves, why then bring a child into this world? Should that be a crime? I don't know how you could punish those convicted of that crime without also punishing the child that was brought into this world by that parent. What magnifies the problem even more is the fact that many single mothers have multiple children. How is bringing five children into this world with no job not a form of child abuse? These kids don't even get a fair chance.

For the record, I will never shy away from pointing the finger directly at myself if I contributed or am contributing to a particular problem. I had a child at fourteen years of age. I had no job, and in fact received a life sentence at the age of fifteen. What do you think that makes me? A horrible father!!!!! I cannot even call myself a father when you get right down to it. Yes I write, get visits, and talk to my son on the phone, but those small portions of time are insignificant compared to what he needs from his father. My actions at the age of fifteen from a criminal aspect aside, are disgusting considering what I did to my son and his mother simply by coming to prison and essentially abandoning them when they needed me most. It does not matter to them that I wanted to be with them, when my actions as a gang banger dictated that I wanted to come to prison. My actions superseded my wants. I do not run from blame.

There is such a huge debate over whether or not to have sexual education taught in our schools. While it is true that teen pregnancy has steadily declined from the levels it was at in the eighties, it is still far too high. Teenagers are still getting pregnant, but it seems that they are just a little bit older. At first glance you would think that sexual education would have nothing to do with the gang problem but if you take a closer look I'm sure you might be surprised. Considering the number of teen parents that have children who have become gang members, there is a clear correlation between teen pregnancy, single-parent households, and gang membership. I will state it again, so many gang members that I have met come from single-parent households in which their mother or father was a teenager them self. This evolves directly from teenagers being unprepared to consider the consequences of pregnancy. Is the correlation not obvious?

If you take household after household with this same mentality and create an entire community full of single-parent households, where then are all of the positive male role models to instill the values in their sons? You have a community of essentially parentless kids. Many children are going to get in some sort of mischief purely from a curiosity standpoint. I don't care if they are an Honor Roll student or Boy Scout, you will get into something here and there. What makes the situation dire in communities suffering from poverty is what comes with those communities. Drugs, prostitution, robbery, crime, and gangs are all alive and well within these communities. There are no grassy yards to play in, only broken bottles and abandoned houses. Can you honestly tell me that this does not take a toll on these children's psyche? Here is an easy way of looking at the situation. How do you feel when you get a new pair of shoes or a new outfit? It is "just clothing", and yet it has the power to make you feel a little better about yourself correct? You feel an added little pep in your step right, a little more confidence perhaps? Where was that pep with your old shoes, your old clothes? Odds are you didn't even notice that this "pep" wasn't there until you put on your new attire. Transfer that same mentality over to your community, your home. How would you feel coming home to a rundown home with no lawn compared to a six figure home within a gated community? That nice new home with the manicured lawn is akin to that new pair of shoes, that new outfit.

Now look down the street at all of your neighbors' homes and they are as run down as yours. Some have bars over the windows; some have boards over windows that have been shot out.

There are no lawns, but rather patches of dirt. Do you not think witnessing this does not subconsciously affect the mind of a five, six, seven, or eight-year-old as they grow up? That same *lack* of a "pep in one's step" that is never noticed until you put on a new pair of shoes, is similar to the feelings one might not know they are experiencing until they were able to move into a better environment. Yes, it's true that not everyone can be born into a home within a nice neighborhood and this is exactly my point. Very few are born into privileged environments. They are called the 1% for a reason. We are the other 99%, some less fortunate than others.

As I said before, it is absolutely no excuse to join a gang simply because one may be born into a poor community, so I hope that it does not appear that I am saying so. I am merely stating various factors in which juveniles find themselves in a situation where they feel joining a gang is a "way out." Whether that way out is perceived or not, makes little difference. The point I am attempting to make is that something is terribly wrong with this country, with certain communities if a child honestly looks at gang membership as a way out. Perhaps it is to late for many of those who have already tried their "way out", but we need to look at why it gets to that point in order to eliminate one of the many elements that leads kids to gangs. In this particular instance I am referring to poverty. All we can do is tackle each of these issue one at a time. It will at first look like we are making no progress until we can begin eliminating most of the issues that contribute to juvenile gang membership, but we cannot eliminate two issues without first eliminating one.

It is clear that the children who are born into poverty are at an immediate disadvantage, both from how it affects them internally and how it affects them physically. They are quickly going to realize that they are a member of the have nots. No one wants to be a member of this group. It may be at a young age that they realize it by not having any of the toys they see on TV or being hungry at school because they did not eat dinner the night before. They may not have the best clothes, but here is where it gets interesting. In an earlier scenario I explained what can happen to a poor kid that is sent to a posh school because their clothes are inferior in looks. In schools where the entire class lives in poverty and very few have high end clothes, what do you think happens? Well, you will now understand why I raised the softball scenario. In that scenario, everyone had a lack of what? Talent. It didn't take long for teammates with that same lack of talent to criticize and put down their teammates so that they can trick themselves into believing they are less impoverished from a talent standpoint. Take that same concept and apply it to those living in poverty. For them, the lack of something is money and or material things. It matters not that no one has a lot of money (*Talent*). It will not be long before classmates (*Teammates*) start to pick on and bully others to raise their stock so to speak. What better way to get ahead than by walking over you? It is unfortunate but true. Kids can be vicious, especially if they already have the mindset of being a have not.

It's interesting to note however, that sometimes parents can have the reverse effect. Some of the best human beings that I have ever met in my life were poor when they were kids. They were not mean; they were not bullies then or now. They did not have that woe is me mentality. In fact, they never took anything for granted. Everything was/is a blessing to them. I've always wondered why that was, and the only real common factor that I saw was that the majority of them had in their own words, great parents. Yes plural, parents with an s. They had great values instilled in them. That type of parenting seems to be almost a lost art form when you take a look at how some of these children are raised today. It makes no difference whether you are rich or poor. Children of today are clearly less respectful, less hard working, meaner, and have far more of an entitlement attitude than ever before. The only real difference between rich and poor that I see is that rich kids have more safety nets to catch them when they fall. When the rich rebel, they are not doing so in communities where murder is merely a phantom statistic or something seen on TV. If the rich kids who rebel were living in communities rampant with gang violence, I guarantee that many more rich kids would be joining gangs. Money isn't the cure all, but it sure can make a difference. Remember, all of what is taking place today will have a compounding effect. It will get worse for at least another generation for sure, two if we are not vigilant. Earlier I spoke on a child and how they view life when their father has abandoned them. They are often bitter and then they have kids. All of these woman that have four, five, and six, kids with different fathers that have never been involved in their lives, what is to become of them? They will most likely be born into poverty. Don't you think that this cycle will continue? Why would it *not* repeat itself? It is already repeating itself in this generation.

The economy is getting worse, so what makes you think that suddenly poverty will cease to exist? A study was just released from New York University that showed children born into a recession are more likely to do drugs and commit crimes than those born into a non-recessive economy. Poverty ridden communities are living in a constant recession. This study is speaking about exactly what I have been referring to in this book thus far.

There are so many more single mothers in America today. What do you suppose is going to happen to all of their young sons that are growing up without a father? What if they, like their fathers start having sex and create more fatherless children? Society is blind if they feel like the cycle will not repeat itself. It will, but the scale will be even larger. Think about that for a moment. The scale will be *so* much larger. I don't claim to have the ultimate answer. I don't think that there is an "ultimate" answer that will solve the poverty problem in this country. I can see however that if we continue on the course we are on, we will not want to imagine what this country will look like in twenty years.

Getting back to the children who grow up in poverty and who begin school; many factors come into play and together create ideal conditions for kids to believe that joining a gang is a way out. These factors might include not having money for decent clothes, having a single-parent, being unsupervised for extended periods of time, and growing up in a community with high crime rates. Any one of these elements for a child would be less than favorable, but imagine if you had to experience every one of them simultaneously. It is the perfect storm for gang membership. Remember Derrick Sanders? Remember who had the nice clothes and new cars? Gang members of course. Far too often these individuals become almost idolized by youth in their communities. These individuals seemingly posses everything that everyone else wants; money, jewelry, fancy cars, beautiful women, status, and power. This idolization begins at an early age and not necessarily for their material possessions, but rather from how everyone fawns over them, how everyone tries to emulate them. It should be pretty simple to understand how this happens when you break it all down. In any community, those who have managed to make money become somewhat popular. In the male centric society that we live in today, this usually means popular with women. This often makes other men jealous and or envious. Some wish to ride their coattails, some want to be like them, and some want to take what they have. Whatever the desire is for men and women, they are the topic of conversation. Children can see this, they are neither blind nor deaf when it comes to who older people are envious of. They notice when so and so comes around that everyone else seems to come around as well. Every neighborhood within the inner city has those few who are "getting money" in a major way by selling drugs. Kids take notice, though I don't know if they are conscious of how these individuals seem to have what no one else seems to have from a monetary standpoint. They learn as they age, but they are oblivious at first. I think they begin to understand when they are in elementary school.

While all of this is being processed in their brains, the issue of not having a father figure is taking its toll as well. There are a number of aspects to this issue alone, because while it is problem enough to deal with no father, there are other issues that arise by default from having no father in one's life. A major issue arises out of a lack of supervision. Children should not be alone at an early age. This would seem to be a "no brainer", but when you have a single mother that works two jobs and cannot afford day care, who do you think will take care of her children? When I was a teenager, I had many friends that had little brothers and sisters who were left alone at very young ages. I remember as a kid I had this fear of not being able to breathe. I hated the idea of not having any oxygen. I remember thinking to myself that for these kids left alone, what if they choked on a piece of candy or something? Who would save them?

Anyway, the lack of a parent, any parent usually a father, gives a child entirely too much time to learn about life on their own. Two parents can barely do the job at times, much less one which is never at home. For now, let's leave all of the emotional damage that is caused from this out of the equation. That in and of itself is damaging, but sadly is not the most dangerous aspect of the situation. Take a child and place them in a community that most adults do not feel safe driving through. They will most likely have friends that are similarly situated. As I said before, kids are curiously mischievous and as the saying goes, "idle hands are the devils workshop", or something like that. Religious connotations aside, the last thing young boys need is an abundance of unsupervised time in a neighborhood where breaking windows and vandalism are the least worrisome options. "Trouble" usually begins small, perhaps by throwing a rock through a window or stealing a Snickers candy bar from the local corner store. There is a small rush that comes from these things. Have you ever wondered why boys like to throw things through windows? There has to be something psychological to this because it does not matter what income level or what race one might be, because I think almost every boy has either thought about throwing something through a window or has actually done it. I suppose adults get somewhat of a rush when they do something wrong, but usually the "wrong" act isn't done solely for the rush, but rather for some other purpose. For a child throwing a rock through a window, they have no other motive other than curiosity and or the rush they get from doing this. Usually as we age, we *should* understand the consequences better of what our actions could bring. You wouldn't know this by the actions of some adults however.

It's interesting; at the time I was writing this page I have gone twelve years without getting into any trouble behind bars. From the ages of fifteen through nineteen, I accrued over sixty conduct reports. A conduct report is given to you when you break any one of a number of prison rules. A small infraction may consist of having too many photographs in one's cell. A major infraction might consist of battering another inmate. I spent years and years in the "hole" (*Solitary confinement*), so I thought the hole would never *scare* me because I had spent so much time there. Awhile back, it was a ninety-plus degree day outside and I cracked my cell door to allow some air to circulate in my cell. Most guards allowed this on hot days because it gets very hot in our cells because the building is made out of concrete. This is a medium security prison so the cells do not have bars for doors that allow air circulation; they are all closed door cells. One day a guard that never worked our unit worked and came by and slammed everyone's doors. He then wrote the entire unit "warnings" for having our doors cracked. A "warning" is one step below a conduct report. Some guards do not give warnings, some do. He was one of those officers that did not get along with inmates or other guards. I was so unbelievably worried about this "warning" because I have spent so many years doing what is right. I thought about what a "wuss" I had become because I had spent so many years in the hole for major violations. I never blinked an eye back then. In fact, I looked at it like badges of honor. Now it is clear to me that I am definitely not cut out for the criminal lifestyle because a simple warning from cracking my door terrified me. The "rush" is no longer worth it for me. It no longer satisfies anything within me. There have been other similar instances where I have come close to receiving a conduct report and then too I felt like I was going to have a panic attack. I suppose it taught me that I no longer felt comfortable breaking the rules. As a teenager however, I would not have given a second thought as to what worries me now.

I suppose in large part having a life sentence has essentially "scared me straight" so to speak. I know that if I am ever given a second chance at freedom, I cannot make a single mistake. It will be like walking on an eternal bed of egg shells. Knowing this is what made me understand the value of life, understanding that tomorrow is not guaranteed to any of us. Had I not been given a life sentence, I cannot say for sure how I would think today. I would like to imagine that I would eventually become who I am today but if I am to be honest, I doubt this would have transpired. I most likely would have continued doing the same illegal things for the rush of it. The rush for me didn't necessarily come solely from doing bad things per se. I rode dirt bikes, I climbed many a tall structure and jumped off of it like every young boy did/does, but eventually I needed more. I think back to the reckless things I did for a rush and wonder if my son does the same thing. The thought makes my heart want to stop. I don't know how I didn't paralyze myself. I recall these memories because many young boys have the desire for this same sort of rush. Some crave the rush more than others obviously. At first, these small stunts like jumping off of a second story house will quench that thirst. As with drugs and alcohol however, the more you do them the more you need to feel the effects of them. Pretty soon, the rush from throwing a rock through a window seems pretty boring. It isn't long before one needs to do something "bigger" to get that same rush throwing a rock through a window once gave.

I wonder if this could be considered an addiction of sorts. I can only speak for myself but I think I was addicted to "the rush" as it were. This is I'm sure going to sound somewhat sick, but it is the truth as to what I felt when I was a teenager. I first realized that I was addicted to "the rush" when I was shot at for the first time. Perhaps it was due to the unusual way that it occurred, but at the conclusion of it my heart was racing so unbelievably fast and I felt a sense of excitement. Not in a sexual way, just in a thrill sort of way. The shooting happened so suddenly that I don't think I had time to be or get scared. I was on the receiving end of other shootings or situations where someone wanted to take my life and fear definitely overwhelmed any feelings of excitement. Those situations were much slower in movement, giving my mind time to evaluate the danger that I was in and coming to the conclusion that I was in real trouble here. Concerning the first drive-by I was involved in. I along with about fifteen other gang members were sitting on a porch because it was raining. Suddenly a car screeched to a stop in front of the house and a teenager puts his hand out of the window and begins shooting at us. It lasted maybe two to three seconds and they pulled off. No one even had a chance to move or get out of the way because we were all so jammed onto the porch trying to stay dry. The odd part was that the shooter ended up hitting the house next door. To this day I do not understand how he could have been that bad of a shot. Perhaps he didn't want to hit anyone and was making it "look good" in front of his fellow gang members. It literally would have been like shooting fish in a barrel because there were so many gang members crammed onto that one porch. Had the house next door not had bullet holes in it, I would have thought he was shooting blanks.

Whatever the reasons, I felt a huge rush, a rush like I had never felt before. I had skirted the hands of death, brushed off the hands of the reapers Grimm. I think it gave me a false sense of arrogance/excitement that clearly set the bar impossibly high for what I would need to do to feel the rush the next time. For other young boys with a plethora of unsupervised time on their hands, it is no wonder they end up in very bad situations. Boys are curious by nature and so they explore. Within the inner-city, what do you think are some of the things they have to explore? Couple this with the fact that young boys are always seeking the approval of older boys in their community. They feel they need to make an impression and the older boys are always trying to show off a little bit anyway. It is the perfect storm once again. I'm sure to some extent; it must make one feel better about themselves to know that a younger person looks up to you, even if it is at the behest of one doing criminal activities.

As I stated earlier, many of the older boys within impoverished communities that are having money, have obtained it by less than Kosher means. Many are drug dealers, many others are gang members. Starting to see where I am headed? It is in them that the younger generation sees the means to a profitable end. It may start off innocent enough, and I have seen it begin many a time. An older gang member is thirsty but does not want to go to the store and buy himself a soda. A little young "up and comer" is asked to go and get it for him. He gladly runs off to the store and might even get to keep the change. It seems like something so insignificant—going to get a soda for someone. It is so much more than that however. There is a desire by the younger male to impress, or make happy the older gang member. It always starts off small. Before to long, going and getting a can of soda for "him" no longer makes the younger kid feel "cool" and turns into going and getting him a beer, or taking a hit on a joint. Anything to be accepted by those he looks up to. It's interesting because it seems as though it is a lose-lose situation when it gets to this point. Older kids can do two different things; on one hand they can tell the younger kid to beat it or to essentially not do what they are doing, sort of like a do as I say not as I do situation. The second option is that the older teenager takes the younger teen under his wing and "teaches him the ropes" so to speak.

Looking at the two options, on a surface level it would seem as though the first option would clearly be the best scenario if you had to pick one correct? The latter is obviously bad; it is just a matter of trying to determine how bad the situation will turn out. I say a lose-lose situation because when young boys are at the point of feeling they need to impress older boys, they simply are not going to "be good" because an older teen told them to. To the contrary, rebellion is another one of those things I describe as an entity like hate, bitterness, poverty, etc. Rebellion is a virus as well, and *IT* cares not whom the rebellion is *from.* Sometimes it can be a crux used in a positive fashion, such as a child that is constantly abused by his parents and vows to never be like them. They rebel against violence. Or take a child who has many siblings, all of whom break the law and are sent to prison. The younger sibling vows to never be like them and does so by refusing to hang out on the "block", not smoking marijuana or choosing not to drink. They rebel against all of the things the criminal life requires to live the criminal life. Those are the rare occasions when rebellion can be a good thing.

Unfortunately the bad variety, the self-destructive variety of rebellion is so much more common. I'm sure at some point we have all rebelled to some extent or another, most likely from our parents. Some of this rebellion has insignificant consequences, some have disastrous. What happens though, when a young boy at the age of fourteen feels he needs to rebel against an older gang member because the older gang member treats him like a child, tells him he cannot hang around him, or tells him to do as he says, not as he does? A variety of things can take place, the majority of them quite bad. One scenario is that the younger boy will transition back towards teenagers his own age. You would think this would be good, but it rarely is. That need to impress is still there. If he cannot impress the older crowd, it is far easier to impress those younger in years. He becomes the alpha male for his age group and he feels the need to do things to impress his peer group. This may begin by him smoking cigarettes, or stealing and evolve into smoking marijuana and bringing a gun to school. There are varying levels of self-destructive behavior, but destructive nevertheless. As before, that need begins small but escalates in severity as one does more and more. I'm sure it doesn't take much imagination to understand what the future holds for him

Another possible scenario for the young shunned boy is that a plan of "shock and awe" will accomplish his goal. This is a very likely probability. The shock and awe can be anything from stealing something to carjacking someone, or to the extreme of doing something violent that results in the loss of a life. Essentially, the younger teen tries to do something that even the older teenagers aren't quick to do. The hope is that mimicry is the ultimate flattery. The hope is that the older teenagers will look at the younger as one of them. There are all sorts of possible and likely scenarios that can occur, regardless of whether the ultimate goal of acceptance is achieved. I don't even think the end result matters because victims are created in the process of accomplishment. Remember the earlier scenario of the eleven-year-old in a previous chapter? The one who went and shot three rival gang members because the older kids were making fun of him and calling him scary. That is a very real situation. I know many personally, who have been on both sides of that scenario. You can even say I was on the younger end of that scenario.

So, the younger boys are usually arrested for whatever act that they commit. If it is serious enough, they are charged as an adult and sent to an adult prison. At this point, their fate is pretty much set. The adult prison system is no place for young teenagers. They are essentially being placed in the worst possible environment and then surrounded by the state's worst and most violent gang members, murderers, rapists, child molesters, etc. What now do you think they have to do to "fit in"? What do you think they have to do in this environment to not become a victim themselves?

Again, in no way shape or form am I saying that there should not be punishment. I hate that I always feel the need to make that disclaimer, but I know if I don't, someone will quote me as being favorable to the criminal when in fact that could not be further from the truth. This entire book has been written to prevent another victim from being born. This is my *only* goal but unfortunately there are many in society that think the only way to do this is by locking everyone up for the rest of their lives. For those who have that philosophy, you are living in a fantasy world. For you, perhaps you should look to the once ultra-conservative Texas prison system that is now acknowledging what I am saying; that we cannot simply lock everyone up and throw away the key. The problem is at a far earlier stage.

I raise this because just last week, there was a story on the news that involved a sixteen-year-old that was arrested for possessing four pounds of marijuana. They charged him as an adult. Should he be punished? Absolutely. Should we charge a sixteen-year-old as an adult and send him to the adult prison system for having marijuana? He will be surrounded by murderers, rapists, child molesters, etc. What do you think he will acquire from them? Sure, it is possible that he will learn nothing from them, that he will be scared straight so to speak but I find that possibility to be rare. I think that society is writing him off by charging him as an adult. I don't know his background but it cannot be that bad if he was still living as a free sixteen-year-old. Society may think they are not writing him off but that is exactly what is being done, and why? Treatment is far too expensive. It is short sided wisdom. Society believes that it is far easier/cheaper to punish him as severely as possible by sending him to the adult prison system and hoping he learns his lesson. They do, and when he gets out he is worse than when he went in. He now will commit a violent crime and that price society was so unwilling to pay for his treatment will now be paid to incarcerate him. Beyond that, now we will pay in pain and tears because someone was victimized. We as a society then act dumbfounded as to why this takes place.

Why wouldn't that sixteen-year-old get out and commit another crime? What has he learned between getting arrested and being released when all that surrounded him was older more sophisticated adult criminals? Combine that with a system that is nearly bankrupt and is staying afloat by cutting more and more educational and rehabilitative programs.

These young boys who rebel, they do need to be punished and some need that punishment to be very severe. It is quite clear however, that the adult prison system is not qualified to do so in a way that does not make the situation worse. If we know this to be true, and I think many in society are finally starting to realize this, then why are we not putting forth as much effort and funding into preventative type programs? Prevention is the best offense. The most crucial time to administer prevention is when these young boys are at the stage when they feel the need to impress older youths.

Expectations play a major role in this as well. In these communities, there is almost a culture of despair, of hopelessness in ever reaching "old" age. Many of today's teenagers living within the inner-city do not expect to live to see their twenty-fifth birthday. They honestly don't. Think of the mindset that this creates in a person that actually does not believe they will live to see the age of twenty-five. I really need you to understand this, understand what happens to a community as a whole when the majority of the youth believe in their heart and soul that they will not live their entire lives. This mindset creates so many problems that seem almost impossible to overcome.

Look at it this way, let's say that tomorrow President Obama holds a news conference and states that NASA has located an asteroid that that will eventually collide with the earth. The asteroid is the size of the moon and will collide with the earth in five and a half years. As of now, there is nothing that can be done to prevent the total destruction of this planet and everyone on it. How would society react? After the initial shock and panic subsided, if it ever would, what do you think people would do? Do you think people would continue paying into their 401k and plan for retirement? Would people continue to eat healthy? Would people continue to sacrifice their time, effort, and money to make this world a better place for the next generation? Would children still go to school? Would people care about getting a sexually transmitted disease or getting pregnant? Would people still adopt children? Would banks still give people loans?

Who would we become as a people? As a civilization? Would religious wars cease? Would Palestine care if Israel told them to relocate? Would South Korea tolerate any more, the provocations of the North? What would happen to the monetary system? Would people still work long hard jobs to pay their bills? Would the entire infrastructure of the world collapse? What would *you* do? Would you care about your future beyond the five and a half years we are expected to live? Would you care about the future of others? Just think about how much would change overnight if we honestly believed that we were going to die in five and a half years.

Now take that same thought process and apply it to the countless teenagers living in violent inner-city communities whom honestly believe that they will not live to see the age of twenty five. How can we not expect them to act in the same exact way the rest of the world would if they believed they were going to die in five and a half years? The only real difference is that the teenagers of today don't believe they are going to die as a result of the earth being hit by an asteroid, but rather at the hands of another in their community. I don't really think it matters what mode of death you will die by, so long as you believe that death is certain. Try and think about all of the aspects in one's life that would be affected by the belief you were going to die in a few years. Now imagine this in the mind of a teenager. There are a couple of easy scenarios to help understand this concept. For instance, let's say you have two boys, both fifteen years of age. One is going to a good school in a good community, the other in a poverty ridden school. They are both going to take a math test and both know that they will need to study very hard if they wish to pass. The boy living in the better neighborhood believes that he will live a long life and that his options are endless so long as he puts in the work. The boy living in the impoverished community honestly does not believe he will live to see his twenties. They sit down to study and it is really difficult. There is so much to absorb. Both want to quit and go do something they would enjoy doing. What do you think crosses each of their minds at this point? The boy living within the less violent neighborhood probably says, "This sucks, but if I want to get into that college, I better grind it out." Do you think the boy living within the impoverished community has that same mindset? Perhaps, but I don't think the odds are high in that regard. Does he wonder what the point is? Why would he study if he won't live long enough to go to college anyway? Whatever the outcome of that particular math test, I think the desire to study hard will decrease until the day when there is no point in studying because he won't graduate anyway. Let me ask you this, when you were in high school and studying for finals, would you have honestly studied as hard as you did if you honestly believed that you would not live to see your twenties? Or would you have spent your time "living it up", doing whatever it was that made you feel good? Perhaps you cannot put yourself in these shoes so maybe this scenario is pointless, I don't know. Personally I think it would be difficult to convince me that you would study just as hard as you would if you believed you had a long life ahead of you. Let me also be clear that it is no excuse to drop out of school, sell drugs, and gang bang simply because one might believe they are going to die in a few years. Whether right or wrong however, the reality for so many young people today is that they will not in fact live to see their twenties.

Instead of dismissing this as wrong, we need to understand why this mentality is created in the first place. So, if you felt you would not live to see your twenties, what would you do? School is pretty much out, right? After all, what's the point because you will not live long enough to graduate and get a good job, right? You do need to make some money however, because nothing in life that feels good comes cheap, right? So what to do? There are a couple of options. For one, you can just take what you want, whether it is money, a car, or other material things. Another option comes via the drug game. Based upon how drugs seem to be so accepted within many impoverished communities, there almost is a mindset of drug dealing is expected. It does not matter of what race the community consists of; drugs transcend all races and communities.

Whatever the means of obtaining money by less than legal means, the likelihood that gang members will be involved in this world is highly likely. As I said before, gang membership might not be someone's initial goal, but after time many often see that the profitable end they are trying to realize can only come via joining a gang. It is the gang members who have the drugs. They often purchase them from other gang members. Some wish only to sell drugs and not indulge in the gang lifestyle but as I said earlier, sometimes they need the protection of the gang to sell their particular product. If teenagers feel that drug dealing is something they wish to partake in and so many drug dealers are gang members, isn't it then likely that they too will consider becoming a gang member so that they may sell drugs? It seems like a logical progression to me. After becoming a drug dealer and gang member, other elements come into play. So many times I have heard the following, "I'm just selling enough drugs to make X amount of money and then I'm done." Greed however, has other plans because I don't know that I have ever met one single soul that said you know what, I have enough money, I am going to stop selling drugs. I have met a few that made enough to start legitimate businesses, but even they didn't go all the way legit. The same greed that exists for those making millions selling drugs exists for those making millions selling stock. It seems that once you have so much, you want just a little bit more. After all, you want to live within your means correct?

It's expensive being rich. Another aspect of this life, of poverty that I have noticed is that if you have had nothing for so long, once you get something it is as though you have to show it off. Many call it different things, whether it is flexing, stuntin', showin' off, etc. It is all the same. One-upmanship is such a deadly disease. I think it is also an addiction. When one cares so much about the material things they have, the less one is concerned with the risk it may take to acquire these things. This risk reward ratio starts getting skewed because so and so has 30's on his car and hell if I'm not gonna get 32's on mine. So what to do? Push the limit, sell more drugs and rob more people.

As all of this is taking place, the long term future is becoming less and less important because you know other people have the same mentality. "They might rob me, so I have to stick them first." They feel the need to live in the moment. The now is all that matters. Later is nothing more than a five letter word with little meaning. At this point, the odds of self-rehabilitation are almost non-existent. The penitentiary and the grave will be the place of residence for many of these like-minded individuals. We have not yet begun to understand the true consequences of this generation's mindset in that regard. What will happen to those that do not end up dead but now are reaching the age of retirement? I am scared to imagine what it will be like. When all of these people with no educations and no retirement savings get to the point when they can no longer work, what do you think is going to happen? What is going to happen to our society as a whole? Who will pay for their health care, their housing? Many people that have worked their entire life cannot even pay for the medicine they need and they have paid into Medicare and social security for years. Do you not see the problem that is going to arise?

Yes, it is easy to say that this is their problem; they should have made better choices. To the latter, yes they should have, but they didn't. Society has taken the approach it has due to a lack of money. The amount of money needed to prevent kids from joining gangs will seem like peanuts compared to the cost of taking care of the millions of gang members who will have squandered their lives and need help when they retire. This is why we need to understand this problem. Even if not one more gang member were created after today, the price it is going to cost society when the gang members of yesterday reach retirement will be astronomical. I honestly don't think people understand the magnitude of this future problem. Unfortunately, there will be millions more gang members created because they are not simply going to stop recruiting, stop existing. There are so many issues that are important at such a young age when it comes to creating conditions that make young teenagers think that the gang life is a way out. Poverty creates the ripest conditions for them to feel this way. Maybe it is too late for this generation; perhaps the problem is too large. We can if nothing else however, learn from this generation's mistakes so we can save the next, or at the very least give them a fighting chance. Do we not owe that to them? Time will tell, and the tale it tells will in large part depend on us and our actions of today.

Chapter Eight

Mentality of a gang member: understanding the psyche

Just as gang members come in many different sizes, ages, and colors, they also come with as many different mentalities. Again, society is given an image of how every gang member thinks and acts. When they think of a gang member, they often think of a psychopathic gun wielding murderer. Some are, but many do not fit this stereotype. Those who do not have that murderous mentality will however try and use that perception for their own personal gain and will try and live off of that image.

Many gang members have a different view of gangs themselves and what the lifestyle should and should not entail. Most likely to the surprise of most, many gang members would in fact go to school and get a good job so that they can one day obtain a good career. Many gang members do admit however, that they are living a self-destructive lifestyle that would lead others not to believe they want to live legit. Many gang members retire as they age because they see that the gang life is no way to live. (*Retire in the sense that they leave the gang life behind.*) When gang members are young, they have the "I don't care attitude", but as they age they realize that gang banging in the verbal sense is plain stupid.

Also, there is a distinction between gang *claimers* and gang *bangers.* These sub groups also have sub groups themselves. They are extremely different even though all exist in each particular organization. Gang *claimers* can be either the type who sell drugs and rob people, or they can be the types who are trying to uplift their race in a positive way and feel certain gangs can give them the platform to do this. The robbers and drug dealers really don't care about the whole gang aspect itself; they view the gang as a means to a profitable end. They do not care whether or not other gang members break the rules or are disorganized. They are strictly in it to make money and have fun. The easiest way to do this in their minds is by being a member of a gang.

Gang *bangers* on the other hand are a completely different breed of people altogether. They are in a gang for one purpose alone; to gang bang and take out all opposing members of other gangs they deem a threat. Interestingly, gang bangers tend to frown on hurting "innocent" people. There is almost an unspoken rule that if you are not a member of a rival gang, they have no quarrel with you. There would simply be no point in quarreling with someone that is not a threat. Gang bangers are always wearing their colors proudly, hoping to run into rival gang members. They are either shooting at rival gang members, being shot at by rival gang members, or spray painting their graffiti wherever they can. These are the ones doing the drive-bys. Gang claimers and gang bangers and their affiliates simply tolerate one another, neither really approving of what the other is doing. It is an interesting relationship to say the least.

Topics and questions elaborated on in this chapter will include:

- o A thin line between love and hate
- o Why do some gang bangers "believe" in God?
- o Who's worse, gang bangers or gang claimers?
- o Here comes the dope man!
- o Trust is something no one has, why?
- o Keeping up the image is a must.
- o Codes of silence?
- o Unwritten rules of the gang life.
- o A silent understanding between sworn enemies.
- o Breaking down the street mentality.
- o Comparing the street mentality to the prison mentality.
- o East Coast, West Coast, why two differing philosophies?
- o The changing views of gangs.

1234567 8910

*   *   *

Many in society if asked would most likely believe that all gang members are created equal. Most probably do not care that different gangs and different gang members within each gang have different mentalities. To them, all gang members are equally repulsive, equally guilty of creating victims. In a way, I can even understand this sentiment. Had I never lived this life, I too may have shared that philosophy. Some in society probably do not want to know the different mentalities of gang members, and I would be alright with that if society did not **need** to understand these differing mentalities in order to truly prevent juvenile gang membership.

Up until now, I for the most part have written about the time period that leads up to gang involvement. More precisely about why it gets to the point that juveniles feel gang membership is a valid choice. I will now speak about individuals who have reached the point where they are officially a gang member. The reasons it has gotten to this point no longer really matter. They will play small roles here and there, but for the most part these reasons are no longer of any real value.

If you are asking yourself why there is a need to understand the differing mentalities of today's gang member, I say simply so that you can steer other juveniles away from what they are. If you do not understand "what" they are, you stand no chance of steering them away from what you do not understand. Only after understanding how these differing mentalities think, can you effectively know what to do in order to keep other juveniles from ending up like them. This is no easy task even if you can distinguish the different mentalities of each gang in your community, but at least you start on a level playing field.

Furthermore, getting grown men to leave the gang life behind will play a role in future gang prevention. It will not be the police, or judges that end the gang problem, but rather future ex-gang members and their particular communities. I'm sure that statement sounds as crazy as the world was round pre-Columbus. This is one way to think about it. The more adult gang members we can get to renounce their gang affiliation, the fewer adult gang members there will be to recruit younger potential gang members. Obviously it is easier said than done, but the theory itself has to fall in the realm of common sense does it not? So if we need to get adult gang members to renounce their affiliation in order to deplete recruiters, the only way to do this is by first understanding how adult gang members think. The only way to accomplish this is to understand the mentality of the gang members we hope to free from the gang life. This should seem pretty straight forward. Understanding why former and active gang members are the part of the solution is a little more complex.

There are a couple of ways to look at this. I don't know if you have had any dealing with Narcotics Anonymous or Alcoholics Anonymous support groups, but if you have, you will know that many of the facilitators are recovering addicts themselves. If you didn't know this, I'm sure it must come as somewhat of a surprise to hear that a recovering alcoholic is treating an alcoholic. Now that I think about it, I wonder who first thought of this concept. Who first suggested that it may be a good idea to have this recovered alcoholic try and teach other alcoholics not to drink? How do you think that conversation went? Were they laughed out of the room? I think whoever thought of this concept was a genius and had excellent forethought and understanding as to how to solve a problem. In hindsight, it seems like such an obvious course of action. Who better to understand what an alcoholic is going through than a recovering alcoholic? I don't care how many degrees one has, how many certificates they may have hanging on their office wall, because every single one of them is trumped by personal experience. Do not misconstrue what I am saying, an education is also needed to help others, and the best of both worlds is in my opinion the answer. I think the best candidates to facilitate certain Alcoholics Anonymous meetings are those that have suffered through alcoholism themselves, but also have the credentials to become a counselor.

From that same philosophy, is where I have taken it upon myself to earn a degree in juvenile psychology, so that I too may have the credentials and life experience to aid in the realm of juvenile gang prevention. Who better than former gang members themselves to get through to today's youth? This is not a new concept, but it has been shown to be effective. The only bad part is that the scale has been entirely to small to show any results. Unfortunately, the main reason for this is a lack of former gang members who are willing to sacrifice everything to dedicate themselves to juvenile gang prevention. There are other problems/factors as well, but for the most part, it is due to the fact that for those that leave the gang lifestyle do not, or cannot "stay around" and prevent what they were once a part of. Some get so sick of the life that they want nothing to do with it. Others have made enemies that care not of their new found change of lifestyle. Others have "left the life" because they were expelled for snitching or other frowned upon practices. They cannot work with active gang members because they have been ostracized. As I said, the gang problem can only be solved with the help of active gang members. A dialogue must be formed, and they will be unwilling to do so with a snitch or any other that has a bad stigma attached to them.

On a side note, I have asked countless active gang members simply why they continue to be a gang member. I have received many different responses, but a recurring one is that, "Rival gang members do not care if I have dropped my flags (*Renounced their gang affiliation.*) It's true, many rival gang members that have been wronged by you will not care that you are no longer in a gang. They want revenge. This is unfortunate for a couple of reasons. Many gang members do not care if you renounce your affiliation if you have disrespected them in the past because certain gang members juxtapose their gang with their own manhood. Remember I spoke on this in a prior chapter? Another example may be if you shot a rival gang members little brother or sister in an attempt to shoot them. They are highly likely to want revenge no matter if you are currently a gang member or not. Even if they do not want revenge, they feel the life *requires it*. They will seek street justice for you. Here is the key. It is this belief that the life requires revenge, requires street justice that causes so many problems. Yes, the act itself does in fact make some very angry, but I think that anger often subsides over time unless there was loss of life. I don't believe all acts of gang violence have that long of an impact from an anger standpoint. The obligation to retaliate often compels gang members to repay the favor in kind. It's an adult form of peer pressure if you will.

I learned this lesson over the years from trying to keep people from fighting each other in prison. I don't like to see people go to "the hole" and setting themselves back. If I see two people about to fight, I will try and diffuse the situation. I don't care if I know them or not. Many fights in prison stem from acts of disrespect that can come in a variety of forms. When one feels disrespected, they feel obligated to rectify the disrespect via violence. Most do not want to fight, but feel that they really do not have an option. If you can give *each* party a high road to exit the situation, you can often keep them from fighting. Taking the high road lets all parties keep their honor in a sense. Some situations cannot be prevented however, no matter the attempts to quell the situation.

This same philosophy applies to gang members who have renounced their affiliation. Many rival gang members "want" out as well, but are afraid to renounce their gang affiliation for the same reasons of thinking "rival" gang members will not care. Unless they have a very personal grudge against you, they are happy to have you as one less enemy they need to worry about. Many more rival gang members than you think will let whatever personal beef they have go. The only bad part is that you just can never be sure. You would essentially have to put your trust in a rival gang members hands, and for some, this is next to impossible to do. Those hands are the same hands that have likely pointed a gun in your direction. They do not feel like very trustworthy hands. To an extent, I can truly understand this. There are a few people I am sure that still wish to hurt or kill me for what I have done in the past. They may not care that I have renounced my gang affiliation. In fact, they may take it as a blessing, because now they can retaliate on me without fear of reprisal from my former gang. I've always thought how fitting that even when you do the right thing, there are always people that will make you pay. No good deed goes unpunished, my father always says. I must have been a farmer in my last life because I sure know how to reap what I've sown.

The first and perhaps most important aspect of understanding how gang members think, is to understand that all gang members think differently. I touched on this in an earlier chapter when I was discussing or defining rather, the different groups, cliques, gangs, street gangs, etc. Gangs on the East Coast think and act completely different from those on the West Coast. In fact, members of the same gang will act one way inside the walls of the prison system compared to how they act out in the free world. Every gang member even within the same gang acts very differently. I will get into all of these mentalities as I move forward in this chapter, but I **need** you to keep in the forefront of your mind, that gang members think very different from one another. One of society's biggest misconceptions is that all gang members are the same. It's understandable to an extent that this misconception exists, but that fact in no way helps us with a solution to the problem. In fact, it is this misconception that is actually preventing us as a society to effectively prevent juvenile gang violence.

I will begin with describing the mentality of gang members outside of the prison system because many join when they are living in the free world. A sizable number join after they are incarcerated, but these individuals are another sect altogether that I will get into later. They too have a particular mentality that is different. They have joined for different reasons than those who joined on the street so you have to expect that their mentality is going to be just a little bit different from the beginning. This does not mean that they do not act in a similar way or believe much of the same things, only that they have a slightly different mentality and this is important once again for the purposes of juvenile gang prevention.

I'll speak about what I felt when I joined a gang. Many people experience different things so I will speak with firsthand knowledge rather than speculation. My mentality evolved as well and this is one aspect that we need to understand too, that mentalities do change over time. This can occur for a variety of reasons, in large part predicated upon exterior influences. These influences can be other members of the gang, the type of community one may live in, or the type of gang one belongs to. For example, let's say that a teenager joins a gang *during* a war with a rival gang. He joins right after people have just gotten shot. His mentality will most likely become serious and violent pretty quickly. Compare this mentality with another individual who joins a small street gang that "just" sells drugs and likes to party. His mentality will often be much less serious, much less violent.

Chapter Eight: Mentality of a gang member

This is my story.

For me, my very first encounter with a gang member occurred when I was about twelve years old. I had met numerous wannabee gang members, but this individual was the first one that I considered to be a real one. I lived on the West Coast so the gang culture was different than it is here in the Midwest. I did not know this at the time however. I had just moved to a new school and the very first "friend" that I met happened to be a gang member, though at the time I did not realize that he was a gang member. He never made mention of this fact at first. Now that I think about it, I suppose that it was possible that at that particular time he was not yet officially a member. He had some friends that I later learned were gang members so maybe he became one at a later date after our first meeting, I don't know.

In any event, one day we were at his house and he showed me this t-shirt. On it was written PSV-XIII. (Park Side Barrios 13) I asked him why he was showing it to me and he said that it was the name of the gang he belonged to. As I said earlier, it surprised me at this point to hear that he was in a gang. At first I thought that he was joking but he assured me that he was not. I really didn't know what to think. I thought it was interesting and I was definitely curious. I had always found everything interesting. I think some people are born to be curious about everything. The weeks went by and he would tell me what he and his other friends would do. It all sounded very interesting but it never got to the point of me joining or even asking to join because a short time later he was shot in the head and killed. Very shortly after this I moved to the Midwest and lived with my grandparents.

When the eighth grade began, I met a kid in my class whom I got along very well with. I really did not know anyone else, so I really only hung out with him. I soon learned that he was a graffiti artist. I had always been a fairly good artist so this seemed like an interesting transition to make. Early in school they teach you that marijuana is the gateway drug that opens the door to using even more serious drugs. One of the things that I explain to the kids that I speak with every week is that same gateway philosophy can apply to one's friends as well. I'll explain. I'm sure you have all had a friend who had other friends that became your friend by association, correct? You begin by meeting them here and there, and the next thing you know they are now your friend as well. That original friend was your "gateway friend" to meeting their friends. Sometimes you can meet good people in this fashion, but other times you end up meeting the type your parents do not want you hanging around with.

This is exactly what occurred in my situation. That first friend that I made who was a graffiti artist had another friend that was a gang member. Again, I didn't know that he was a gang member because he was a graffiti artist as well. He and I got along very well and so we hung out all of the time. I cannot remember exactly how I learned that he was a gang member, but it was fairly early after I met him that I found this out. Keep in mind that this is all transpiring over a matter of a couple of months, two at the most. I was fourteen years old at the time. Shortly after new years of 1995, I felt like running away from home because I felt like I was being treated like a young child. My new friend said that if I ran away I could come and stay with him, his mom would not mind. So I did.

As I look back, that was probably the most fatal of all my decisions up to that point. It turned not only mine, but so many others lives around. Such a haphazard decision; to run away. If only I could have known that decision would eventually lead to so much pain and victimization. People always ask me if I could make one decision over, what would it be. Obviously I would not commit my crime, but the choice I would take back if I could, would be running away because it led me to becoming a gang member and eventually committing my crime. It was my gateway choice to other self-destructive choices. Of course I am aware that had I not ran away I still could have ended up a gang member, but at least the circumstances would have been a little different. Perhaps I was meant to experience my gangland destiny, who knows?

I am on the run now, and also am aware that my friend is a gang member. He had three uncles that were also gang members and kept asking me when I was going to "come home." Come home meant to join their gang. Everyone always wants to know why teenagers join gangs. Society as I said earlier, always gives the generic answer of fulfilling a family void. This most certainly was not the reason why I joined a gang. Nor was it the reason many of the other gang members that I know joined a gang. I had a great family. I couldn't ask for a better family. Another answer frequently given was that teenagers join a gang to fit in. I searched for my truth as to this question for years and came to the conclusion that this did not apply to me either. I had a great group of "popular" friends if you want to look at it that way. My girlfriend at the time was beautiful so it was not to impress females. In fact, all of my female friends were the most popular and finest females in the school that I went to, so I had no one that I wanted to fit in with besides them and they did not in any way approve of the gang life. For the most part they were all taggers themselves and/or hung around with taggers. Taggers are graffiti artists. When they learned that I had joined a gang, they told me that I was stupid. My girlfriend was definitely not happy.

I've always been a very curious and impulsive individual. This is a horrible combination if there were any. I evaluated whether or not I truly felt pressured to join a gang by my friend's uncles. They were older and seemed to have that fast life allure. As I said earlier, I was always searching for that rush in life. I suppose joining a gang seemed dangerous and exciting. I believe that it was a combination of these last two elements that led me to join a gang.

What a horribly sickening decision that was to join a gang. I've hated myself for a long time for that choice. That hatred made me contemplate suicide at times over the years in order to punish myself, but I could never build up the courage to do it. I have to still

be careful and remain in control of my negative feelings for myself
or they do get out of control at times. I **chose** to become a gang
member, nobody forced me, no one threatened me and I made that
choice of my own free will. Even though at the time of this writing it
has been over thirteen years since I renounced my gang affiliation, I
still find times when I look in the mirror in disgust. I went from an
Honor Student to serving life in prison in less than a year's time. So
much potential and I threw it all away. That is one tough pill to
swallow at times.

My particular initiation consisted of a six minute violation
from neck to toe, meaning that they could hit me everywhere but in
my face. This was done by my friend and his uncles. I've always
found the whole violation process to be somewhat interesting if you
look at it from different perspectives. You would think that if
someone was informed - "Do you want to hang out with us? Then
we will have to beat you up first", any rational human being should
think "yeah right", like I want to go through that just to hang out
with you. Why would anyone want to get beat up just to hang out
with another group of people? You'd think gangs would try and
implement a better marketing strategy rather than, "Hey, we have to
beat you up but then you can be one of us." My particular violation
was not as bad as some that I have witnessed or heard about. I ask
myself now however, why the hell would I agree to get beat up just
to become a gang member? Interesting, I have never asked myself
that before. I understand the reasons behind why these violations
occur. Some believe it is to show that you can take punishment, by

proxy proving that you will not run if you and your comrades are ever ambushed by rival gang members. Perhaps these days one should get shot to prove whatever because it seems that very little fighting is going on in this day and age. Most gang members are trying to shoot and kill other gang members, not beat them up.

Other people say that the violation is to show solidarity with your "brothers." I guess in an odd way, knowing that everyone has endured the same punishment to claim what you now claim can give the illusion of feeling like a group. In a way, getting violated into a gang is no different than the hazing that occurs in some college fraternities. Beyond them, if you believe in all of these secret societies like Skull and Bones, Bilderbergers, and the Freemasons, they too have pretty out there initiations.

There are other initiations that people can go through as well. They are different for every gang. Some have to go on a mission, (A drive-by on a rival gang), while some have to kill someone to be a member. There are certain prison gangs in the federal system that have this initiation. Some gangs have female sects and they are initiated in a sexual way, though this is predominantly frowned upon by all of your larger organizations.

Back to why I chose to get violated to essentially hang out with another group of people. Obviously I would have rather not gotten violated but that was not an option to become a member. There was a part of me that wanted to show that I could take whatever they could give, that I was willing to sacrifice something (pain) in order to be a part of the collective group. I did it to show that I was not a coward.

In retrospect, the oddest aspect of the whole violation process is that after these individuals beat you up for X amount of minutes, they immediately embrace you and call you their "brother." It would from the outside looking in, appear so strange to see a group of people violently beating up another for a period of time then suddenly stop and embrace the apparent victim of an assault. It would be interesting to take that violation out of context, by videotaping it without sound, then showing it to some focus group in a foreign country and listen to their interpretation of what they see. Remember, there would be no context, all they are told is to watch this video. What do you think that they would think?

Thinking back, after the violation and the older gang members were shaking my hand and giving me my congratulations, I did feel as though I was a part of something bigger. I did not know of exactly what, but I definitely felt different. It obviously sucked during the violation, but after its conclusion it felt worth it as sick as that must sound. I received my first two tattoos that night.

The next morning when I woke up, there was a little cockiness that I felt within. I was still a runaway at the time, so I wasn't in school. Over the next few days, my girlfriend and graffiti artist friends found out what I had done. I honestly did not expect their response. They did not take it well. I remember questioning my decision at this point, wondering if I was stupid. I did, but felt I was past the point of no return. My decision seemed innocent enough for the first couple of weeks because I really had experienced no violence up to that point. Call it luck or whatever, I don't know. There were a lot of parties with everyone having a good time. I guess it was the calm before the storm in a way. I was on the run for about a month before I was apprehended and sent to live with my mother who lived a few blocks away from my grandparents. I went back to school but was expelled very soon for spray painting inside of the school. As I write this, I can only shake my head in disgust, in sadness.

I was sent to an alternative school where the entire class was comprised almost completely of gang members. I spoke on alternative schools in an earlier chapter. They were essentially breeding grounds for gang activity. If you were not a gang member when you started, you certainly became one in a short period of time. Birds of a feather as they say.

After a couple of months the allure of that life had worn off for me. My curiosity was met as it were, and I realized that being a gang member was not all it was cracked up to be. I started creating excuses to not go to meetings or hang out anymore. It was a slow process, apparently to slow for my girlfriend at the time because she gave me an ultimatum; her or the gang. I remember pretending to be mad at her for "making me choose", but in reality it came as a relief because I was searching for an excuse to leave anyway. I also loved her very much and did not want to lose her. I stopped hanging around them and was eventually given a violation of fifty to the chest *for this behavior. This meant that someone held my arms behind me while other gang members punched me in the chest. I thought about running from this violation, but figured it would catch up to me eventually. I ended up being sent to the hospital for this. I told my mom that I had been randomly jumped by a group of teenagers. Now I was sure I wanted out, as did my friend as "luck" would have it.*

I went with my friend to one of his uncles houses where there were a few other gang members. They told my friend that he was first to get a violation. They took him into one of the bedrooms and proceeded to beat him badly. This violation was from head to toe and also lasted about six minutes. In retrospect, going second was horrible. I had to listen to them beat him, knowing that I was about to feel the same thing in a matter of minutes. The anticipation was almost worse than the violation. Mine was six minutes from head to toe as well. There was no embracing afterwards.

When finished, I went home. I really thought that I was done with the gang life. As I am sure you are wondering considering that I am in here for a gang-related homicide, obviously I was not done with that life.

My girlfriend ended up getting pregnant. All of this is taking place as I was fourteen years old mind you. Everything was happening so fast. She was about five months older than I was, and I didn't know what to do. My girlfriend wasn't even allowed to have a boyfriend at the time so her pregnancy obviously came as a surprise to her family. Needless to say, her parents were not thrilled with me. I didn't know how to be a father, how to support them. I wasn't even in high school yet. Looking back, I clearly started pulling away from everyone; my family, friends and girlfriend. I was trying to distract myself with other things. In my heart I honestly had the plans to get a job so that I could pay for an apartment and take care of my child and girlfriend. My actions however, clearly told a different story. I talked at length in the beginning of this book about actions superseding want. I wanted to take care of my girlfriend and child because I loved her very much. My actions showed however that I ran from my responsibilities and acted like an ass. I did not deserve her, and she rightfully dumped my coward little butt.

A month or two went by and my mom took my same friend and I to a lake some two hours away from Milwaukee. While I was there, a female's voice called out my name from behind me. This surprised me because we were out in the middle of nowhere essentially. There were lots of people swimming at this lake, but I did not recognize any of them. I turned and it happened to be my friend's ex-girlfriend. The odds of this encounter had to be next to impossible I thought. This encounter would be the first time that I would later ponder destiny vs. free will. I am not speaking in relation to my friend's ex-girlfriend whom I met at the lake, but fate in relation to my eventual gangland destiny. I'll explain. She gave me her phone number and told me to call her when I got back to Milwaukee. I ended up calling her and she told me to come over to her house. My house was on one end of the south side of Milwaukee, hers the other. I walked to her house but a block from her house I

heard someone yell my name from the house I was passing by. As
fate would have it, it was the leader of the gang that I had belonged
to. At the time I looked up to him much as Derrick Sanders looked
up to the older members of his gang when he was young. He had all
of the money, status, women you could want at a young age. He also
had more power than he knew what to do with. His tone of voice
surprised me because he did not sound angry or hostile towards me.
He asked where I had been, why he hadn't seen me for a while. It is
somewhat hard to explain this, but in an earlier chapter I described
that many organizations had different sets or hoods even though
they are all a part of the mega organization. Chapters would be a
good way of describing them. They are all the same thing, but each
neighborhood had their own particular leaders and subordinates.
They all fell under the leader of the entire organization. There are
different chapters all over Milwaukee because it was such a large
organization. I was a Spanish Cobra that claimed allegiance to the
South Side. The leader I was speaking to was a North Side Cobra
but decided to start another set on the South Side. His Brother was
the overall leader. The individuals that violated me out I was told,
were no longer Cobras either. They had been caught stealing from
incarcerated members so they were X'ed out. (Kicked out of the
organization) It became clear that the leader did not know that I was
violated out because he appealed to my ego and told me that he
needed my graffiti talents. He wanted me to spray paint COBRA'S
down the side of a building. The building was on one of the busiest

streets on the South Side and was about eighty feet long, so the letters had to be massive. He showed me a bag of spray paint.

And there it was, that fatal moment. Who knew the end of my victims life, and the destruction of so many more hinged on a few cans of spray paint that he held in a worn out grocery bag? I've reflected so much on this moment. So many things were pulling me in opposite directions. I didn't want to do it because I didn't want to be in that life anymore. On the other hand here was this powerful man asking me for a favor, stroking my talent ego. It was at this point that the need for that rush crept back in, coupled with my desire to escape the emotional things that were going on in my life like becoming a father. I also was worried what he would do to me if I told him no. I had witnessed him do many violent things to people who did less. Fear is no excuse, but it was an emotion that I felt at the time as I thought about turning him down. I was only fourteen years old still, and he was in his twenties. He was also a lot bigger than I was. It seemed that the only thing that had power enough to distract myself from what I was going through was something very self-destructive.

I wonder how different so many lives would have been had I the courage to turn him down. What if I had never met my friend's ex-girlfriend and walked to her house? What if I had walked one block over instead of taking the path that I did, never walking past the gang leader's house? Was it my fate?

I grabbed the grocery bag from his hands. Had a movie been made of my life, in this scene, producers could have superimposed the hands of the Grimm Reaper's over his as he handed me the grocery bag, because essentially that is when my victim died.

At the end of the day it was my decision, and mine alone to make. I have absolutely no excuses for why I took that bag. I offer no excuses of feeling pressured or desire to distract myself. It was all me. It is difficult to not blame anyone, but I have learned in life that one can never move forward without first taking full responsibility for one's actions. It is a sad reality that so many young people are faced with similar such decisions every day. These decisions are being made by ten, eleven, twelve, thirteen, and fourteen-year-olds. Unfortunately they have very little life experience to give them the tools to make a logical decision, but the tragedy of the situation is that the streets do not care how old you are. They force you to make certain decisions no matter your age. Our only recourse is to decrease the conditions that propagate these types of decision making scenarios. We have to get through to them before it gets to this point, because sadly many teenagers will fail this test in life. It is a point of no return usually.

So, with a can of Krylon in my hand, I began my gangland destiny and spray painted Cobra's as big as I could down the side of the building. I'm amazed at how little forethought I put into my future at that moment. I never even considered how my actions of that day could dictate the choices I would face tomorrow.

It's odd; it has taken me a very long time to write this last paragraph. It isn't because it is difficult writing, but rather I keep gazing out my cell window really reliving that day for the first time. I've thought about that day before, but I really never put everything into thinking about that day. A bag of stupid spray paint!!! That's all it took for so many lives to be ruined. Robert would still be alive, his family never relieved of their tears. My son would have had a father, his mother a husband to share life with. My family would never have suffered and blamed themselves for what I had done.

After I spray painted the building, everyone was impressed with how it looked. The leader said, "Bro, I want to go over to 2-1 hood and tag up their shit." (A rival gang) They were warring with the Cobras at the time, so we went over to their "hood" and spray painted all over. That was a rush; going into a rival gangs neighborhood and spray painting all over their houses and garages. At any moment we could have been seen and shot. I didn't have a gun at the time, and I didn't ask if he did. All I knew is that we were in serious trouble if we got caught. It's crazy; the fear of getting caught by the police never once crossed my mind. This was exactly the type of distraction that I thought I needed from what I was facing in life. As long as I was focused on these self- destructive behaviors, I didn't have to face my own reality. Once again, this is no excuse, only my way of rationalizing things at the time. Clearly in hindsight I was delusional.

Of course I was told to come back the next day, to kick it and hang out. I did feel that little tug within myself that this is not what I want but honestly, that feeling of seeing how proud everyone was of me going into a rival gangs neighborhood and tagging it up with no gun made me feel good. I did not feel like a little fourteen-year-old. I went back the next day, and it was this day that I was first shot at when we were all crammed onto the small little porch. Something in me changed that day after I let my mind catch up to the day's events. It was a rush, but after I came down I was like, "They just tried to kill me!" They wanted to take my life. I think it was then that I thought I had a vested interest in the gang life.

I went back day after day. I was so much younger than everyone else. It's odd now that I think about it. I don't remember anyone close to my age. Everyone was in their twenties it seemed. I think that was part of my downfall. Everyone always made a big deal over me because I was so young. All of the older females fawned over me in a way because I was always the youngest around. So many wanted to take me under their wing so to speak and this only furthered what my ego wanted.

Over the next couple of months I witnessed much violence, many shootings. All of these things should have made me leave that life but they only made life seem surreal at fourteen. It was like living in a movie. It should have culminated when I was kidnapped by rival gang members, but even this did not make me leave. Earlier I had spoken on my friend's uncles that were X'ed out of the gang; they were the ones that had previously violated me out of the gang.

That isn't where our paths crossed for the final time however. They "flipped" which means they became members of a rival gang after they were no longer Spanish Cobra's. They became Latin King's, whom are bitter rivals of Spanish Cobra's. To put it into context, it would be akin to a Crip becoming a Blood. I had heard about flipping but I really didn't know what I thought about it because I had at that point never met anyone who had flipped.

A few weeks before I committed my crime, I was forced to face my friend's uncles that were now King's. One night I was sitting on the porch of an older women's home that let us hang out there. She knew all of the old school Cobra's and was more than happy to let them stay at her house. It was exactly 11:00 pm because I could hear the "Married With Children" music on her TV. It was a warm summer night and I was just relaxing on the porch waiting for some other gang members to come back from the house across the street. I don't remember what I was thinking, but I was always aware of my surroundings because we were once again at war with the 2-1's. Being "at war" means that two gangs are actively trying to hunt the other. It's interesting though, because King's and Cobra's are always trying to kill one another but are rarely described as being at war. Perhaps it is because it is a perpetual war that has no ending, sort of like Palestine and Israel. There is never "peace", just periods of less violent war. That is an odd way of wording it as I read it back to myself, "Less violent war?" Can there be such a thing?

"We" were at war with the 2-1's, who we usually were aligned with to fight the Latin King's, but had fallen out of grace with. I placed "we" in quotes because at the time of the incident I was a we, but now I am a me, and I don't want to in any way ever again be considered a "we."

As I was sitting on the porch, a car came flying down the street and did a "French Connection" type donut in the middle of the street. I couldn't see in the car but knew that it couldn't be good for me. The gang members that went across the street were going to get a few guns for protection from the 2-1's, so I was left without any protection. I needed no other incentive to go into the house to seek cover. I could hear people yelling but the words they were yelling were not those a rival gang would yell, but rather those of other Spanish Cobra's. Every organization has certain things they yell to represent themselves to other gangs. Verbal representation if you will. I turned around just in time to see three men run into the house behind me; my friends three uncles. If looks could kill, I surely would not be here writing this book today. I instantly knew that I was in a horrible situation with no apparent way out. I was fourteen years old, probably 5'2" tall at the time and weighing less than 120 lbs. They were all in their twenties and were much bigger than I was. The older lady whose house I was in had five or six little kids sitting on the couch, and I didn't know where any of the doorways led, so I didn't know which way I should go. It was a matter of seconds before they swarmed me and began beating me. There was not much I could do. The kids were screaming, and the woman was yelling, "Not in front of my kids, not in front of my kids!" In an instant, they were dragging me down the steps of her porch and throwing me into their car. I honestly don't even remember my feet ever touching the steps. I was trying to free myself, but to no avail. They threw me in the car and the oldest jumped in with me while the other two jumped up front. We sped away, and I thought that I was breathing my last breaths.

The situation was made more bizarre because of the relationship the oldest uncle and I had. He had been a Latin King for many years, unlike his younger brothers who were Spanish Cobras at one time. When I ran away he let his nephew and I stay with his wife and kids. He was in his thirties so he wasn't into gang banging and didn't care that we were Spanish Cobra's. He and I got along great. He felt like my uncle in a way. So I couldn't understand why he was doing this to me. Honestly I didn't know how any of them could do this to me because just as few months earlier I lived with all of them and their grandparents when I was a runaway. I understood that they were no longer Cobra's, but them being X'ed out had nothing to do with me so I held no ill will towards them. The feelings were apparently not mutual however.

As they drove off, the younger uncle that was driving would stop at every stop sign and red light and turn around to punch me as the older uncle held me. The oldest was holding me so that I couldn't move, but it was almost like he didn't want them to punch me as much as they were because every once and awhile he would say, "Enough." We must have gotten twelve blocks or so, and I remember consciously thinking to myself in the midst of everything that was going on, "man, there sure are a lot of damn stop signs and red lights!" I don't remember there being that many stoplights when I walked over here before. As I said, every time he would stop, he would turn around and punch me. At the time it did not dawn on me that he was following all of the traffic rules so that we would not get pulled over by the police. I'm sure you have seen a movie where someone is carrying a large amount of narcotics in their car and they are sure to follow the speed limit and use proper driving techniques so they did not attract the attention of the police. I'm sure that is what the younger uncle was thinking, but I was thinking, "really, now you want to use blinkers and follow stop signs?!" Stupid stop signs I thought to myself. I hated me a stop sign at that moment.

The two up front kept yelling something at me, but to this day I cannot remember what they were saying. I just remember tasting blood in my mouth and trying to understand how I would free myself from the situation. It was odd, everything was moving so fast, but my mind seemed to process everything even quicker which gave me the opportunity to have a sort of conversation with myself. It's hard to describe, but everything was sort of muted and yet I could hear my own thoughts quite clearly.

In the last chapter I spoke upon being shot at and not being scared because the event happened so quickly that my mind didn't have time to be afraid for my life. This was not like that situation; I was definitely scared during this event. The rush of it all was definitely overrated. I kind of freaked myself out with my own thoughts. In this calm dialogue that I had within my mind, I started to picture myself being tied up in a chair in some non-descript basement. It was at this moment that I started to understand that if I didn't get away before then, I was going to die. Who knows what they had planned. This wasn't like the movies, I knew Steven Seagal was not going to bust down the door and rescue me. I knew that my best chance at escape was when they tried to get me out of the car. I was trying to picture ways of doing this, trying to understand what they were yelling at me, all the while trying to dodge the driver's stupid fists.

I remember thinking that I was quite surprised all of this was happening to me. Was I actually being kidnapped? It still sounds weird to me to this day when I say that I was kidnapped. I thought that only happened to other people. A few blocks later we came up to a stop light coincidently in front of my son's mother's house. There were about fifteen people out front. I couldn't focus on any of their faces. I knew that I should yell for help, but what could they do? As I was thinking about this, the passenger opened his window and began yelling to the crowd as if he were still representing himself as a Spanish Cobra. He was throwing up Cobra signs and everything, even though he was clearly a Latin King. In a split second, everything clicked. He was "false flagging." False flagging is when a member of one gang will wear the colors of one of their rivals as well as verbally represent themselves as a member of that rival gang to get unsuspecting gang members to represent themselves. They do this to lull them into a false sense of security, to make them think that they are safe so they can get close enough to kill them. Here is an example of how and why false flagging takes place. Let's say that you have a gang member walking down a street but he is not wearing any identifying colors. A car rolls up to him and throws up their gang's sign. They are rival gang members. The walking gang member is unarmed and knows that those in the car are likely to have a gun if they are rolling up on him like this. Some individuals when faced with this scenario will say that they aren't a member of any gang so they will not get shot. The reasoning behind this is when a car full of gang members rolls up on you and asks you what you are; nine times out of ten they are armed.

Everyone knows that this can happen so to get around this, gang members will wear the colors of their rivals and pretend to be whatever their rival is. The hope is that the walking gang member will think that they are members of his own gang so that he will represent himself as such. When he does, he has essentially fallen into their trap. This same tactic has been utilized in many urban combat wars in the Middle East. It should come as no surprise that today's gang members employ much of the same tactics.

Back to my situation; I knew the passenger was false flagging. I knew he was trying to get someone else to admit to being a Spanish Cobra. I understood that they were going to kill someone. What if my son's mother was in that crowd? I prayed no one said *that they were a Cobra. The light turned green at this point and the one driving noticed that on the other side of the stoplight was an unmarked detective's car. (Gang squad as they were referred to as by us) The older uncle held me down even tighter. I had no chance of getting the attention of the passing detective. We started to move and all three of them were clearly spooked. I couldn't really understand why. I understood that it was a serious situation, but there was no chance the detective was going to see me so I couldn't understand why their entire demeanor had changed. All they had to do was just drive normal and they would be free and clear of the oncoming detective. As we passed the detective's car, they all turned to see if he was going to follow us. I couldn't see what the detective had done but the very next street we came to, we turned and the driver slammed on the breaks. The two up front kept yelling, "We gotta' go, we gotta' go!" They jumped out. The older uncle snatched me out of the car, but while he did so whispered, "I have to get you out of here; my brother is going to kill you." My feet hit the ground around the same time he said the word "you" and he did not have to tell me twice. I saw that the other two were at the front of the car, so I ran as fast as I could the other way. Or so I thought. I tried to run so fast that my feet left without the upper half of my body and I fell. I must have looked like one of those cartoon characters that go nowhere but make that silly little running sound. As soon as I hit the ground however, I was back up and gone. I think at that moment I could have kept pace with Mr. Bolt from Jamaica. I could hear the* older uncle behind me asking for me to wait up. The other two I could no longer see. I didn't know where I was running, where I was, I just kept running. I could still hear the older uncle way behind me asking for me to wait. There was something in his voice that made me stop. I don't know why, but his voice didn't sound as though he meant any harm. After all, he had just freed me from his brothers. I was more than a block away from him so I waited for him to catch up. I felt a little safer out in the open because I clearly demonstrated that I could outrun him if I felt I was in danger again. As he approached, he had his hands up saying he did not want to hurt me. I remember asking him why? He said it had nothing to do with me. I was just at the right place at the wrong time.

He kept telling me to relax and come back to his wife's home. I told him he had to be kidding. There was absolutely no chance that I was going to go back to his house. My trust wasn't going to allow me to go that far. He assured me that his brothers wouldn't be there. He also told me that they were just involved in another shooting a half hour earlier, and that is why they were so alarmed when they saw the detective's car. It had nothing to do with me. I didn't ask any questions. As far as I was concerned, that was more incentive to not go with him to his house. It made me want to get away from him as well. I just wanted to blend into the shadows and find my way home. I thanked him for helping me get away but told him I had to go. I didn't know where the other two were.

I was probably eight blocks or so from my home so I started running through yards when I stopped dead in my tracks. My bearings must have come back because I became aware of what could happen if I kept running in the same direction. I lived on 20th and Grant. The oldest uncle lived on 16th and Grant. My luck, I would end up running into all three of them in some alley on the way to my house. We were all running to the same street, just to a place four blocks apart. They were on foot too, and I could only assume that they were all going to 16th and Grant to hide out. I remember standing there thinking you have to be kidding me. I wasn't going to take any chances, so I ran all the way back from where I came, figuring this is where they were running from so I shouldn't run into them. I then took the long way home. I don't know what time I eventually got home, time had lost all meaning at that point.

My mom was sleeping. Of course I did not wake her. I remember laying there as I tried to sleep thinking that they are only four blocks away. I was arrested a short time later so I never ran into the two younger uncles again. I did run into the older uncle some fifteen years into my incarceration. He was not at all thrilled to see me because of other events that occurred that same night.

Remember when I said that they dragged me into the car? The other gang members I was waiting for were coming out of the house across the street just as we were driving away. They did not know what had just transpired. They recognized the car, but that was about it. They were explained the situation by the woman that asked them not to beat me in front of her kids. They immediately retaliated by going to the older uncle's house and shot it up. They did not know that the older uncle had helped me escape. They only knew that the three of them all hung out at his house. This was the house four blocks away from mine. The shooting must have occurred as I was trying to escape because I did not hear about it until the next day. I felt horrible because the house that was shot up belonged to the uncle that had help save me. His wife and kid were there when the shooting occurred. Thankfully no one was hurt.

As I said, I eventually ran into the older uncle some fifteen years into my incarceration. He knew that I was not the one who did the shooting, but did not know if I had ordered them to do it. I explained to him the situation; that it made no sense for me to have the house of the one person who helped me that night shot up. He and I knew what transpired and he eventually realized that it would not have made sense. He and I left on good terms.

As far as me, the next day I went to school as if nothing had happened. This incident did not make me rethink anything, or second guess my choices up to that point. Perhaps I was too young to understand the seriousness of what had transpired, how close I was to being killed, I don't know. Obviously in hindsight I can see the situation for what it was, but back then I did not. The only logical conclusion that I can come to is that I really did not want to see the situation for what it was. I was so terrified to be a father at fourteen that the gang life provided the perfect distraction from what I should have been facing. In retrospect, that aspect alone made me deserving of a life sentence. My actions contributed to what I now know is one of the leading factors of eventual gang membership by *young teenagers; single-parent households. My actions took me away from my son's mother, leaving her alone to raise him by herself. I was part of the present and future problem.*

My son is already years older than I was when I came to prison, but thankfully he has not followed in my footsteps. His grandparents and mother are solely responsible for that. I will never be able to show my appreciation for that but I am grateful beyond words that they were there for him.

I was only a gang member for about six months before I committed the crime that led me to prison. I changed so many lives on September 26th, 1995, three days after my fifteenth birthday. As I first wrote this book, I broke down the events of that day, intending to include them in this book. I then thought about it and thought that it would be disrespectful to my victims and their families to do so. In short, I am guilty of 1st degree intentional homicide and attempted first degree intentional homicide. There is and was absolutely no justification for my actions of that day. There is absolutely no one to blame for what I did other than myself. Furthermore, I take full responsibility for those actions and can only hope one day to show my victims that I am sorry with my actions over the course of my life. I do understand that nothing I will ever do can bring Robert back. I can never un-cry their tears or relieve them of their pain. I can dedicate myself to preventing what I was once a part of in the hopes that another family does not go through what I put them through.

While this in no way makes up for what I did, I feel it is the only way to atone for what I have done.

I have shared what I experienced so that parents can understand how quickly they can lose their child if they are not vigilant. You can be the best parent in the entire world, but still lose your child to the gang lifestyle if you are not cognizant of what they could be going through. Many parents think that it can never happen to their child. I was an Honor Roll student and played two musical instruments. I participated in math competitions and spelling bees. I never skipped a single day of school, other than when I ran away and was not able to go to school. I was accepted into the young astronauts program. I had all of the potential a parent could hope to have for their child. A year later I had a life sentence. That is how quick a parent can lose their child.

This chapter is about the differing mentalities that gang members have. These mentalities derive from somewhere, usually the events in one's childhood. I am trying to show that gang members come from all walks of life. I did not come from a single-parent household. I was not abused as a kid. From an income standpoint, I was definitely not rich or anywhere above average. My father always tried to instill the best values in me. He came to all of my sporting events and award ceremonies. He was everything a son could want, and yet here I sit serving a life sentence. Any child can fall victim to the gang life. This life discriminates against no one. It cares not of one's income, race, or intelligence level. Society has this stereotypical image of not only what a gang member looks like, but also of what a gang member's mentality consists of.

I will get back to my mentality later as I proceed through the prison system because my mentality changes as well. Most mentalities change after coming to prison because it is a different world. The culture changes and you have to change with it.

For now, I will focus on the street mentality alone. In this chapters opening statement, I briefly described a differing philosophy/mentality between gang claimers and gang bangers. Every gang can have both types of mentalities as members. In fact, some can start off as a gang claimer and become a gang banger or vice versa. I have often asked myself who is worse? I suppose it is one of those lesser of two evils type of scenarios. I have gone back and forth on this question for years and will most likely continue to do so. In one respect, the answer can change depending on the culture at the time. I have tried to stress in this book that everything is in constant motion. The gang culture is continuously evolving and changing. We need to understand this so that we too may change with it from a comprehension standpoint. Gangs of the seventies and eighties are almost unrecognizable in philosophy from how they are today. It's so important to keep up with the times. Juvenile gang prevention relies on this. It is almost pointless to use the tactics that worked in the seventies to prevent juvenile gang violence on the youth of today. They have a different mentality; the culture has a different mentality.

To answer the question of who is worse, gang claimers or gang bangers, we first have to understand the mentality of each. My gut response to my own question was that gang claimers were worse for society because they had more innocent victims than gang bangers have. By innocent, I mean that they were not themselves a member of a gang. Let me be clear, just because someone is in a gang does not mean that they deserve to be killed or are not innocent from a victim's standpoint, only that they understand the life they live. They are living it with the understanding that their gang membership will likely increase the odds of death. Remember, gang bangers are more interested in taking out members of rival gangs rather than robbing old women and hurting young children that have nothing to do with the gang life. Do they cross that line and hurt innocent people? Absolutely, they do it all of the time but there is a distinct line and while it may be crossed, does exist nevertheless. Gang claimers on the other hand, usually are more interested in making money whether by selling drugs or robbing people. Do they cross the line and commit drive-bys and spray paint their insignias all over the place? Sure, but again, it is not their focus. You can look at it this way. Many people want to go to college but have a hard time deciding what to go *for*. Usually at some point, a major and minor are chosen for the particular careers they are interested in.

That same philosophy can be used to understand how gang claimers and gang bangers are different. A gang banger if attending GU (Gangster University), might choose to major in drive-by's while choosing to minor in the sale of marijuana. A gang claimer on the other hand might major in narcotics marketing but minor in graffiti. As I said, some might choose to change their "major" at some point as they progress through college. So to do the mentalities of gang members as they progress through gangland.

I never run from asking myself difficult questions, so I asked myself if I considered gang claimers to be worse than gang bangers because I would have classified myself as a gang banger. I am sure subconsciously that there is some smoke to that fire so to speak. On the other hand, being that I do go back and forth and am very hard on myself, I usually come to the conclusion that gang bangers are far worse because so many more lives are lost at the hands of gang bangers than by the hands of gang claimers. At the end of the day, it matters not that the majority of the lives taken by the hands of gang bangers are other gang members. Loss of life is loss of life.

As people join gangs, I believe age has a large impact on one's mentality/philosophy. Juveniles aged between twelve and nineteen or so, I think are more likely to be gang bangers rather than gang claimers. Those above the age of nineteen usually realize or have started to realize that gang banging in the verbal sense is pretty stupid. By this age, they are likely to have seen shootings, stabbings, and many deaths. They have also witnessed many of their comrades receive life sentences for their roles in this behavior. This has an impact on people whether they are conscious of it or not. There is a reason we don't see to many fifty year olds out doing drive-bys or spray painting their gangs graffiti all over the place. I would have to imagine that most gang-related shootings are committed by those aged between sixteen and twenty-one. There are always exceptions. I am one for instance, I was barely fifteen years old and my codefendant was in his mid- twenties I think.

Let me also be clear that when I stated that thirteen to nineteen-year-olds are more likely to be gang bangers, this is also relative to one's mental maturity. There are some twenty-year-olds that *act* as though they are fifteen and vice versa. These numbers on either end of the spectrum are given in approximation. It is the younger gang member that seems willing to fight, shoot, spray paint, and gang bang. This should come as no surprise because many younger teenagers are often looking for that thrill or rush. These types of activities will often give one a rush. This behavior often gives a juvenile the means to earn one's stripes. This desire to earn one's stripes or show one's loyalty gives birth to the gang banger mentality. You can easily see who has this mentality if you know what characteristics to look for. For those that don't truly have it, a few things can happen. Some get violated out of the gang because they appear to be weak or "scary." Some try and play the role of the tough guy, acting as if they are all hard core. Sometimes they can convince others that they are "hard" but often the gang life has its ways of bringing one's true colors into focus. Many times it is these individuals that get caught committing other crimes and are so quick to turn states evidence against their fellow comrades. For them, depending on their damage control ability as far as their reputation is concerned; they can sometimes maneuver themselves back into their gang's good graces. It is somewhat hard to explain how this can be possible considering that very few things in the gang world are worse than 'snitching'. At least this used to be the case. I have noticed that snitching is much more prevalent these days than it was in years past. I can only assume the reason for this is twofold. **1.** Because everyone is telling on eachother it seems, and **2.** *Because* everyone is, it no longer comes as a surprise when someone is told on by their fellow gang members. You will never get people to admit that "everyone" is telling because by default that would include them.

There are those that will still go down with the ship so to speak, but I believe these individuals are rare. I don't know what has changed over the years, but I am confident that police officers and District Attorneys have welcomed this change. Why has this changed do you think? This chapter concerns the mentality of gang members so I suppose snitching is a part of that mentality. If I had to break down why snitching has become so prevalent, I would begin by stating that in large part it stems from the philosophy of the "entitlement generation", or the "me, me, me", generation. I think if I had to date them, the fatherless generation as I have called them, would pre-date the entitlement generation by one generation. This attitude of me, me, me, seems to encompass today's generation in all areas of society. Why shouldn't it then translate to the gang world as well? It should really come as no surprise now that I think about it. Why would those in the gang world be the only sect in society to not put "me" first? It would make no sense. What people have failed to see however, is the affect this "me" mentality has had on gang violence. I'll explain. As I said in an earlier chapter, one mentality born out of growing up in the gang lifestyle is one of, "I have to kill them before they kill me." That mentality still exists, but now another has been added; "I have to tell on him first before he tells on me." Now if that is where it ended, it would probably be best in the eyes and minds of those in society who want to end gang violence because eventually everyone would tell on each other and pretty soon all gang members would be in prison or stop committing crimes out of fear of being told on. Unfortunately there are elements or byproducts of this mentality that people either can't or don't want to understand. I think there are those in both camps.

This mentality has contributed to an increase in violence altogether because now gang members understand that they essentially have a get out of jail free card as long as they have "dirt on someone else." Think about this for a second. Take a gang member with the "me" mentality and he cares only for himself. In large part, this stems from the belief that everyone else has this same mentality so it only furthers his desires to put himself first. Violence surrounds this gang member on a daily basis so it doesn't take long for him to witness or hear about who has committed certain crimes in his neighborhood. This is not top secret information because gang members and criminals in general love to boast of their "accomplishments." All of this is a part of his mentality. He finds out that one of the individuals he knows has committed a murder. The police do not know who is responsible. Think about what this gives the gang member the ability to do. He can essentially commit any crime short of murder and if caught, simply give information to the police about who committed a murder. He will either be set free or have his sentence shortened greatly. Now imagine a whole community with that mentality and what that mentality could contribute to. Now apply that mentality to communities all over this country. What furthers this behavior is the fact that "snitches" aren't even automatically excommunicated from their particular organizations anymore. Snitching has essentially become acceptable behavior because so many people are doing it.

For those who are X'ed out or kicked out of their gang for any number of reasons, a few things can happen as well. Most likely they still have a criminal mindset and are unwilling to respect their fresh gang free start. Fresh start in that they are no longer a gang member. Oftentimes these individuals will go and become members of a once rival gang because the rival gang is not likely to know the reasons they were kicked out of their previous gang. They "flip." This means they go from one gang to another. This is also called "pan caking." I have known individuals that have done this three and four different times! At the time I was writing this, I have been incarcerated for going on eighteen years and have had the "luxury" of witnessing countless individuals get released as a member of one gang and come back as a member of one of their would be rivals. It is interesting to see the looks on their faces as they tell me what they are now. I can see that they are clearly embarrassed, but not embarrassed enough I suppose or they wouldn't have flipped. This used to surprise me but now it is a regular occurrence. I no longer assume someone is what they were when they left. I notice that they make me angry. Not because they have flipped, but rather because they came back as a different gang member. This means that at some point no matter how short in duration that they were not a member of any gang. They have to renounce their affiliation from one to become another and I just don't understand why they would want to continue living that particular lifestyle. I always try and keep in perspective that I feel this way because I have squandered my life for the sake of gang membership. I ask myself sometimes if I had come to prison for some smaller crime and only received a year or two and then was released, would I have still continued to gang bang? Probably if I am to be honest.

Concerning gang bangers once again, there is an interesting philosophy that they live by. Their mindset evolves as well, almost like "gang banger 2.0." (*Sort of how the iPhone evolved from the i Phone 1 to the iPhone 5.*) I am sure many will choose not to believe this but for the 2.0's, the desire to gang bang is still there but different rules are followed. Gang bangers will not spray paint their graffiti on a church for example. I've always found that to be one of the most interesting moralistic juxtapositions. How can one choose to gang bang and tag everywhere but choose to draw the line at not doing so on the walls of a church? There have been people shot on church steps, but there will be no spray painting on church walls. I was a graffiti artist before I was a gang member so after I became a gang member, I used to spray paint even more. I remember seeing these huge white blank walls that almost seemed to tease me. They would have been a taggers dream canvas, but they belonged to a church. I never spray painted on one. Many gang bangers do not consciously target those who are not in rival gangs. While it has changed somewhat, gang bangers used to give you a pass if they caught you while you were with your child or mom. They wouldn't shoot at all of you just to hit you. Some have chosen to violate this unwritten rule over the years. These violations have however, led to some of the most violent gang wars in this country's history. I have noticed that the gang banger of today is less likely to care who you are with if they happen to catch you. There is becoming a mentality of anarchy. Anything goes these days it seems. This is a scary thought.

This new street mentality is one of utter disregard for anything. Society thought the gang members of old were bad, but this new breed cares of nothing. It is entirely cut throat. Because of this, the entire complexion of gangland is changing. It used to be that these mega organizations like the Bloods, Crips, Gangster Disciples, Vice Lords, Latin Kings, and Spanish Cobra's had huge numbers and all fell under a chain of command. They all had one leader. Over the years of "generation me, me, me," selfishness has prevailed leading to almost a mentality of every man for himself. This in turn spelled doom for the traditional mega organization. They still exist but look completely different than they did fifteen and twenty years ago. Essentially, the once large numbers are still there, but they are now broken down to smaller sets or blocks almost. Many of these "sets" view thier former comrades in no different light than they view their most bitter rivals. I have often wondered why they don't then change their name to something other than their original mega organization name. It is clear that they are not on the same page anymore. They sometimes add a particular street before their original gang's name, or some other small way of differentiating themselves, but they usually keep their same name. There are so many different sets out there now that it is difficult to keep up with all of them. It seems as though everyone is something different.

The streets allow people to be whatever they want to be and do whatever they want to do. You can party, do drugs, be cut throat, snitch, have fun or whatever else you want and really not be held accountable if you can blend in well enough. There is always room to run from repercussion. The street mentality takes a drastic blow however, when one finds themselves within the adult prison system. Culture shock does little justice in trying to explain the drastic difference one faces and feels when they leave the streets for the prison system. Even to this day after living over half of my life in prison, I am in awe at the difference between the street and penitentiary mentality. At first I had chalked up the difference to me coming off of the street and being blasted with a different environment. I realized that this wasn't true when a couple of years ago I was sent back to the county jail for a court hearing. Believe it or not, there is a difference between the mentality of those in the county jail and those in the prison system. I will try and break it down. When someone commits a crime, they are arrested and sent to a county jail within their city's limits. This is not prison. It is within the county jail that people await trial and sentencing. A person gets very little property in the county jail setting. It depends on the jail, but most do not let you have personal clothing but rather mandate that orange or tan jumpsuits be worn. I only note this because in gangland, colored clothing is the easiest way to identify the particular gang one might belong to. This type of identification process is eliminated in the county jail environment.

From a gang perspective, some county jails ask what your particular affiliation is. I'm sure most in society would find this to be an odd question to ask an inmate, thinking they will not be honest and admit that they are in a gang. I can understand why many would think this to be true. In a city that has a very violent gang problem, officials will try and segregate opposing gang members as best as they can. They do this because it lessens the violence within the county jail. If rival gang members are allowed to mingle, there will certainly be a chance for violence to occur. The same philosophy applies to beta fish if you have ever had one; you cannot place more than one in a tank or they will fight. Let's say that you are a member of one gang and do not tell authorities what gang you belong to when you are brought to the county jail. You are treated like every other inmate and sent to a random cell block, pod, or housing unit. What if the unit you are sent to is the unit that authorities have placed all of your rival gang members in? I can assure you that your stay will be short and unpleasant. This is why many gang members will in fact tell the authorities what particular gang they may belong to because they do not want to end up being placed in a cell block with rival gang members.

In other cities where guards are unable to entirely segregate all of the different gangs, there is a high propensity for violence. Imagine living within the demilitarized zone between North and South Korea. The stress would be extreme. There are no guns, but it is very difficult for many gang members to simply forget some of the acts committed by their rivals just a short time earlier when they were free. Within the county jail, the street mentality still exists for some time. The county jail forces you to confront many of the people you were out there robbing, shooting, stabbing etc. What do you think is likely to happen when two enemies meet within the jail? Suddenly they will choose to peacefully coexist? Not likely.

A few things come into play simultaneously. On one hand your freedom is at stake. Depending on the particular crime one may be charged with, there will be the hope that you can beat the charge and go home. If this is your thought process, there will be a part of you that does not want to fight someone who is your enemy because the judge will surely use any violence committed by you in the county jail as a reason to increase your sentence. Due to this, you might be willing to let certain things go, whether it be disrespectful remarks, looks, or other actions by a rival gang member you are in the county jail with. You choose to look the other way in a sense under the guise of going home. On the other end of the spectrum, if you are freshly arrested for committing a triple homicide and are facing the death penalty, you know your chances of ever going home are slim to none. What type of mentality do you think this breeds within the county jail? One of utter disregard for anyone including their own. When there is a belief that one will never go home, there is nothing from an incentive standpoint to not try and make a name for oneself. If you are wondering what is in a name, a reputation; the answer in here is everything. In the prison system, your reputation precedes you wherever you go. If your reputation is poor, then your time will only be that much more difficult because other inmates will treat you accordingly.

A stay in the county jail can last anywhere from a couple of hours up to about a year and a half. Unless you have a really high profile case, the odds of staying at the county jail any longer than a year and a half is not likely. As I said, for those fresh off of the street, they still have that me mentality of selfishness. You couple that with the hatred many have for rival gang members and then put them in the same living unit together and many violent things are likely to happen.

There is not very much structure within the county jail system either. Structure in the sense of gangs being organized. The stays of people in the county jail are usually not long enough to establish any lasting structure. If it is established and everyone there at the time eventually gets sent to the prison system, then they have to start all over again when the next batch of the same gang comes through the county jail. Because of this, there is essentially one big power struggle. If each particular gang is not organized, then they will not be organized in how they interact with one another. This stands in stark contrast to how the prison system is run. There is also a lot of violence between members of the same gang within the county jail. This should come as no surprise. Consider two gang members getting arrested for a homicide. As I said, it is almost a guarantee that one of those two will try and turn states evidence on the other. Word if this will travel, and whoever is thought to be doing the telling will suffer many violent consequences.

In the long hours of anticipating what will or might happen during trial, many are forced to take a strong look at the decisions they have made in life. You have so much time to think, though I have learned that most people do not want to self-reflect. No one wants to look in the mirror. They think if they don't think about what they have done or are doing, somehow they will not have to deal with it emotionally. Little do they know that the longer they try and suppress what they are feeling or feel, the worse it will eventually come out at a later time. This must be a product of the free world because sadly, almost all of the free people that I know are clearly choosing not to deal with many aspects of their life out of the fear of facing their emotions. I couldn't live like that personally. You can try and run from the past, but the past will never get tired of chasing you. It is tireless.

Many newly incarcerated individuals can only think of ways to remove themselves from their current plight. Anything would be better than this. It's interesting how many at this point will try and make deals with God. "Please God, just let me go home and I swear

I will never do anything bad ever again!" I expect that most people go through this, but I don't think God makes deals to free people from certain plights. I have also found it interesting how people living within the county jail swear up and down that they will never be back if they are let out this one last time. Yet all they talk about is getting high, selling dope, and playing females. I have come to the conclusion that this is delusional thinking. I think they actually believe they will not come back but are unable to see that their mindset has not changed, but rather is just being manipulated by the beast of incarceration. The mental toll incarceration takes from an aspect of wishing one were in any other situation than "this", is enormous. This will create a false belief that they will never come back. Many can actually convince themselves of this, but they are delusional. Their hatred for their current physical plight gives a false sense of desiring to change. Change can be born out of the loins of hardship, but the hardship must be more than a few losses of physical activities.

For those that think they do broker a deal with God and somehow catch a break, their desire of change is built on a foundation of sand. It is likely to crumble when the memories of incarceration gradually begin to fade. When this happens, the "true you" slowly starts to come back into focus. If one never faced their issues of narcotic use or desire to gang bang fully, soon that brokered deal with God will cease to exist as you begin what you used to do. And the cycle continues.

For those that do not catch a break and are sentenced to prison, a few more things are placed on one's plate. Bitterness towards God often takes place for a time with thoughts of, "Why did you do this to me, I really would have changed if you would have given me one more chance!" The larger the sentence, the less one will likely care about doing the right thing at first. I guess this could be described as shock to an extent. People are very likely to lash out because they are unable to cope with the idea of spending huge amounts of time behind bars. This is especially true for those sentenced to life sentences. Hope seems bleak, retreating like light from darkness at sunset. When that hope fades, despair is born. Out of this; anger, rage, fear, and hatred. People can understand anger and it often becomes one's only companion, a friend to ward off despair.

Anarchy rules the street, but despair rules the penitentiary. There is no place to run in here, both from a physical and mental aspect. Everything catches up to you. **Everything** becomes so unbelievably serious in here. In prison, many people will never see the light of a free day ever again. When you leave the county jail and enter the prison system, you enter *their* home, their life for the duration. This is an important aspect because structure now becomes an issue. This can be very bad for some, as well as falsely good for others. For those gang members that have snitched on their fellow brother in arms, tough days are in store. It is arbitrary dependant upon what state one is sentenced to, as to what will happen when a "snitch" arrives in the prison. Prison systems are definitely not created equal. Some may die very quickly after arrival, while some may just get beat up or escape completely unscathed if they are lucky enough to never be found out.

When I was arrested, I had no idea of what to expect. I had never been to jail or prison before, so I had only word of mouth and what I have seen on TV to go on. I had the added stress element because I was so young. I was the youngest and smallest inmate at every single place I went up until I was in my later teens. There were no special units for young inmates at the time because there weren't any other inmates as young as I was. It was a weird feeling to never see a single person younger than I was for the first four or so years of my incarceration. Not one! I can remember sitting in the van in the sally port of the first adult prison I was sent to. I will not lie, I was scared. All I had in my mind were images I had seen in the movies. Beyond that, I had the words of other inmates and the sheriffs that told me I would be getting raped in the adult prison system because I was so small and young. I had no reason at the time to think they were not telling me the truth. What they said correlated with what I saw in the movies. I was scared of being raped more than anything else. I didn't care about getting beat up or even stabbed that much, just being raped. I was eventually placed in a holding cell after I got off of the van. There were about fifteen other inmates in the cell with me, all of them adults. I was very uncomfortable. I remember seeing in the movies that you had to make a quick name for yourself if you hoped not to become prey. I didn't know if I should just start punching people so they would think I wasn't scared or what. One of the other inmates asked me how old I was. When I told them, everyone was kind of shocked. They wanted to know what I did, why I was in there. I didn't answer any more questions.

I was placed in a cell after my intake procedures were done. No more than forty-five seconds later, a pack of cigarettes came sliding under my door. I couldn't see who slid them under my door, but one of the things I was told while in the county jail is to never accept anything from another inmate because you will then be in their debt. I quickly kicked the cigarettes out of my cell. A second or two later, they came sliding back under. I still couldn't see who was out there because my cell door was solid, not barred. I kicked them out again and then this huge white inmate appeared in the cell window of my door. I don't know if he was huge, but I think the situation made my mind think he was like seven feet tall. He probably was of normal height. Before I could say anything, he bent down and kicked the cigarettes back under my door while saying, "These are yours." He barely got the word "yours" out before I kicked them back out of my door and told him I don't smoke. He kind of looked at me with a quizzical look upon his face and then it must have dawned on him what I was thinking, why I kept kicking those cigarettes back under the door. He chuckled and said *something*, I didn't know what because I was too busy trying to determine whether or not he was trying to buy me or not. I said, "What?" He said, "Relax, do you know Rico C?" I was trying to slow my mind down because I knew of someone that had this name, but I couldn't understand how he would know to ask me that, so the context really was not forming for me. He asked me again. Why the hell was this guy asking me if I knew Rico C? Hesitantly I said yes, and asked what about him. He said that he was on another unit and knew I was coming. He then told me that cigarettes were a form of currency. He said that Rico would meet me when we had recreation so that we could talk and asked me if I needed anything else in the meantime. I told him no, but thanked him for giving me the message. I hated cigarettes and the particular unit I was on happened to be a smoke free unit, but that did not stop me from going to the window and smoking a cigarette in the hopes of calming my nerves like people say smoking does. Needless to say that my nerves were not calmed.

As I sat there alone, I wondered how they knew I was there. I was only in the cell for a moment. I knew that people in the prison I was eventually going to go to were waiting on my arrival, but I did not think I would have been expected at the intake prison. I later found out that word was put out to watch for me when I got there. In one sense I was lucky to belong to a large and powerful organization. I do not condone ever being a gang member, but I would be lying if I did not benefit from a safety standpoint because of what organization I belonged to.

My mentality was about to change from one of the street, to one of the penitentiary. At the time, a few different things were going through my mind. On one hand, the fact that there were a lot of powerful gang members whom were legends on the street that were waiting on me, made me feel important. Let me be clear, my mentality over these next four years was one that I am not proud of. I do not condone what I did or thought, but feel that I have to be honest in what I felt to help you better understand the prison mentality. I compounded horrible decision upon horrible decision. Honestly, I am disgusted with many of those behaviors, however I cannot change the past and I do not run from what I did. I accept fully, everything I did after I have come to prison. If I could un-ring that bell I definitely would, but alas I cannot.

My ego was boosted because so many people knew who I was. It gave me a false sense of pride. I had this life sentence over my head that I was trying so hard not to face, that I took solace in anything that I could. As the days progressed, I simply refused to acknowledge that I could spend the rest of my days behind bars. I was clearly in denial. That very first day I made a "shank." (*A knife that I manufactured out of a sharpened toothbrush.*) Obviously this was a rule violation and I make no excuse for doing this, but my reasoning was that I thought that this is what one did upon coming to prison. This is what they did in the movies. The reality is that I was scared for my life. I honestly thought that I was going to get raped. I knew that I had rival gang members that were also waiting to catch up to me for what I had done, so in the mindset of survival of the fittest, I made a shank. As I think back, I can only shake my head. I was just thrown into the adult prison system. I wasn't old enough to even have a learners permit, and here I was faced with all sorts of things a teenager should never be faced with. I will be the first to admit that I and others like me need to be punished, and I deserved everything that I experienced those first few years of incarceration, but there has got to be a better way. There was no rule book of what to expect, what I was supposed to do in certain situations. Yes, the prison officials give everyone an inmate handbook with prison rules, but that book did nothing in the way of helping me with what to do in countless other situations.

I was in a daze, almost in an auto pilot sort of trance. There were a couple of surreal moments when I would almost see myself from an out of body perspective, trying to contextualize the situation. I remember filing one end of the toothbrush down and then stopping for a second. "Am I in a movie?" I wondered. "This has to be a dream!" "Am I really on my hands and knees sharpening a toothbrush?" "I was just on the honor Roll not to long ago, a Boy Scout for God's Sake!" "What the hell happened?!" And then back to sharpening, and sharpening, and sharpening. It took me what seemed like forever, perhaps because I was trying to be quite so those in the cells next to and below me could not hear what I was doing. I was also looking out for guards every once in a while. I didn't know what to make of them at the time. I honestly thought that they would treat me different because I was so young, but they didn't. In the movies, prison guards seemed to be as bad as the inmates, so I was extremely wary of them as well. Loneliness and I became bitter friends.

I was found by other members of my gang at chow and on the recreation field. They informed me about what was going on in that prison and that we weren't currently at war with anyone. There were a few individuals that I was told to keep an eye on for however simply because they were Latin Kings.

This is one aspect of prison that has changed. Back in the seventies, eighties, and nineties, the prison system was much more serious than it is today. It is still a violent place today, but nowhere near as violent as it used to be. There are a few reasons for this change, most notably because of all the new segregation units that each prison has built. There has also been a boom in the creation of so called "Supermax" prisons across the United States. In the earlier days of my incarceration, if two inmates were to get into a fight, they would only spend three days in the hole as punishment. The only way you got more time is if you stabbed or jumped someone. With the penalty being only three days for fighting, there was really no disincentive to fight others. Three days was nothing. Now when two inmates get into a fight, they will get anywhere between ninety and three hundred and sixty days in the hole. Half a year spent in the hole is incentive for many to not be as serious. Don't get me wrong, plenty of people still fight, most just in the hopes of not getting caught. This has affected gang violence in the prison system to some extent. In many ways, it has curtailed the *amount* of gang violence committed solely for gang-related reasons; however it has also increased the severity of the violence. It has done so by creating a festering environment if you will. When the punishment for fighting was only three days, many people did not feel the need to hold their grudges in. Just like when you shake a can of soda, when it gets opened it explodes all over the place. Now that gang members know that if they fight they will serve long periods of time in the hole, they feel they might as well get their "money's worth" and really try to hurt the other individual.

I spent about two months in the intake prison before I was sent to the hole myself for the first time. The reason epitomized my juvenile attitude at the time. An officer felt that the shirt I was wearing was to large and ordered me to wear a smaller one. In my mind, the shirt he gave me to wear instead was entirely too tight. I ended up throwing the shirt at him and was subsequently taken to the hole. Needless to say, I did not come out victorious in that little battle. I remained in segregation until I was transferred to a maximum security prison where I would spend many of my next years in life. At the time, this prison was referred to as "Gladiator School" because all of the gang bangers were sent there to do time. I was actually happy to be sent there because this is the prison I had individuals waiting for me at. Earlier in this book I detailed my first day in this prison. After that day, all of my fellow gang members were locked up and placed under investigation because of the day's events. My name had yet to cross the desk of the gang Captain because I had just gotten there the day before, so I was not on the temporary lock up list. I thought you have to be kidding me. I was all alone. It was quite a humbling feeling. That is when the loneliest place on earth became an overcrowded prison. I will never be able to find the words that describe those feelings and emotions. I had to shut off everything inside of me. Emotion was weakness I learned. It gave other inmates an upper hand. I suppose a part of me died in those days because I don't know if some of the emotions I had to turn off can ever be found again. I look at those emotions as casualties of war however, the war to keep my sanity. If I stopped to evaluate my then current situation, I would surely have gone mad.

I wonder at times if that is what the judge had in mind when he sentenced me. For years I was incredibly mad at "the system" for essentially throwing me to the wolves. There were situations that I found myself in that no teenager should ever go through. On the other hand, I deserved every single second of those moments for my actions as a fifteen-year-old. My victims did not get to choose their circumstances, so why should I be given that luxury? I was curious about what being in a gang meant. Well, my curiosity was certainly quelled. Now I knew what it meant to be a gang member, to play with the big boys so to speak. I had finally gotten what my actions dictated that I wanted. My victims did not get a second chance, so how could I cry for one? These thoughts made me begin to hate myself. I began mentally punishing myself during the day, begging God to take my life at night.

This was my life now. My hopes of being a fighter jet pilot— dead, that young astronaut and Boy Scout—dead. All that was left was an empty reflection in the mirror. Remnants of my once great potential. Later I rationalized this time as needing to lose myself before I could find myself.

I was all in at this point, or so I had to make myself believe. I felt as though I had to trick myself into finding a way to cope. I knew I had a life sentence and by default that prison would be my home for the rest of my life. One of the first lessons that I learned was to never believe you would ever go home. I know it will be difficult for any who have not experienced what I have to understand that, but believing you will die in prison makes it easier to forget about what could have been, what will never be. It is a way of pushing freedom as far away from one's mind as possible. After all, what good was freedom anymore?

It was difficult for me to do this at first because almost every other inmate loved to reminisce about the past. I really had no past to reminisce about. I hadn't really lived life yet, had never drove, had my own place, or even gone to a high school dance for that matter. All of my memories came from birth to eighth grade, and I really couldn't remember much from my first couple of years of life, so…….. My memories and dreams quickly became those of prison life. I felt as though my only course of action was to lose myself in this life completely. The gang culture back then was so serious. There were no games played in those days. You had better not even look at someone wrong or they would make you taste your own blood. One such gang war lasted three years between the Cobra's and the Black St one's. Hits were ordered all over the state. When someone got out of the hole, they were immediately beaten again. It went back and forth until finally a truce was called. The stress from that war aged me beyond my years. It really did not even stem from the actual acts of violence, but rather the mental strain from constantly being on alert. You could never let your guard down or show the slightest sign of weakness. If you did, your own kind would take a strong look at you first of all, never mind what the opposition would do to you. Everything was about perception. If one was viewed as weak, then all were viewed as weak, so the weak were quickly ostracized. Every time I left my cell I had to look over my shoulder. If we went to shower, we had to wear our tennis shoes and carry our shower shoes just in case something occurred. One cannot fight very well in shower shoes. I'm sure people think that inmates would not fight naked, but that would be a wrong assumption.

There were so many rules. There were the prison rules given to you by the guards, the rules given to you by the gang you belonged to, and then the unwritten rules of penitentiary living. The rules given to us by the guards were the ones cared about the least. When you violated the other ones is when you paid your dues. These sanctions could be physical, monetary, or both. Sometimes instead of you getting a physical violation for breaking the rules of your gang, you were told to go and beat up a rival gang member. This is when things really spiraled out of control, not that there was ever really any true control. Every organization was different from a structure standpoint. Some were very strict, like the one I belonged to, others not so much. I found this out the hard way on a couple of occasions. I was young and wild. I felt this need to always have to prove myself because of my size and age. I felt I had to gang bang harder than the next man to prove I wasn't just some little kid. Tattoos were one way of representation. I had a few prior to coming to prison, but received many more while behind bars. Some of these would take hours at a time. This was done by switching cells with other inmates without the guard's knowledge. Inmates would switch for the night sometimes because certain tattoos took so long to do. If a guard walked by, you just turned around and acted like you were washing your hands. When they did their counts, most of them just looked for a body and not for a particular face.

Anyway, my "enthusiasm" to gang bang harder than everyone else caught up to me one day when I went to the library and did some graffiti on one of the walls. I was disrespecting another organization. It was huge and I thought it was just another way to prove that I was not afraid to go that "extra mile." Yea, that didn't work out to well for me. I got violated by my own gang before members of a rival gang could do anything to me. As I said, prison is all about respect. My actions placed every single one of my fellow gang members at-risk for retaliation. They did not know the graffiti existed at first, so if a rival gang member saw it and decided to attack the first Spanish Cobra that he saw; it would be on my head. It would have stemmed from my careless actions. Beyond that, who do you think had to clean that graffiti up? Not an officer, that's for sure. It was the inmate custodian for the library that had to clean that up. Now he was an enemy because I made his job more difficult. Had he been a member of a different gang, that incident could have sparked a war.

I am sure much of this seems impossible to comprehend. None of it is sane or rational behavior. It is all insanity at its finest, but the reality is when you take everything from man, they will find something to garner control over. This is why prison was so serious.

In this chapter's prologue, I explained that on the street, many gang members were not forced to complete school. Some did not want to be seen learning anything anyway because they suffered from an image crisis. In the prison system however, there comes a change in that behavior, especially for those belonging to the more structured organizations. There are many organizations that mandate that you go to school and get your GED. There are many gangs that mandate that you work out, stay fit, and not smoke or do drugs. In prison, it is no longer cool to skip school, to not have an education. I won't lie; this surprised me as I learned all of this. I expected that prison would be the opposite, that no one would care if you went to school or indulged any other vice you wanted. Now let me be clear; there are many more gangs and organizations that do not enforce any of these things on their members than do, so please do not think that. These gangs are not well-structured however. Unfortunately or fortunately, I guess it depends how you view the situation, institutional staff really aren't concerned with these gangs because they are cut throat and disorganized. Solidarity worries prison officials, not anarchy.

For those that do belong to very structured organizations, the violation of their rules brings swift punishment. The reason is similar to why the military has such strict protocols. Military command has to ensure that there is a high discipline standard. Chain of command is strictly enforced. Orders are expected to be obeyed. They do not want their soldiers questioning their superior officers in the heat of the battle because people can die. This holds true for gang leaders as well. Gang life is a constant war of sorts; with very little time for peace. When things hit the fan so to speak, a swift response is carried out to show strength. All prison systems are different. Some prisons do not have any murders. In other systems, people are murdered and stabbed numerous times each month. In the federal system, respect is paramount. Each organization and race polices themselves. There are very few random unsanctioned fights between rivals because this behavior can quickly lead to a war. I don't think that society has a clue as to how violent the federal system is. Many in society think if you simply mind your own business, you won't have any problems in prison. This may hold true in many state prisons, but not for the federal system.

There are countless people that have come to the federal system with only a few years to do for a sentence, and end up dying or receiving a life sentence for murdering someone. Sometimes there are situations that only allow one person to walk away alive. You do not have to be the aggressor or instigator, merely there. There is absolutely no excuse to take someone's life, but there are often many situations that are no fault of your own that lead you to either kill or be killed. It is not right, or justifiable, or moral, but rather reality.

Moving on, there are many gang members that do want to free themselves from the grips of gang membership, but are afraid to—for various reasons. As I said earlier in this book, I have spoken with many gang leaders that have told me personally that they wished they were no longer in a gang. They do not renounce their affiliation for many different reasons however. For some, it would be like abandoning their family and subsequently like being abandoned by their own family. Regardless of your own personal moral thoughts on the gang life, you have to understand why it is hard for some to leave that life. You can look at it this way. Let's say that you are an American diplomat living in South Korea. You are likely to view the North Koreans as somewhat of the enemy because many of their actions and practices you view are evil. The North Koreans however, do not view themselves as evil. In their minds, they are in the right, they are "just." They would die for the sake of their country out of patriotism, even though to you, it seems as though they are on the wrong side of right. If they sought asylum in another country, they would feel as though they betrayed their country. I am not saying that gang members are like North Koreans, but you can look at it in the same way. Regardless of whether or not their "war", their "life" is justifiable in your eyes, does not mean that they view it the same way. This is how you have to look at the situation to understand it.

Many are quick to simply say that gang members know that what they are doing is wrong, so they can just stop. What if they actually do not believe what they are doing is wrong? Remember, perception is everything. *Your* reality and theirs if believed to be different, creates a different set of rules to play by. Of course you believe *you* are right, but wouldn't they have to believe that they are right in order to do what they do?

I have asked many gang members why they do not simply renounce their gang affiliation if they no longer want to be a gang member. They give a plethora of excuses that perhaps even they themselves believe. The real answer is really a very simple one. The street is a far easier place to renounce their gang affiliation. The street gives an individual numerous places to hide from repercussions. In prison you are forced to face every single decision you make. There is no place to run. If you renounce your gang affiliation while still incarcerated, there is a one hundred percent chance that you will face the consequences. Different gangs deal differently with those who renounce their gang affiliation, none of them being pleasant however. I don't even think it is the physical aspects that most individuals face, but rather the psychological effects from being completely ostracized. If one were living the gang life, it goes without question that they most likely have been beat up before so they really aren't too worried about bruises that will most likely heal.

I'm sure that many would think that the physical would far outweigh the mental, but again you have to look at it with the mind of a gang member. Often they have spent much of their entire life being a "we." It becomes a comfort, a falsified belief that that no matter where you are, you are not alone. The human nature aspect of seeking the opposite of solitude comes into play here. Very few people in this world truly want to be alone, regardless of duration. Why do you think so many kids hang out with so many "friends" their parents do not want them to associate with? They want to feel accepted. Once accepted, the euphoria experienced from believing they are a part of something larger tends to stifle that little voice in one's head that says these are not the type of friends that I should be associating with.

After years and years of convincing oneself that they are a "we", there comes a sense of panic at the thought of being an "I" rather than a "we." I again will use a military analogy. When soldiers face life and death situations *together,* they form a bond. When a soldier's tour is up and they are forced to go back stateside, they often do so with feelings of guilt for leaving their fellow brothers behind. The guilt can be overwhelming at times, sometimes leading to alcoholism, abuse and violence. The same holds true for many gang members who contemplate leaving the gang lifestyle. Gang members often face life and death situations with one another. You must remember that just because these life and death situations are not justified in your mind, this fact doesn't change anything in their world. Of course they should not be in these situations, but we are beyond that point now. You cannot look at their situation through *your* eyes, with your life experiences. If you do, then the gang problem will continue to be as it is.

Why wouldn't a gang member feel a similar bond towards their fellow gang member just like soldiers feel towards one another? To understand why it is hard for a gang member to renounce their affiliation while still behind bars, you can look at it in this way. Think of the soldiers right now in Afghanistan. They are in a battle but one of them decides that he no longer wants to fight or be a soldier. The reason doesn't matter. It could be that he no longer believes in war, just had a baby or whatever. What comes next is purely a hypothetical scenario, at least as far as the physical location of the soldier.

The soldier is allowed to "quit" if you will, but he is not allowed to go home until the rest of his units tour is up, 18 months later. This soldier is forced to live in the same barracks as the rest of his fellow soldiers. He still must eat in the same mess hall and use the same recreation facilities. He is in the middle of a desert so like many prisons; there is no place to run. He is forced to look in the eyes of every single soldier that had previously put their life on the line for him. Put aside your judgments that he is getting what he deserved. Yes, he might be but that is besides the point for this scenario. How do you think those eighteen months would be for that soldier? It might help to break those eighteen months down into 13,140 hours. Take just one of those hours that are given for one of his meals. The ex-soldier takes his tray through the line and puts it on the counter for one of his once fellow soldiers to place some food on it. How will that exchange go do you think? That soldier serving the food knows he quit on them.

Someone has to give him his mail, clean his clothes, and sleep in the bunk above or below him. These small seemingly insignificant blocks of time are all minutes where he is forced to interact with those he is ashamed to look in the eye. Eighteen months is 788,400 minutes. If he slept a third of that away, he would have 525,600 minutes left in which to interact with soldiers that look at him with disgust. Do you think there would be no physical retaliation, no theft or damaging of his property? Those 525,600 minutes would be hell, would seem like forever. Do me a favor; count to sixty in your head. Seriously, stop reading this page and count to sixty for me.

Did you do it? Good, only 525,599 more blocks of time like that and the ex-soldier's tour will be up. *Your* sixty seconds were not however, wrought with violence, intimidation, and ridicule. I'm sure you understand the time spent doing something that you enjoy goes much faster than time spent experiencing something horrible. Those

525,600 minutes would feel more like five years than eighteen months.

I raised this to ask if a soldier knew he would have to endure those hardships if he decided to quit, do you think he would still quit or wait until his tour was up when he would no longer have to be surrounded by his once fellow brothers in arms? I have learned in life that most people choose the path of least resistance when it comes to potential emotional mental/physical hardship. I have learned that many human beings are weak and do not want to face what they themselves have created. We are all guilty of this to some degree, some just more so than others. Some learn that to take the easy way out now will surely make it more difficult to face in the future. I found that out the hard way. Now I purposely look for the hard way out because I know it will only get easier for me in the future. It is one of the single greatest lessons that I have ever learned. With this strategy, I no longer run from the past. As I said earlier, the past will never tire from chasing you.

Now take that same soldier scenario and apply a similar philosophy to an incarcerated gang member contemplating renouncing their gang affiliation. The situation is quite a bit different however. The soldier didn't have much incentive to "quit", but the gang member has even less. Depending on the state, system, and gang, the gang member has this to look forward to upon renouncing his gang affiliation: beatings, stabbings, shame, protective custody, banishment, rape, or murder. Prisons are not the barracks. People will go out of their way to make you suffer. They will squeeze enjoyment out of this. Those eighteen months, or 525,600 minutes are often ten, fifteen, or twenty years plus. Literally millions and millions of tortuous minutes would be spent enduring whatever your former gang members had planned for you. I am sure it has lost all perspective for you once I started saying millions of minutes, but this is the reality.

Let's say that one gang member wishes to renounce his gang affiliation and has only ten years left before he goes home. I say *only* ten years because quite honestly, ten years is a small amount of time for a gang-related crime. Ten years is about 5,256,000 minutes. To try and put that into perspective, a football game on average lasts about 180 minutes. Ten years equates to about 29,200 football games. There are only 256 football games played in the regular season each year. If you watched every single football team play every single game, ten years would be the equivalent of watching 114 whole seasons straight. Watching football is time spent in enjoyment, so the time goes rather fast. Now imagine watching those 114 seasons of football, but every single game was the worst possible game you have ever seen. Beyond that, for every play that you watch in those 114 seasons, imagine that those are moments also spent worrying about what others will do to you, and enduring what they *are* doing to you. That is a stress that you cannot imagine, and that is for only ten years. I can give you all of the analogies I want, but nothing will fully put the situation into perspective. Imagine the most horrific, violent, stressful moment in your life. Now imagine feeling that same exact way for ten years without any real sense of a break. If gang members know that the next "ten" years would feel like that, can you start to understand why there are so few gang members willing to renounce their gang affiliation while still behind bars? As I said earlier, we are beyond "they made their bed", at least if we truly want to make the situation better. We are beyond the blame stage. We have to be to solve the gang problem because unfortunately, change really only comes via two avenues in my opinion. **1.** One day you look in the mirror and hate who you are more than the hardships that you will endure if you change, or **2.** You are blindsided by a tragic event in which you lose everything. This is when change is the hardest; because often times you have very little options at this point. Usually you have dug yourself in quite a hole, both emotionally and mentally. Many people give up at this point because they feel it is too difficult to ever recover. Many feel that their life is over anyway so they might as well go down with the ship. If you do not believe in an afterlife, then what point is there to change one may wonder? I will speak more on change in an upcoming chapter.

As far as gang members renouncing their gang affiliation prior to being released from prison, I hope you can see why it is not as easy as one might think. Again, I am making no excuses. To the contrary, I guarantee that I am less tolerant than you are on the subject because I renounced my gang affiliation when I was more than twenty years away from my *first chance* at parole. *(That is a lot of football games.)*

Honestly, I think a very good gauge to judge the extent of someone's desire to leave the gang life is whether or not they renounced their affiliation while still incarcerated. I am a firm believer in the theory of nothing good in life comes without toil. Yes, it is much easier to leave the gang life after you are out of prison. I explained what many face physically and emotionally if they renounce their gang affiliation while still incarcerated. These consequences are ***huge*** disincentives.

The prison gang world thrives on fear and intimidation. If there were no consequences to renouncing one's gang affiliation, many would do so. I know this is hard for some to believe and you do not have to if you do not want to, but it is the truth. Very few enjoy being ordered to go beat up or stab a rival gang member and receive more time in prison. Very few enjoy having to constantly be on guard. That is a stress you can never begin to comprehend. It sucks the life out of you. Dominance and control are what in theory, lead to a better stay while incarcerated----at least from the standpoint of those who are calling the shots. The means to this end comes along the pathway of violence, both physical and mental. The larger each organizations numbers, the easier it is to control the situation. Gang leaders understand that if they lose the numbers, they lose their power. They will use unspeakably violent means to ensure that their numbers stay large. This does not bode well for the gang member contemplating renouncement.

I believe that one has to almost despise the lifestyle in order to face the consequences of renouncing their affiliation while still incarcerated. Think about it, what other incentive is going to outweigh the negative disincentives? Doing the right thing? Yes, but many people are in prison because they were unable to do the right thing. You truly have to hate what you were or are a part of to do this while still in prison.

It's interesting, I have known a few individuals who have renounced their gang affiliation while incarcerated and then went home. Their recidivism rate I have noticed is unbelievably low. Beyond that, I have never met a gang member who renounced their affiliation while incarcerated, got released, and came back as a member of a different gang. I'm sure that there are some who do this, but I have personally never run into them. Why do you think this is? To understand this, you have to go back to what I said about really hating what you had become, as well as taking into account what one most likely endured after they renounced their affiliation prior to being released. If they didn't hate being a gang member before, I'm sure what happened to them after brought that hate on. I have seen some really horrible things happen to those who have renounced their affiliation while still incarcerated. I can guarantee that the desire to participate in that lifestyle again is not high on one's priority list.

Beyond being done with the gang life itself, often comes the desire to leave the criminal life behind all together. This comes from a new mentality that is formed out of self-reflection. In order to "volunteer" for the consequences that will be suffered if one renounces their gang affiliation while still incarcerated, there is a good chance that the individual in question has been doing some serious self-reflection on their choices and decisions. They have certainly begun to take a real good look at themselves; who they were, who they are, what they want, and what they don't. With these thoughts comes the realization of pain caused to others by you, their victimization via your hands. This is a difficult phase, but it often gives one the courage to want so badly to never inflict that sort of pain again. Beyond that, these former gang members know that if they commit any crime and are sent back to prison, their former gang will be waiting for them. They will be thrilled to see their return. Out of this fear often comes the desire to live a better life.

It is so unbelievably difficult to understand the many different mentalities in gangland. Unfortunately, we as a society have little choice in what to do now. We must try and understand them all because the key to true prevention lies within this understanding. It will be an uphill battle to say the least, but a necessary one.

Chapter Nine

The Warning Signs: knowing what to look for

Many families simply do not know what to look for when it comes to identifying possible warning signs of gang involvement. So many juveniles could be saved from the grips of gang membership if their families knew what to look for. This does not necessarily mean that the parents in question are not paying attention to their child, but rather that they have an inability to understand what they are seeing.

Essentially, I went from the Honor Roll to serving a life sentence in a very short period of time. Some parents believe that because their child is doing well in school, they couldn't possibly be involved with any sort of gang activity. My family really had no reason to look for the warning signs of possible gang involvement. Even if they were looking for signs that I had joined a gang, they would have had no idea what to look for.

Unfortunately, parents today have no reliable source of information that can be easily found. The information that a New

York parent needs compared to that of what a Dallas parent needs might be completely different. Different areas of the country have different fads, different ways of thinking, and different ways of representing one's gang affiliation. Some of the simple external signs a parent can easily spot are things like the color of a child's wardrobe. In most cases, gangs identify themselves with certain colors. It is usually a combination of two colors in the Midwest, with one of the colors normally being black. There are many exceptions and this is exactly my point. There is no one set look all gang members have. If a parent was to buy their child some clothes and the child tells the parent that they hate that color, it is *possible* that they are involved in some gang activity. Now does this mean that every kid who wants to wear a certain color is involved with a gang? Of course not, perhaps the child just likes a certain color.

Another thing to look for is if a child no longer wants to go to a certain area of town with their parent. Perhaps this area is in an area occupied by rival gang members. Again, this is no sure thing but rather a possibility. There are numerous signs that a parent can see as long as they know what they are looking for.

Topics and questions elaborated on in this chapter will include:

- o Colors do matter.
- o Sports logos and their hidden meanings.
- o Drug use.
- o Late for dinner or early for death?
- o Friends over family?

1 2 3 4 5 6 7 8 9 10

*   *   *

A parent's love is often blind. This is good in many respects but can also be a detriment. No parent wants to believe that their child is bad or evil. A parent wants to believe that their child is good and that they have been raised well by them. Out of this "want", sometimes comes a belief that their child can do no wrong. "Not *my* child" they say to themselves. Parents have a tendency I have noticed, to get very defensive when someone accuses their child of doing something wrong especially if the child says their accuser is lying. Parents blind themselves to reality it seems, and this can have serious consequences later in life for the child in question. What often happens is by the time the parent comes to grips with the fact that their child isn't as innocent as they once believed, much damage has already accrued.

For the record, when I speak of parents I am implying caretakers in general. This could refer to parents, grandparents, aunts, foster parents, etc.

I have asked myself what constitutes a good parent. What makes a good parent? Is there a specific definition? Can we make this determination while their child is still a child, or do we have to wait until they grow up before we can answer that question? Here is something interesting that seems like such an obvious statement. I don't know what made me think it, or become surprised as I pondered it. I have found only one thing that every single gang member that I have spoken with has in common. Every single gang member has a parent. I know, I know, a parent is more than giving birth to a child or impregnating a woman who gives birth. I'm not speaking of a parent in the verbal sense. Let's say that there have been five million gang members to have ever existed over the course of time. Would you say that by default, every sing parent of those five million gang members would have to be labeled as bad parents simply because their child ended up as gang members?

If you as a parent have a child that becomes a gang member, are you automatically a bad parent? Now that I think about it, I am really curious as to what your opinions of this question are. I'm sure there would be many that would most certainly say that yes, you would have to be a bad parent if you allowed your child to become a gang member. I think most of these people however, are the type that cast stones in glass houses, but I guess I could make an argument for that philosophy. I could also make an argument against automatically deeming every parent of a gang member as a bad parent. I think these are dicey waters because there are so many things we do not understand about the human mind, body, and soul. Without certain facts, no one but God can deem a parent good or bad, at least categorically. Obviously if a parent beats a child, they are bad parents. So many things come into play with this argument. The human nature question once again pops into my mind. Are we born good or evil? Are we formed by our circumstances? I don't know what your belief is. I raise this to say that if you believe some are born evil, then that child could have Saints for parents and yet they would still be labeled as bad parents if their child grew up to become a gang member. If a child is born evil, can they have good parents? If so, how would you define them as such? We do not know who is born evil or if some are, so we will never know whether the child became evil as a product of bad parenting or because they were born evil. Also, the question of free will comes back into play as well, somewhat mirroring whether or not some are born evil. Again, if one's fate is set, are their parents capable of being either good or bad? Are they simply parents without the capability to mold the soul of their own child?

We cannot know for sure some of these questions, and because of this inability to truly know, we as a society have to essentially take the safe route and error on the side of caution *if* we have to error. We have to assume that a parent does in fact have the ability to shape the morals of a child's soul, that they are not born evil. With this belief, we have to give parents all of the tools to identify early warning signs that a child might show. These signs are often very subtle and almost indistinguishable from other childhood misbehavior caused by normal rebellion. I don't think rebellion has to always be criminal in nature. I think most kids at some point in their life rebel in some fashion.

Childhood is ripe with change. Change will be born out of curiosity. This stems from wanting to identify who we are in life. Unfortunately, we have to often make mistakes along the way to finding out who we are. It is difficult to sometimes distinguish "normal" childhood rebellion from the warning signs a child might give off if they are gravitating towards gang members. The very first thing that *every* parent needs to do is tell themselves that it is possible that their child can join a gang. Every parent needs to say this. I can understand the hesitation to do this because after all, "My kid could never join a gang", right? If you are a parent, you can choose to not believe that your kid can possibly become a gang member. This is your right. If this is your stance, I think this makes you a bad parent by default. I'm sure this must sound disrespectful, but I assure you that I do not intend it as such. I am not saying that you should think it probable or even remotely likely, but rather only possible. I say this because if a parent is steadfast in their belief that their child will never join a gang, they will have blinders on. They will see only what they want to see. They will make excuses for what they really see and not even be aware that they are doing so. Many parents can convince themselves that the situation is not as bad as it appears. I can understand this concept and would probably be guilty of it myself had I been free to raise my son.

This does not make it alright however. A parent cannot have the mindset of, "If I ignore it, maybe it will fix itself." I have talked to many gang members and non-gang members and asked them what their first rebellious act was. It seems so many of them were clear cries for help. Clear in the "hindsight 20/20" variety. I think if many parents look back at certain events they once thought as insignificant, they might see them in a different light. This really does not matter much anymore because we cannot change the past, regardless what light we shine on it. I only raise it now so that parents today do not have to experience what the parents of yesterday did. I believe that a parent has to believe their child is capable of anything, both good and bad. It definitely works both ways. If you believe your child is stupid and will amount to nothing, then they will probably have higher chances of doing just that. Your actions will enforce that belief.

I was re-reading the last page or so and realized that much of what I have just said should be of the common sense variety. As I have stated, sense it seems however, is definitely not common. As I am thinking about it, most people should know much of what I am writing. I think the problem comes from the fact that most people do not see how important all of these little events are. Most people cannot see that the gang problem is a culmination of so many seemingly trivial issues. Individually yes, they are trivial. Put them together however, and you have a massive gang problem.

I think that there is a difference between a parent believing their child is capable of anything (*Becoming a gang member for instance*), and a parent believing their child has the potential to become an astronaut. I am not saying that you should believe your kid will become a gang member, but rather that if care is not taken; your child *can* become a gang member. You can be the "best" parent in the world from a potential standpoint, but if you have blinders on, you are asking for trouble.

There are a lot of ways to begin understanding "the warning signs." Let me be clear, there will be no neon arrow over a child's head that says they are a gang member. Many gang members do not fit the stereotypical Hollywood profile of what a gang member should look like. In fact, many who look like the stereotypical gang banger are not gang members at all. This is something I think is important to note. I have noticed that those "not in the know" have a tendency to over assume that everything is gang-related. I have seen this in the prison system from many of the staff, as well as with many of the teachers that bring kids into this prison to speak with inmates. I think this occurs for two completely different reasons. It's actually quite odd that you get the same result from two very different walks of life. In prison, the entire world is gang infested.

Because of this, prison officials look for everything that can be used to represent oneself as a gang member. This could be from the way a person tilts their hat, to the amount of creases in one's shirt.

For the teachers that bring kids into the prison for the morning to meet with us, they have very little experience with gang activity. They will come up to me and say that this kid or that kid is a gang member. It might be because they are wearing a "hoodie" or a certain bracelet or whatever. They are wrong in many instances. In these smaller communities, there is a fear that there will eventually be a gang presence, (*Rightfully so*) so they try and nip it in the butt so to speak. Great intentions, but believe it or not this can have the opposite effect. I think that it is very possible for communities to bring a gang presence upon themselves by accusing kids that are not in a gang, of being gang members. Think about it. Let's say you have a community that truly does not have a single gang member in it. Teachers, guidance counselors, police, etc. all want to keep their community gang free. They start creating rules like no groups of teenagers are allowed in the park. Many larger cities do not allow more than five teenagers to group together. This is called "mob action." This was done in an attempt to minimize gang members loitering in large numbers together. In prison, inmates are not allowed to stand in a group larger than six for the same reasons.

Another rule the gang free community might enact is to not allow a child to roll one pant leg up higher than the other. You definitely cannot do this in prison either because some use this to identify themselves as a member of this group or that.

All of these rules are being enforced on the juveniles of this community but remember, none of these kids are gang members. Some time goes by, the kids feel a little harassed because none of them are in a gang so they do not understand why they cannot do the things they used to do, whether it was hang out in the park or roll a pant leg up. The community does in fact have good intentions. They really are making these changes because bigger cities are doing these same things.

A few different things begin to take place simultaneously. A mystique is being created, a glamorization almost of gang members. Teenagers see a way to rebel against the establishment. Every community will always have these boys that want to act out in an attempt to "look cool." It doesn't help that this behavior is further enforced because many of the school's little females all think the bad boys are cute. Once the adolescent male understands that getting into trouble equals girls, it's a wrap. There is nothing a boy won't do if he thinks it will impress a girl, and what is the new way to get into trouble in this community? Hang out with more than six other kids in the park, rolling up one pant leg, and breaking whatever other rule has been enacted to prevent gangs from forming. I don't think these boys do this because they want to become gang members, but rather because it is a rule that can be broken. I refer back to an earlier chapter when I asked the question, "What is a gang?" When I speak to classes brought into the prison system, I ask them what their definition of a gang is. I get a plethora of responses, most of them wrong. As I said before, a gang in its simplest form can be described as a few kids that hang out and get into trouble. They do not even need a name. I'm always amazed as how many people think you have to call yourselves something to be a gang. I look at it this way. Take any gang that you have heard of, the Bloods and Crips for example. Let's say that one day the Crips say that they are no longer going to call themselves Crips. They do nothing else different; just quit representing themselves as Crips. Do they cease to be a gang? Are they no longer a gang because they have no identifying name?

A bit of irony I have always found, is that the police almost have a bigger need to give a group a name than the group does. In the early stages of pre gang creation, let's say that you have a group of teenagers that sell drugs and commit other various crimes. They do not label themselves, but the police in the neighborhood might call them the 35th Street boys because they need a way to identify this group to other law enforcement personnel. Well now this group of boys does have a name, given to them by the police. I know a few instances where a group was labeled by the police as this or that and eventually began calling themselves this name. In most cases, it was simply the street name. I always found it odd that more creative names were not come up with. I always thought, "Really, you couldn't come up with anything better than that?" It's like whoever invented the "egg beater." Really? That's what you're naming it? You couldn't come up with a name like "the scrambler" or "yolk emulsifier"? (*Tangent, I know.*)

I have always wondered what is in a name. I read something a long time ago about naming your child a certain name with the hopes their name would steer them in a certain direction. Seinfeld also did a bit on this, saying that if you named your child Jeeves, you have destined them to be a butler. Obviously he is making a joke out of the situation, but I think that there is some truth to this as crazy as this must sound. I won't apply this to human names, but rather on how gangs name themselves. I have been going through many gang names that I have heard of over the years. Do you think the name of a gang has the potential to make them more violent? Can a simple name have that type of power? Let's say that you have a gang that calls themselves the "Lonely Boyz", and another that calls themselves the "Death Squad." What's in a name? Do you think that gang members might feel the need to live up to their name? Absolutely! I know some individuals who have been given a nickname because of the things that they have done or how they act. I have personally asked an individual who had the nickname "Murder", whether he felt like he had to live up to his namesake. Without any hesitation he said yes. He stated that he was in prison for murder and to this day feels that he has to gang bang just a little bit harder to keep his name up. Is this true? I don't know, I suppose he could have been lying to me, but I don't see the point in him doing so. He wouldn't have had the need to lie about that.

As far as the gang with the name of Death Squad, I believe these individuals do feel a need to live up to what they call themselves. The reason is no one will take them seriously if they simply spray painted their gang name but only fought occasionally. Rival gangs would laugh at them, telling them they have never killed anyone, why do they call themselves "Death Squad"? I know of a few gangs that have similar names to Death Squad and many of their members are stomp down killers. They do not play any games whatsoever. I also know of other gangs that have more passive names but they too are stone cold killers so I am not saying that everything is in a name, but rather that the name can have more of an impact than you might think.

Back to the community with no gang presence. The boys are thinking that they are pretty cool for breaking these new gang prevention ordinances. One day they come up with this great idea to call themselves the "Crazy Boys." They decide to all wear a certain color to represent themselves as "Crazy Boys." They all tilt their hats to the left and spray paint "Crazy Boys" all over the park.

Well, how about that? The community with no gang presence now has a full blown gang in their midst. One of their own creation. If you think that this is an unlikely scenario, it is not. I know for a fact that this has happened. I do not know in how many communities, but I know it has happened in more than one. I first found this out when I was speaking to one of the school classes brought into the prison every Wednesday. I asked a thirteen-year-old boy if any gangs were in his school. He surprised me by saying yes, and that in fact he was a member. I asked the name of his gang but I had never heard of this group before. I questioned him about it. His explanation was the one I gave about the previously gang free community.

Once his gang was created, it wasn't long before a second group was created to keep from getting bullied from the thirteen-year-olds gang. Sometime later, a few more kids moved into the city and claimed to be members of a "real" gang. They became rivals of the "Crazy Boys." Now this community does have a gang problem and it was born out of the fear of getting a gang problem. The violence may begin small with a few beatings, but will I'm sure escalate as the community grows. Victims *will* be created. It is so surreal to witness how the gang problem has migrated over this state. I have spoken with school classes for years from all over this state. The gang presence has slowly migrated from the bigger cities out into the less populated ones. When I first began speaking to these kids, certain areas really had no gang presence whatsoever but as the years have passed; gangs have made their presence known in these small communities. It's odd; I see how some of these kids dress, the type of shoes they wear, how they talk, and what grades they get. I say to myself that there can't possibly be any gang members in this school, but I am wrong on more occasions than I would like to be. I wonder how these communities will be in ten to twenty years. Will these so called wannabee gangs have become full blown murderous gangs like those in larger cities?

I began this topic with the warnings that society should be careful to not over label everything as gang-related. Even in prison this occurs. Shortly after I was arrested, I was in school. I had finished my work so I decided to draw a picture for my son's mother. I was drawing a rose when the teacher came up to me and snatched the paper out of my hand. She said the rose was a gang symbol. I looked at her thinking at first that she was joking. She began ripping up my picture so I could see that she was serious. I didn't know what to think, I honestly was only drawing a rose and it was not gang-related. Well, I lost that battle and was sent back to my cell. Sometime later I asked her why she did that, trying to explain that a rose was not gang-related. She informed me that she had been given gang identifier training and that a rose was a symbol that was classified as gang-related. She was given bad information. Many staff have either never been trained in what to look for or have been trained wrong in what to look for. One cannot understand the gang life by taking a couple of gang intelligence courses. It often takes years and years to fully understand the gang life. This is why I am writing this book, because people that have the power to make a difference sadly do not understand well enough, the problem. This inability to understand nullifies any effectiveness in prevention.

From a prevention standpoint, those who have the power to make the largest difference are parents, teachers, social workers, counselors, and former gang members. When law enforcement has gotten involved, the first four lines of defense have already failed in most instances. There are some law enforcement officials that view potential juvenile gang members with an eye towards prevention rather than punishment, but for the most part, the law enforcement angle is usually one of punishment. Unfortunately, sometimes it gets to the point where this is necessary. When all of these lines of defense fail a child, incarceration or death are the final two steps. It is extremely difficult to free a child from the grips of gang membership at this point. Many times a child that goes into prison will come out much worse. If the child is sent to a juvenile prison, there are very violent gangs there too. People are killed in these prisons as well.

Juveniles waived into the adult system do not have an easy time. Trust me. Society can say what they wish, but when a juvenile is sent to the adult prison system, they are being thrown away. I will not mince words on this subject. Yes, I know that juveniles that commit serious crimes should be severely punished. I will not get into the lengths of sentences because that is a whole other topic, but I will speak on placement because there is a direct correlation between gang membership and juveniles waived into the adult prison system. While I understand the need for society to be tough on juvenile crime, why many say if you do an adult crime you must do the adult time. Unfortunately this is where society wishes to end their focus. Society does not want to know what happens to many of these juveniles after they are sentenced as adults. They do not want to picture these young teenage boys getting extorted, raped, and murdered by their fellow adult inmates. Some of these younger inmates do not stand a chance. For those who do not want to admit that this goes on in the adult prison system, I ask that you simply read one of the many reports compiled by either Amnesty International, or our own government concerning the rape and murder statistics for young inmates in the adult prison system. You will not believe me if I read you their numbers, so please, read them for yourself. I promise that the numbers will shock you. Why do you not hear about these rapes and murders on the news? If a fifteen-year-old boy was raped and murdered in the free world, it would be headline news, and yet we hear nothing about all of the crimes that transpire post-conviction. Is it because society does not want to know about it? I think this does play a role, but not for the reasons you may think. I think the juvenile crime issue is such a difficult issue to resolve. Worrying about what happens to these juveniles convicted as adults is more than most in society seem to want to worry about. Perhaps society does not care what happens to these child killers, I don't know.

I only raise this topic because these young juveniles that are sent to the adult prison system, who do they have to turn to for "help" when they are being beaten, raped, and extorted? Gangs. I don't know what the statistics are for juveniles that are sent to the adult prison system who are non-gang members compared to those who are, but I know that every single juvenile that I have personally known that was waived and sent to the adult system became one if they already weren't one. 100%!!!! I am not exaggerating; I do not know a single juvenile that was waived into adult court that did not eventually become a gang member. I was already a gang member prior to coming to prison, so I did not have to face that scenario. Had I not been a gang member, I surely would have become one. I hope you can understand how hard it is for me to admit that. I hate that I was a gang member but I am also a realist. I was fifteen years old and was barely five feet tall and weighed about 120 lbs. I wouldn't have been able to defend myself if attacked by some of these huge adult inmates. I don't know what my prison life would have been like had I not been in a gang when I first came in. I can assure you that it would not have been pleasant. Please understand that I am making no excuses nor am I condoning anything, but people do not know how violent this prison system was in the early eighties and nineties. In many other states it is still extremely violent. Inmates are murdered all of the time in the Federal system. This particular prison system has changed drastically with the building of the new super maximum prison, but other states have not. Many of these kids have no choice. It angers me when people who do not know any better say that you always have a choice. "Just mind your own business" they say, or "Just keep to yourself." Tell that to the teenager who is getting raped every day. Tell that to the teenager who gets all of his food taken and is made to be some other inmates wife. Society has no clue what happens to these young teenagers sent to adult prison. All they care about is that they are doing the "adult" time they were sentenced to.

I am not saying that every single juvenile that is sent to the adult prison system is raped or extorted, every situation is different. I'm sure that there are some prison systems in which the juvenile would not have that hard of a time.

What if you were getting beat up every day? What if someone was taking all of your food? What if grown men were gang raping you every day? What would you do? If you cannot physically defend yourself, what are you going to do? You have to spend the next thirty, forty, fifty, and sixty years in prison. This is your home now, what are you going to do? Seriously, actually put some time into thinking about the literally thousands of juveniles serving life sentences in the adult prison system, and what they are forced to face. It is not a hypothetical situation for them. If joining a gang came as a "reprieve" from the violence that others are inflicting upon you, do you think you will not consider joining? Trust me, it is a lose/lose situation, but you have to choose something. You can choose to check onto protective custody, but for how long? In protective custody, you are essentially sent to segregation or the "hole" for twenty-four hours a day. I don't know where society gets this *twenty-three* hours a day nonsense from. There is no law at least in Wisconsin, which states we are allowed to come out of our cell for an hour a day. Perhaps it is this way in other states but it is not like that here. I was in the hole from 1999 until 2002. I was not allowed to leave my cell for nine months straight and only then because I was transferred to the newly opened "Supermax" prison. It was not until the last six months of my almost four-year "hole" stay that I was allowed out of my cell for recreation. I will get more into this later in the next chapter as it relates to change.

In the context of young people spending years in segregation, it is not good however. I witnessed grown men go insane because they could not handle segregation. I remember one such occasion that still haunts me to this day. I will never forget it. I was eighteen years old and was in the hole for my fifth time I think, so the hole itself was nothing new to me. They placed a man in the cell next to me who was in his mid-twenties I think. He seemed normal but I really didn't talk to him so I really did not pay much attention to him. Our cells had showers in them so there was literally no reason to leave the cell. Twice a week officers would turn the showers on for five minutes. Before they did, they would hand out a rag the size of a wash cloth to wipe up the water when we were done. I am not exaggerating. There was no partition on the floor between the shower and the rest of the cell, so when the water was turned on it just covered your entire cell floor and we had to wipe it up when we were done. I guess we didn't have anything better to do right?

Anyway, many inmates would try and keep their rags so that we could get a pile to wipe up the water. Trying to soak up an entire floor of water with a single washrag took forever. Some guards didn't notice if you kept your rag but most did. The man next door to me was accused of keeping his rag. He said he turned it in but the guard wasn't hearing any of it. I don't know if he actually turned one in or not. At the time I think I just assumed he was keeping his like the rest of us were trying to do. They went back and forth, the guard and inmate. They both got a little disrespectful. The dinner cart was coming and they told the inmate that he would not be getting a tray until he gave them the rag. He kept telling them that he didn't have a rag but was apparently not very convincing. He did not eat that night. This was really no big deal at the time. Little things like this happened all of the time for this or that. The next day came and they didn't feed him again. At this point the rest of the tier began to get agitated. The way we viewed it, he was on his own the first day because no one knew if he really kept his rag or not, but into day two we didn't care if he did or not, he needed to be fed. The tier began kicking their doors and supervisors were called in. They came and talked to the man next door and he was written up for not handing a rag in. His sanction was being placed on "seg-loaf", or nutri-loaf. Seg loaf is when kitchen staff takes everything from that day's meal and places it into a mixer and adds eggs. They then bake it in a loaf shape. This is done so that an inmate has no tray he can keep or throw at officers. Seg-loaf began to be used as a punishment for various reasons for thirty days at a time until inmates filed a law suit. The courts found that it was cruel and unusual punishment to place inmates who did not abuse their food on seg-loaf. They also ruled that for those who are placed on it, can only be placed on it for seven day increments. Seven days may not seem like a long time to you but trust me; it seems like forever when you are in the hole. I unfortunately speak from experience. I was placed on it but simply could not manage to get it down. The only way I can describe it would be to say that it has the consistency of a very dense bread pudding but it is not sweet at all. Some days it smelled worse than others. If there was tuna casserole and white cake, well it was all getting thrown into a blender and baked. I tried it again on day five because I thought I was going to pass out from a lack of food, but I still couldn't get one bite down. I know people say that if you are hungry you will eat anything. Well, I remember getting to my seventh day without eating a single thing and the mere smell of that stuff made me gag. I don't know how much hungrier I could have gotten without passing out, so......Gandhi was a machine, I'll give him that. I couldn't go thirty or forty days without eating, I don't know how that would be possible.

On a side note, just one of those as luck would have it things---everyone in prison has a meal that they feel is the worst, one that they will never be able to eat. Mine was a breakfast called creamed beef over toast. We called it "shit on a shingle." I can assure you that you never want to eat a prisons creamed beef over toast. You would be better off ordering sushi from a gas station. When you are on seg-loaf, of course all you can think about is food and it was torturous. When my seven days were up, it was breakfast and I ran to my cell door when I heard the cart coming down the hallway. I promise you that I was not going to miss this meal. The officer opened my trap and set a Styrofoam plate on it. You already know what was on it. Shit on a shingle of course. I just looked at it and kind of gave one of those laughs we do to keep from crying. What were the odds? I had never so much even breathed a breath of that meal before but I tell you what, I inhaled it that morning. I was so unbelievably hungry. It was like ambrosia upon my tongue. I remember my throat being cut from the crust of the toast either because I was eating it so fast, it was really hard, or because my throat was not used to solid foods for a week. Nothing but water and toothpaste for me that week. The funny thing was that every single time that meal came up again, I demolished it every time. It must be a psychological thing because I'm sure it is still nasty but it was my first meal.

Anyway, I have gotten off topic. Back to the man next door that was just placed on seg-loaf. Apparently he could not stomach it either because he refused to let guards give it to him at meal times. A few days went by and he had eaten nothing. It was lunch time when he finally snapped. He starting yelling and screaming hysterically, as well as pounded and kicked his sink and cell door. At first I thought he was just blowing off some steam but you could hear something in his voice, something had snapped in him. Other inmates tried to talk to him but he was incoherent. His words were like babble. It scared me. Not because I was worried about anything happening to me, but rather because I was eighteen years old and here was this adult next door to me who was going crazy. We were in the same situation but he could not handle it. I thought to myself, "Well if he can't handle this and he's an adult, how am I going to manage?" At the time I think I had been in the hole for only two or three months.

He was never the same after that day. Mentally he was gone. I remember lying down and looking at the cell wall that separated us and wondered what his eyes looked like. I know that must sound odd but I've always heard that the eyes were windows into our souls, so I wondered if you could see "crazy" in a grown man's eyes. What does insanity look like I wondered? I looked at my eyes in the mirror, wondering if I was going to go crazy as well. Of course I couldn't tell anyone what I was thinking because I did not want to look weak. I took all of my fears and just ate them all the while "kept it pushing" mentally. I just had to walk it off so to speak. After all, what could I do about the situation? It was difficult I found, to not wonder if I was going crazy because I had nothing else to do. I was in the hole with no books, magazines TV, radio, etc. All I had was a pen insert, paper, and a Bible. I could not see outside, go outside, or use the phone. I was in the hole because I had broken the prisons rules but these are the same conditions that a juvenile who would check into protective custody would experience. Each state is different so each juvenile would be allowed different things in their cell. I brought this up when I asked what you would do rather than joining a gang if you were a juvenile in the adult prison system.

If you do choose to join a gang, odds are that you will end up being sent to the hole anyways because you will be told to go beat up a rival gang member for your initiation. Each gang in every prison system is different however. Some gangs in some states require you to kill another inmate before they will let you join their gang.

This is only the beginning however, now you are a gang member. Now you are also a rival gang member to other inmates. Now you are a target for the next juvenile that comes in and who has to prove himself. There are so many instances where these juveniles end up receiving more prison time because of what they did after coming to an adult prison. I'm sure that there will be those that use this as a chance to say, "See, we told you he belonged in an adult prison!" Unfortunately there is a kill or be killed mentality in many prison systems. When it gets to this point for an incarcerated juvenile, hope is merely a four letter word with no meaning. It's sad. Many of these juveniles will never again breathe a breath of fresh air because of what they had to do to survive in this system. It is not always possible to "just walk away." I am making no excuses. I am justifying nothing, merely explaining the reality.

I understand that punishment needs to be severe for juveniles that commit serious crimes, but there has got to be a better way. I can only really see one route that satisfies both victim and inmate. Prevention. Every penny, every minute needs to be spent to prevent the situation from getting to a point where there are no easy answers. Prevention does not come cheap. The good news is that the first two lines of defense are relatively cheap; good parenting and good teachers. Cheap in relation to the cost of victims and lifetime incarcerations that society will have to pay anyway. Again, this is easier said than done because I believe that parents are out of touch with their children these days. I don't know if it is technology or what, but there is definitely a disconnect between child and parent. If a parent is out of touch, they will not know what warning signs to be searching for. The same holds true for teachers.

As I said, the first line of defense in fact begins at home. I want to once again express the importance of thinking that every household is different. Because of this, the warning signs will be different as well. I don't believe that prevention should begin at a certain age. I think it is a misconception that many parents have in thinking that they do not need to worry about gangs until a later age. My aim in this book has been to show that gang involvement isn't just some individual factor that is unrelated to other societal ills. Gang membership is a by-product of other issues that most in society would not directly relate to gangs. As I discussed in earlier chapters, I am referring to poverty, single-parent households, failing schools, peer pressure, etc. These issues affect juveniles *before* adolescence. If gang prevention begins at adolescence, we are already beginning in the hole. I believe "prevention" at this point is a misnomer. We should instead be referring to it at this point as damage control, even though the child may not even know any gang members yet. The virus is already alive and well. For many children, the traits that will allow them to fall into the hands of gang membership will be learned at a young age and will lie dormant within the subconscious until conditions are ripe. At this point all we can do is minimize the damage. It's sad that many in society cannot understand that juvenile gang prevention begins at birth. I love the analogy of building a skyscraper on a foundation of sand and then building braces to sturdy it rather than beginning with a solid foundation. Catastrophe is inevitable unless of course your leaning tower is in Pisa. In fact, that is a good visual now that I think about it. Go and find a recent picture of the Leaning Tower of Pisa. Do you see all of the cables and lines that are holding it in place? That is exactly what gang prevention looks like when you begin at adolescence. As each day, week, and year goes by, imagine snipping one of those bracing wires until there are none left. Then *act* surprised and ask yourself," Why did the tower come crashing down?"

Political correctness plays a role as well. I can't worry about being politically correct or sensitive. It is a fact that children within the inner-city have a far higher chance of joining a violent gang than a child living in a small town out in the middle of nowhere Iowa. It does not matter the race, but if you wish to receive that as a racist statement then please, continue to veil your eyes to reality and point the finger at everyone but yourself. Keep living in communities wrought with violence wondering "why." I bring this up not to ridicule but rather to help. I raise this to say that parents living within the inner-city need to be even more vigilant, even more perceptive. Is this fair? No, but it is necessary because life is everything but fair.

Narrowing it down even further, some cities are obviously more crime ridden than others, so the steps taken in these communities compared to those by a family in North Dakota will be drastically different. Many kids have already been born in situations that are ripe for future gang membership. We can't change that nor can we wait for communities to get better so that prevention becomes easier. We have the last couple of generations to thank for that.

Those most at-risk are single-parents that live in the most violent communities. Those who have children in the poorest funded school systems with the highest dropout rate need to be extra watchful. I believe that the children born into these circumstances stand the greatest risk to join a gang at some age. Prevention needs to especially begin at birth for them. Yes it will be time consuming and expensive but at the end of the day, who is more important than your child? We say that they are most important to us, but remember that actions will always speak louder than words. How important is the next generation to you? Time will tell I suppose.

There are I believe some universal warning signs that a parent can look for at a very young age. Again, please do not think that every child that exhibits these behaviors will become a gang member. If you do see some warning signs in your child, at the very least begin a dialogue. Remember, at the early stages of life we are not looking for any signs with gang connotations. Instead we are looking for behavioral traits that if learned, will smoothly coexist with gang membership at a later age.

Again, the first thing a parent needs to acknowledge is the fact that it is possible for their child to become a gang member someday. It does not matter where you live, what race you are, or what tax bracket you are under. All of this means nothing at this point. Every child has the potential with the "right" conditions to become a gang member. If you are still hesitant to believe that your child can become a gang member, it really comes down to whether or not you want to give your child the best chance at life. Sure, maybe you live in a gated community in a million dollar home and your child might not ever join a gang from a statistical standpoint. Let me ask you this however; let's say that the odds for your child are one in a million that they will join a gang. Sounds like great odds right? Those odds mean absolutely nothing to the victim of that ONE in a million. How does that mother feel? How does she feel about those odds do you think? Is it any consolation that the odds she lost her son were one in a million? Of course not.

I've always found it "odd" that society thinks the odds of something bad happening are for other people. If the odds of getting struck by lightning are one in 2.4 million, people automatically assume that they will not be that "one." Why? Why do we assume that we will never be that "one"? On the other hand, people play the lottery knowing the odds are one in sixty million, and think they have a better chance of winning than being struck by lightning. This is insane to me. Odds are useless in my opinion because people see what they want to see. I believe odds give us a false sense of hope. I wonder if parents would change their parenting tactics if they could know the odds of future gang membership based on certain behaviors. For example, what if you read the following statistics: Children who are not read to by their parents are sixty times more likely to join a gang than those who are read to every night; families that do not eat together have children that are seventy-five times more likely to join a gang than those who do; seven out of ten kids that are raised by a single mother will join a gang; three out of five kids that go to a failing school will join a gang; or, if you are reading these statistics, your kid has a 100% chance of joining a gang. Parents still wouldn't want to believe. They would say, "Not my child!" No one wants to believe that their kid will someday join a gang and it is out of this that prevents parents from seeing what they need to see.

I understand that it is difficult for parents to want to see the bad in their child. No parent wants to admit to themselves that their child might be a bully for instance, because that would reflect on their parenting skills. There is no easy way to parent. Parents just have to do what they need to do and look for what they have to look for. At least this way change is an option if a child is in some sort of trouble. The alternative is to wait until it is too late.

When a child is very young, I believe you can start to see tendencies, especially when they begin interacting with other children. Does the child like to play with others or do they prefer solitude? Do they hit other kids? I'm sure most kids go through the hitting stage, but for some it is more than a stage. Parenting is critical at these stages in life. It seems obvious but apparently it must not be that obvious with the amount of bullying that is going on in this countries school system. Bullying is a direct result of parents looking the other way, parents not caring, or parents instilling horrible values. These values consist of a lack of respect for others. As I am writing this, I find that I am once again shaking my head because it is so clear to me that juvenile gang membership is so unbelievably correlated to the environment a child grows up in. It makes me wonder if juvenile gang prevention as society defines it, is even viable if the damage is already done. So much of who we will be is determined by a few of our younger years in life. This is incredibly unfair to so many children. I think that this may be one of life's greatest tragedies. Nothing like being born behind the eight ball.

It is this line of logic that scares me because I label this generation the fatherless generation and that can only spell disaster for the next generation. Parenting has gotten worse over the years. Parents are only concerned with themselves it seems. The statistics showing the number of single mothers raising a family are alarming. Why would parenting all of a sudden get better with a worsening economy that will result in a worsening education system? Crime rates will surely go up because the economy gets worse. Why will it get better? How would it get better? This is not a hypothetical scenario, the economy is getting worse. Please explain to me how the gang problem will not get worse when all of the contributing factors that lead a child to gang membership are also getting worse.

It is frustrating because it seems the deeper that I try and explain why the gang problem exists, the harder I realize it is going to be to fix it. I didn't plan on using the word fix; it just came to my mind. I only note this because in order to "fix" a problem we first have to understand the problem. How can we get society to understand such a massive problem? How can we get people to understand that so many different factors lead a child into the arms of a gang? How can we help parents understand that both the intelligent and unintelligent can join a gang? That the bully and the bullied can join a gang?

We can do it by being perceptive, by opening our eyes, by holding each other accountable. We do it because we are tired of kids killing one another simply because they wore the wrong colored shirt to school one day. Parents need to begin by instilling structure and discipline in their child's life. Discipline does not mean that they have to beat their child. That is behavior that will help a child become a more violent gang member someday. If your child exhibits violent behavior, you have cause for concern. Does your child exhibit destructive behavior? Do they break all of their toys or destroy the house? Some of this is nothing more than a phase but if not corrected, it can lead to similar behavior in the future as they age. As your child ages and begins to make friends, all parents should make it a priority to get to know these friends. A child's friends are so very important to whom they will become in life, fortunately or unfortunately.

When I speak to juveniles that are brought into this prison, I tell them that I am about to ask them the single most important question that they will ever be asked in their life; do you have any friends that your parents do not want you to associate with but you do so anyway? I never expect the kids to be honest but that is not the case. I would say on average, that seventy-five percent of every single class raises their hands. Seventy-five percent!!! For the other thirty or so percent, I ask them if they didn't raise either hands because they are good judges of character, or listen to their parents and stop associating with bad friends, or is it possible that they are the kid their friends parents don't want their child hanging around. I love to see the looks on their faces when they grasp what it is that I have just asked. There is another possibility why a child won't raise their hand and unfortunately this is probably the most likely reason. Many parents do not get to know their child's friends well enough to make the determination of whether or not their friend is a bad friend. If I could choose one thing for parents to spend more time on, it would be getting to know their child's friends. Yes, there are countless circumstances that will lead a child into the arms of a gang, but all of those circumstances lead them to a couple of "friends" first. It is those friends that then lead them to the arms of gang membership. The only other route is if a child has a sibling that is in a gang and wants to follow in their footsteps. Think about it, how do you think a child becomes a gang member? They just don't go up to a group of people they do not know and say, "Hey, are you guys in a gang and can I join?" It's all about friends, especially if the parent has not done a good job instilling good values in their child.

The word "friend" I believe has lost almost all of its meaning, especially with the advent of Facebook. You can be "friends" with a gas station if you so choose. A gas station? Really? I ask every single student that I speak with to define the word friend. The age bracket I speak with is from twelve to eighteen. The definitions are truly sad. If I don't press them I usually get a simple, "Someone that I have fun with." I let them give me their definition at first and tell them to just be honest. I speak to both boys and girls and you would not believe the difference between their answers. Girls tend to give better definitions, using words like trust and loyalty. They usually say, "Someone that will keep my secrets." As far as the boys go, anyone walking down the street could fit their definition.

I press them, asking what would make a *good* friend. It's interesting how the definitions narrow considerably. Now it's someone who will keep me from doing wrong or someone who is loyal and trustworthy. I have asked this question thousands of times and without fail the answer to "what is a friend" compared to "what is a *good* friend" are always different. I don't know why there is a need to preface the word friend with "good" to get such a different answer. After we talk about what a true friend should be, they always agree that they have a new definition for the word friend. So I ask them with their new definition of the word friend, how many of them have friends that their parents do not want them associating with. They almost always say yes if they had said yes previously, and they wonder why I am asking them the same question twice. They don't see that I was trying to be "too cute by half." I then ask them if their friends fit their new definition of the word friend. They think and then it usually dawns on them that they in fact don't have any "friends" that their parents do not want them associating with, but rather have people that no longer fit under their new definition of the word friend. Now they have *associates* that their parents do not want them hanging out with, but no "friends", at least under their new narrower definition. Of course I am playing semantics with them but there is a point to this. Kids seem to have this sense of loyalty to their "friends", regardless of their definition of the word friend. They have a hard time letting their "friends" go if they consider them to be *friends*. I know this might sound confusing, but bear with me. If we can help them see that these kids are not in fact their "friends", there is a good chance that they will be less loyal to them. There is a chance that they will on their own, choose to unfriend them or begin the disassociation process. Trying to force a child to stop hanging out with someone they consider to be a good friend will be difficult. We need to help them see their friends for who they are, not for who they think they are.

So how do you know what friends are good and what friends are bad? Interaction with them is the ***only*** way to find out. There are some things to be aware of. Obviously if the neighborhood you live in has a high crime rate, you should take even more care. Use more caution, be even more vigilant. If you start out paying close attention to your child's friends at a young age, it will be so much easier as they grow, I promise you. How are their parents? Are they a single-parent? Do they work more than one job? Do they have other older children? Do their older kids get into trouble? Are they known for being trouble makers in the community? Do they hang out with gang members? If yes, it is likely that their younger sibling will try and emulate them. If this happens, now your child is friends with someone who wishes to emulate an older sibling gang member. You should be picking up what I am putting down I hope. These factors raise the odds that your child will become a gang member. Does this mean that they will become one for sure? No, but why increase their odds?

Something else to look for is if you have moved to a new home in a new area. This means that your child will undoubtedly be searching for new friends. I think this is a high risk time because unfortunately it is often difficult to make new friends in a new school. It varies with the school however, some are easier than others. Every school has their own set of cliques as I have already discussed in an earlier chapter. There are "outcasts" in every school that are willing to accept the "new kid." This can be a good thing or a very bad thing, depending on the school. Some of the outcasts are those that are considered to be the troublemakers; potheads, skaters, taggers, gang bangers, etc. Many of these cliques have the mentality of not caring about doing the right thing. They think this makes them "cool."

Another danger comes from the new kid feeling he needs to prove himself to his new classmates. Teenage boys have this need to act tough it seems, or be the "badass." They have this macho man complex that requires them to make a name for themselves. The route they take to accomplish this has many lanes, from merely being disrespectful verbally, to physically fighting with others. Again, the particular school has much to do with what tactics are used. In a very bad school, disrespecting a teacher is not going to go far in building a reputation. Not when kids are bringing knives and guns to school. Here the tactics could begin with criminal behavior and escalate into high levels of violence.

Drug use is another area to be hyper-conscious about, but not for the reasons most are worried about. Obviously drugs are very bad from a health standpoint, but I don't think this is the worst aspect of using drugs believe it or not. What I think of first when I hear about an individual using drugs, is *where* they got them from, or more importantly, *from whom*? As I discussed earlier, the financial livelihood for gangs is the sale of narcotics. If your child is either using drugs or has friends that are using drugs, there is a very high likelihood that that their path will cross with that of a gang member. True, not all drug dealers are gang members, in fact a huge number of them are not but again, all it takes is for your child to meet just one of them to develop a relationship. Beyond the obvious once again, the aspect of this relationship that worries me the most is not the drug use, but rather the relationship that could possibly be formed with the gang member. Depending upon the circumstances, there might be other gang members at the location where your child might be purchasing drugs. If they are buying marijuana, one of the gang members will surely ask them to "fire it up." (*Smoke with them*) What if they get along? What if they have a good time? Maybe the gang member tells your child to come back tomorrow and he will return the favor and "fire one up" with him. A relationship can be formed at first by getting high, but I can assure you that it will escalate into something else. There is a high likelihood that your child will become intrigued by that life, by the gang atmosphere. Whether they eventually decide to join a gang is up to them, but they will probably at the very least consider doing so. Perhaps your child won't want to join, who knows? There will be some sort of peer pressure to fit in and whether it is real or perceived makes little difference. The power of peer pressure is much harder to withstand than society believes I think.

The gang aspect of drug use aside, addiction may also come into play. Again, this may sound wrong but I don't feel that the actual addiction is what should be worried about the most. It is where the addiction will likely lead. I'll explain. When someone is addicted to a narcotic, it will not be long before funds start to run short. If one hasn't the money to feed their addiction, they often turn to theft. All of the situations this can consist of are still not the most worrisome aspects of addiction. They will likely get caught and be sent to jail or prison depending on the crime they are caught for. Whether they are sent to a juvenile facility or adult facility, their odds of being surrounded by gang members will nearly be one hundred percent. I described earlier what it is like for young inmates in the prison system. Time will appear to be *easier* if they join a group or gang. Just think, gang membership via this route all began with that first joint smoked. They call marijuana the "gateway drug." I believe this is true, but not only in regards to opening the door to other more severe drugs. Marijuana can be the gateway to bad friends as well. Drugs bring the most unlikely types of people in contact with one another. Drugs can acquaint a senator with a biker, or a gang member with an Honor Roll student. Fact is stranger than fiction in this context.

Now are you starting to understand why the health consequences pale in comparison to the other *side effects* of drug use? Parents should always be on the lookout for signs of drug use. The obvious signs are physical, i.e. bloodshot eyes, fatigue, being very hyper/paranoid, being unable to sleep, being very hungry or not eating at all. Is there a sudden drop in grades? A sudden loss of interest in what they used to enjoy? Are they suddenly asking for a lot of money? Have you noticed that valuable things are turning up missing in your home? It is easiest to steal from home. Has your child made a lot of new friends lately? Do they bring them over or are they always going to their house? Are they buying different clothes all of a sudden? Do they refuse to wear a certain color all of a sudden? Do they have a sudden interest in a new sports team? If so, has this particular franchise won a championship lately, or do they have a popular player on their team?

I know this must sound odd, but think about it for a second. I'll use an easy example. The St. Louis Cardinals baseball team has a big "S" and "L" emblazoned on their red hat. The S and L stand for St. Louis. There is a gang out of Chicago that calls themselves the Spanish Lords. One of this gangs color is red (*Like the St. Louis Cardinals*). Obviously Spanish Lords begin with an "S" and "L", (*Like St. Louis*). What better way to represent their gang than by wearing a St. Louis Cardinals hat that is red and has the initials "S" and "L" on it? Many "Spanish Lords" wear St. Louis Cardinal's gear. Countless other gangs use other sports teams in the same fashion.

Now St. Louis is a moderately successful franchise, so a juvenile might just be on their bandwagon so to speak and not know anything about the Spanish Lords. What if however, you are living in Maine and your child started wearing nothing but Cleveland Browns gear? This should raise some red flags because the Browns are a horrible unsuccessful franchise and unless you live in Cleveland, you will probably not be a fan of theirs. Why would your child be wearing their colors? Why this sudden interest in a failing sports team? This would be a time to ask your child what's up. Parents can call their local police department and ask to speak with gang officers. They can ask them if any gangs in the area are known to wear Cleveland Browns gear. These officers know what gangs wear what colors and how they identify themselves. Parents need to investigate. What would be the harm? At worst you realize that you were being paranoid. So what!?

If parents are the first line of defense, teachers are I believe, the second. I know it is unfair for us to ask more of our teachers, but they are really the eyes and ears of the parents of today who are busy at work. In fact, I believe there is a huge opportunity that can be taken advantage of if done correctly. Teachers do not have many of the biases and blinders that parents have. They can see the child for who they are, not for who they want them to be. Teachers see students as those who can go either way, good or bad. A parent only wants to see the good. Teachers see a child for a third of a day. They can see how they interact with others, who they interact with, and how that group as a whole is perceived by other students. Teachers actually have more "eyes on" time with your kids than you do. Kids sleep for another third of the day and you probably work a good portion of the last third. Some parents only get a few moments before school and a few hours after dinner to parent in the verbal sense. So given the fact that parents don't really get to spend that much time with their children, extra care should be taken. Personally, I believe so much more needs to be done at school outside of what is being taught in normal classes. I think that there is so much potential if we can begin thinking outside of the box. I understand that the school day is limited and certain classes must be fit in, but I truly think that there should be a class dedicated to one's friends. We need to create a class with the same format as math or science but with the focus being on helping the child learn the importance of friendship and social behavior. Of all the kids that I have spoken with over the years, the overwhelming majority of those that have committed a crime have done so with one of their friends. Very rarely do these kids commit crimes by themselves. If we know this to be true, why is there not more care being taken to help kids better choose their friends? It baffles me.

Also, there needs to be a way for parents to ask teachers about the type of friends their child is hanging around at school. Teachers are not blind. They see who talks to whom in class or in the hallways. Most schools now have some sort of officer or police officer that is stationed in the hallways between classes. They know with a pretty high degree of certainty who is getting into trouble. They know who a lot of the gang bangers and drug dealers are. It is their job. Why can't we come up with a system that allows these officers and teachers to interact with parents about the friends their child is associating with? Children are at school for a *third* of the day. This is a huge portion of their lives and it is essentially a time that a parent knows nothing about. Is that not crazy?

Many argue that teachers already have more than enough on their plate, and I don't disagree with that per se. Yes, asking teachers to notice who hangs out with who might be asking a lot, but I believe there is an opportunity to make a huge difference at school. Kids lie to their parents all of the time about who their friends are. Parents are often at a disadvantage because they do not know who their kid sits with at lunch or on the bus. They do not know who they walk to class with or drive home with. Unfortunately, juveniles do not possess enough foresight to understand the consequences that can come from having a *single* bad friend. Just one bad friend, that's all it takes. One bad friend can take your child from the Honor Roll to a life sentence in under a year. Trust me. My situation is a perfect example for parents to look for all of the warning signs their child might give off. I can promise you that my family never in a million years would have thought I would one day end up in prison serving a life sentence for a gang-related homicide. It can happen so fast. The warning signs might only be exhibited for a few months. A few months!! I can still remember what the judge stated as he sentenced me to life in prison. He spoke on this very subject. He stated that he doesn't know what you say to a parent that has a kid who is on the Honor Roll, how you get them to understand that their kid might join a gang and kill a rival gang member. It makes me sick to my stomach every time I re-read my sentencing transcripts. It's true, it seems like an impossible task to try and get a parent of a kid doing great things to believe that they can so quickly join a gang and destroy countless lives.

I think back to my circumstances and what signs I was giving off. I don't know how many parents would have been able to see my "warning signs." Even if they could see them, I doubt that there would have been a conscious thought of these signs predicted gang membership. Why would they?

Are you starting to understand why I preached the importance of admitting to yourself that it is possible for any kid to join a gang? Am I not proof of what can happen if you do not admit this? It's frustrating because I can spot a gang member a mile away, but I think back to me as a young fourteen-year-old gang member and I really gave off very few warning signs. I was a very private individual that didn't feel comfortable talking to anyone. I held everything inside. I had many family members that would have gladly listened to what I was going through but I really didn't feel as though they could understand me. The only person I ever opened up to in my whole entire life was my son's mother. She was my best friend as well as my girlfriend. She was only six months older than I was however, so she couldn't offer me an adult's point of view. As I look back however, she always told me to do what would have been the right thing, but obviously I didn't listen to her. Beyond her, no one ever came close to seeing the real me.

Concerning teachers, I believe that they should be given some sort of training to detect certain warning signs. They should be taught what colors the active gangs in their school district wear, what sports logos etc. Yes it will cost money, but as I said before, society is going to pay in one way or another anyway, so why not pay to prevent rather than pay to incarcerate? Society is reluctant to spend any money on anything besides punishment. Society feels as though harsher punishments are the answer and I agree that juveniles should not get a pass. They need to be severely punished if they commit serious crimes. What angers me however, is when all the focus and funding is on creating prisons to house inmates, more victims are being created. Does society not understand that if we spend more money on prevention, fewer victims will be created? Here is a visual way to look at the situation. I'm sure you have heard about the old saying that speaks about lemmings following each other off of a cliff. Imagine today's youth are lemmings walking towards a cliff. At the bottom of the cliff lies a prison. Every time a lemming walks off the cliff, a victim is created via that juvenile's crime. The lemming falls to his/her punishment and lands in prison. Keep that visually in your mind and think about this. Society is watching these lemmings walk off that cliff, one after another and they have a decision to make. It is a long way down from the top of the cliff to the prison at the bottom so it costs taxpayers $30,000 to catch each lemming and safely place them in the prison at the bottom of the cliff. It also costs taxpayers $30,000 to take care of each lemming every year they are held in the prison below. Society feels that this is a bit steep but feels that it is justified because with the lemming in prison, it will not walk off of another cliff and create another victim.

There is something that society does not know however. For only $5,000 dollars, they can divert the lemmings *at the top* of the cliff. This $5,000 can be spent on after school programs, another teacher, a big brother/big sister program, and or other prevention based programs. Not only does society pay a mere $5,000 per diverted lemming, but that $5,000 is only a one time fee. The $30,000 dollars it takes to hold each lemming is a yearly fee. (*It costs roughly about $30,000 dollars a year to house one inmate.*) Beyond all of this, one less victim was created when a lemming is diverted from walking off of the cliff. This should be the incentive. I am not saying that every single lemming will be diverted, some will still walk off of that cliff and create a victim and need to be incarcerated, but do you not see the logic in prevention rather than punishment? That $30,000 it costs to house a healthy inmate for one year is going to skyrocket as the prison population ages and requires medical care. All of these juveniles serving life without parole sentences are going to get old, get cancer, and need treatment just like the rest of free society. Who do you think is going to have to pay the tab? None of these inmates are going home. I can assure you that the $30,000 will seem like pennies compared to what it will be in years to come. In decades past, it was rare to see an individual that served more than forty years in prison because so few were given life without parole sentences.

There are **thousands** of juveniles alone that are serving life without parole sentences that they received at 13, 14, 15, 16, and 17 years of age. Yes, thousands. This isn't even counting all of the fifty, sixty, and seventy year sentences that juveniles are serving. For all intents and purposes these are life sentences as well but are not technically labeled as "life" sentences because they have a parole date. It makes no difference that they will never live to see these parole dates; from a legal standpoint they are not considered life sentences. Now factor in the other tens of thousands of adults that are serving life sentences and you start to see what is going to happen to the corrections budgets over the next few decades. As I have said, we really have seen nothing yet because the prison population is still relatively young, wait until all of these inmates need medical care. Beyond that, say a juvenile gets a life sentence at the age of fifteen. He doesn't have to worry about dying young via a car accident, work accident, natural disaster etc. Life expectancy will be quite long for him and others similarly situated. He will probably live into his eighties or nineties. That is about seventy-five years of good health spent behind bars which will cost taxpayers $30,000 each of those seventy-five years. It will come to about $2,250,000 to house that juvenile for the rest of his life. This is assuming he will never need a single pill, operation, or other medical services. This is also not taking inflation into account. Obviously in seventy-five years, it will cost much more than $30,000 to house an inmate for a year, but I am keeping it at $30,000 just to give you a rough idea best case scenario. Realistically, that $30,000 will probably be closer to $60,000.

Now multiply that $2,250,000 by the tens of thousands of inmates serving life sentences right now today. Think about that for a second; the numbers I have given you so far are simply for the inmates *already* serving time. Now factor in the tens of thousands of life sentences that will be handed out over the next seventy-five years while that fifteen-year-old is still alive. Even if not a single crime was created from this day forward, the budget that will be needed to take care of those already serving life sentences will be massive. Remember, I am only talking about "life" sentences. I haven't even figured in the numbered sentences that will exceed the life expectancy of many inmates. Just that one *healthy* fifteen-year-old will cost taxpayers over two million dollars to house him for the rest of his life. Couple that with the victim that he created and the price he will cost society is enormous. Now how does that $5,000 dollar prevention program sound? Over two million dollars saved and a victim never became a victim. Even if the prevention program cost $250,000 *per* juvenile, society would still be saving two million dollars plus a victim's life. The numbers are so large that they seem unbelievable, but all you have to do is add it up. Remember, I have used the numbers from today, not the inflated numbers of the future. To understand that we could spend a quarter of a million dollars on a prevention program per juvenile that would prevent a juvenile from committing a murder and still save two million dollars seems insane. Society must not be looking to the future, because if they just did the simple math I think they would have a heart attack when they realized the budget corrections will need to exist. We won't be able to afford just those that are serving sentences now, much less those that will be sentenced over the next seventy five years. How many more victims need to die before we decide to pay for preventative type programs that will keep someone's family member alive?

The third lines of defense are youth counselors, recreational center staff, and other similar individuals in the community. These individuals do not understand how important they are. These community workers, no matter their title, are essential to the front lines of gang prevention. They are like the marines. They are directly in touch with all facets of the community, or at least they should be. Resolving the gang crisis hinges on the success of these individuals. Funding for these individuals needs to be first and foremost on the list of what to do first. These community centers are in the trenches. They have a vested interest in their own community because they themselves live there. It is them who hear gunshots at night. It is their garages that gang members vandalize. It is their children who are caught in the crossfire of a gang-related shootout. You think they don't care? Do you think that there is not more that they wouldn't do if they had the funding to do so? Many of these individuals have to volunteer their time because the wages are deplorable. These community centers do so much with limited funding; just imagine what they could do with a larger budget that allowed them to pay for what they need. It is the community centers that try and bridge the gap between citizen and police officer. There is mistrust between the police department and many citizens within these inner-city communities that others in society do not understand. Both sides need to grow up in my opinion. Each has valid reasons to mistrust the other, but where has that gotten us? What is this doing to solve the gang problem?

I have met many gang members that still know the name of a counselor at a youth center they went to. They are often an adult figure they trusted because many of them have grown up in the same neighborhood. They know what the gang life is about. They know what gangs are in their community and how they act and recruit. What they know is not taught in the pages of a psychology textbook. What they know comes from growing up in the same communities as the youth they are trying to reach. Many of these youth workers know the older brothers and sisters of the younger generation, giving them credibility to speak with the youth in their communities. They have a rapport with both gang members and police officers and can often be the "go-between." These individuals are invaluable but unfortunately there are not enough of them. Some of these individuals are ex-gang members themselves and there are studies being released that are showing the productivity of these individuals. There is a group in Chicago that calls themselves Ceasefire. They are former gang members that have dedicated themselves to preventing what they were once a part of. They work with the community and law enforcement and have had very positive results. They go around the community and squash conflicts between rival gangs as well as counsel young gang members as to the pitfalls of gang life. They have the credibility to say that they have lived that life but have decided to make the necessary changes for a productive life.

The fourth lines of defense are social workers. Once it has gotten to this stage, there will be some red flags that should be visible. When a child has a social worker, something has occurred that is outside normal childhood parameters. "Normal" in the sense of what we want our children to go through in life. If a child has a social worker, either the parent has abused the child or the child has behavioral type problems. There are a lot of reasons a child can have a social worker, but I don't think a child receives one for positive reasons. A social worker needs to be in the community the juvenile lives in I think. This may seem like it isn't high on the priority list, but I would disagree. I believe that all social workers should go through some form of gang awareness training that helps them identify certain warning signs that a parent or teacher might not be able to see. Beyond that, I feel the social worker should investigate what types of gangs are prevalent in the child's school and home neighborhood. Remember, I have preached above all else, that gangs are not created equal. They think and act differently in different areas of the country. Because of this, the warning signs will be different for every neighborhood. Some might say that social workers already have too many children on their case load or that there isn't enough time and money to devote the necessary training. I agree that these caseloads are too heavy, but I ask that you revert back to that $2,250,000 it will cost to house that fifteen-year-old gang member if he takes a life. We are going to spend money regardless, the only question is how much and how many lives we are willing to sacrifice in the process. This is an area that needs funding. When a child has a social worker or probation officer, it is highly likely that they are one step away from incarceration. This is exactly the type of situation where that $5,000 can be spent to prevent juveniles from joining gangs. We have to look to see where the money is being allocated.

Parents, youth workers, social workers, teachers, and ex-gang members will need to work together in order to give communities the ability to spot the warning signs many young potential gang members will give off. I understand the hesitancy of some to want to work with former and active gang members, but the reality is that in order to effectively deter juveniles from joining gangs, we will need the insight of former gang members who have now dedicated their lives to gang prevention. There should be many checks and balances put into place because there will be many wolves in sheep's clothing. There will be many gang members that claim to have left that life but have yet to do so for whatever reason. It should not be easy to gain the trust of those that they need to work with simply because we need to see who is serious and who is not. I don't care how long it takes me to prove myself because if I was on the other end, I would want to make sure that my motives were in line with the rest of society.

Chapter Ten

Changing the culture: change begins with one

The biggest problem in trying to get juveniles out of gangs is a lack of an individualized plan of attack. What works for one child is not likely to work for another. I cannot stress this point enough because this is really the heart of the entire problem in relation to gang prevention. I have stressed this point throughout the previous chapters but I will now go into detail on this subject.

One of the biggest mistakes that parents and law enforcement make if they are trying to keep kids out of gangs is to slander gang members and the gang lifestyle in general. This is having a negative impact and in fact, is leading many kids straight into the arms of gang members. There are various ways to get a child to renounce their gang affiliation; on their own, via advice from a former gang member, advice from other friends, or via their parent's intervention. With the way society is approaching the gang crisis, the least likely to succeed are the parents. This is so because parents tend to panic and think with their hearts and not their mind. The only way a parent can help their child get out of a gang is to educate their child as to the pitfalls of gang membership. Treat them like an adult and show them respect. This is a difficult task I know, because obviously the child is not acting like an adult. The ultimate goal however, is to make the child want to renounce their gang affiliation and unfortunately this is not an easy task.

Parents have to first educate themselves on what it means to be a gang member. They need to talk to former gang members and try to understand what they were thinking, as well as what roles their parent's played in their own gang involvement. If parents can help their child see that most gang members end up in prison or dead, it begins the doubting phase. Parents should take their children to visit former gang members who are still in prison. Most scared straight programs however, are a failure. These programs try and scare the kids via yelling and disrespect, hoping that this will turn them from the gang lifestyle. THIS DOES NOT WORK!!!!! There should be an "*educate* straight" rather than scared straight philosophy. Having a former gang member that is still incarcerated tell a juvenile respectfully what gangs did to their life, hopes, dreams, family, and friends can have a very significant impact. A parent should not simply enter their child into one of these programs without first investigating it themselves. They need to speak with theses inmates before their kids do to see if they feel comfortable with the situation. They have to be 100% involved in every step of the process. Parents will shop around for months to find the best deal on a house or car, why not spend that same amount of time trying to find the right individuals that can possibly save their child's life?

Were it not for a retired gang member that helped me see the error of my gang ways, I don't know what I would be doing at this moment. Once I realized that gang membership offered me nothing but pain and suffering to not only myself but my family and community, I wanted to get out. The key word was *want*. Once I had that urge to get out, I never had to worry about regretting my decision because I genuinely wanted to change my life. No family member, social worker, police officer or prison guard was able to get through to me. The only one that I even cared to listen to was a retired gang member.

Topics and questions elaborated on in this chapter will include:

- o The golden rule.
- o If you give respect, you will get respect.
- o Unconventional help indeed.
- o Never take away the hope.
- o Burn the blanket approach.
- o Subliminal messages can be effective.
- o Don't be a cool parent, just be a parent.

123456789 10

*   *   *

Rock bottom.......Two simple words that were coined by whom I wonder? Many people who have let life spiral out of control truly come to understand these two words intimately. Others think that they have hit rock bottom but I suppose to each, a different sort of bottom exists.

There was a moment in time, an exact second where I felt myself hit rock bottom. It was one of the most surreal moments of my life. It was nauseatingly humbling. I just turned nineteen years-old and was once again the youngest inmate to be sent to the newly opened "Supermax" prison. There were twenty-two inmates housed in this prison for the first month or so, with us being labeled as the "worst of the worst." I was strapped down to a concrete slab with only my underwear on. I had nothing else in the cell with me; no sheets, blankets, books, or toilet paper. I literally had nothing but my underwear. I was in control status. There are a few ways to be placed on control status and get strapped to a slab of concrete we had for a bed. You had to be placed on suicide watch or extracted from a different cell forcefully. Extracted meaning officers dressed in riot gear would run in your cell and physically bring you out. I was not under suicide watch nor have I ever been, but I was extracted from my cell by officers. The chain of events that led up to this was as follows.

I was just transferred to the new prison and I was put in my cell. I had to use the bathroom but all of the cells had cameras in them. We were under twenty-four hour monitoring. I had been in the cell for about five days at this point and still hadn't used the bathroom other than urinating. I am one of those people that have a hard time using the restroom in front of someone. I don't know why. The camera was above the toilet and I will just be honest; having to wipe myself after using the facilities with a camera right over me made me feel less than a human being. So I kept holding it and holding it though I knew nothing was going to change in the foreseeable future. Yes I'm sure this is too much information, but there is really no other way to say it. I decided that I was going to cover the camera while I used the toilet. This was an obvious rule violation but it was one that I felt I had to break because I have that shy bladder syndrome. This is no excuse mind you; I am merely stating what I was going through.

In this particular cell I was allowed writing paper, envelopes, a bible, and a pen insert. I picked out a piece of caulk from the window jam because it stayed sticky, and placed a few pieces on a small sheet of paper. (*The cell window I got the caulk from did not face outside, but rather into the hallway. We couldn't see out of our cells*.) The cell was pretty wide and the camera was on the back wall. In order to reach it, I was going to have to balance myself on the sink and leap off of it while sticking the piece of paper to the camera lens. In hindsight I can't help but laugh because I'm sure it looked funny to whoever was watching me on camera. There was nothing to grab onto for balance, so it was hard to jump off of the sink while sliding along the wall in the air trying to get to the camera. I had no brakes to slow my momentum from slamming me into the opposite wall of my cell. I remember hearing my skin screech across the freshly painted wall as I slid across it. My first attempt failed because the caulk was not sticky enough to hold the paper to the lens. Stupid caulk! Clearly it was not made to be used as an adhesive. After I slid across the wall and slammed into the other wall, a voice screeched across the intercom, "Hey, what are you doing?!" Each cell was equipped with an intercom that allowed officers to communicate with inmates. The voice came from an officer that was in the control booth watching me on camera. I can only imagine the look of concentration upon my face as I flew past the camera. Clearly not one of my more graceful moments.

The officer informed me that I was not allowed to cover my camera to which I replied obviously. He ordered me to essentially cease and desist or I would get a negative conduct report. I can't remember what I said to him at this point but all I knew was that I had to use the bathroom and he could do what he had to do. I got back up on the sink and tried again. The officer was still yelling for me to stop as I was about to jump when I had one of those quick contextualized moments we get in life. I remember thinking that this was not on my list if things to do in life. Anyway, I jumped and stuck the piece of paper to the camera, crashing once again down the wall. Success! The officer was still talking so I asked him to guess how many fingers I was holding up. I hinted that it was less than two. Yes, I was immature and stupid and have no excuse for acting that way. Hindsight is 20/20.

Immediately officers came to my cell door and ordered me to remove the paper from my camera. I proceeded to cover my cell window at this point as well; I was all in. I quickly realized that my plan had backfired however because officers were now at my door and window yelling for me to uncover everything. No chance of using the facilities at this point. I was irritated now, so I refused all of their orders to uncover my camera and cell window. I also refused to come out of my cell so that they could uncover everything. I gave them no option other than to suit up in riot gear and forcefully run in my cell and extract me. It was not much of a fight because I was still pretty young and small and the officers that participate on the extraction team are all of the biggest ones in the institution. After we scuffled for a minute or so, they shackled me and carried me to the control status cell or observation cell as they also call it. They cut all of my clothes off as they strapped me to the bed, leaving me with only my underwear. Definitely couldn't use the bathroom now.

Well, that was quite the experience I thought to myself, now alone in my cell. Now what? Time began to slow down, along with my pulse from the previous events I just went through. I don't know how much time elapsed because there was no clock. It felt like hours and hours as I laid there strapped to the bed, freezing. These cells were always freezing.

I had been in the "hole" for eight months or so at this point and I don't know what made this day different than any of the others. Perhaps it was being strapped down that refused my hands from pulling the "wool over my eyes" anymore. I had been running mentally from all that I was experiencing. I had been essentially sabotaging myself mentally and emotionally so that I didn't have to face the reality of what I was going through. From having a kid at fourteen to receiving a life sentence at fifteen and being the youngest inmate in the adult prison system. I misbehaved in prison with the hopes of further distracting myself from my true reality, but "hole" time made it difficult to distract oneself from the truth. Some people lose their minds in the "hole" because they are forced to deal with everything they have been running from mentally. There are very few distractions in the "hole." You think you know yourself, but I promise that months and years spent only with your own thoughts will help you see who you really are. Think about it. In the free world, life prevents people from truly getting to know themselves. Think about how many distractions bombard your senses each and every moment, from the TV, radio, traffic, family, friends, work, birds, kids, goats, sports, etc., etc., etc. Every single one of these things that you see and hear distracts you from your inner thoughts. When you hear, touch, see, taste, or smell, your mind puts effort into dissecting what it is that you have just sensed. Without even knowing it, your mind is dissecting every single thing you experience. You are not conscious of it; your mind just does it automatically. Every single one of your senses is distracted by something and when you are, you lose a little bit of focus from your innermost true self. If the distraction is large enough, you can silence any feelings of guilt, shame, anger, sadness, love, or any other emotion you are running from or care not to experience. Many of these emotions are born out of selfish acts we have committed but want so badly to not feel the consequences of.

I believe that we as human beings have two forces that drive us, both of them having needs; the physical and non-physical. Physical needs are fairly easy to understand as well as satisfy. They can be as simple as the pleasure one gets from eating a great meal, or the satisfaction one receives after a sexual encounter. I have always felt that physical needs are satisfied in very short periods of time but can often jeopardize the more important non-physical needs we all have. Non-physical needs can be of the spiritual variety, the heart and soul, or needs of inner peace. These needs far outweigh any physical needs but seem so unattainable to many. Life's distractions also mask the true needs we have as well. It is also my opinion that many people self-distract in order to trick themselves into believing they do not have any non-physical needs because let's be honest, non-physical needs do not have a quick reward for the sacrifice. Here is a really easy example of what I am speaking about. One spouse cheats on the other to satisfy a physical need. On the other end of the spectrum, a priest chooses to be celibate and live an extremely chaste life in order to be closer to God. Each is satisfying a need, presumably sacrificing one for the other. What need if fulfilled, has a higher degree of satisfaction? I suppose it would depend on someone's philosophical background. To each their own perhaps? I don't believe so. I tend to keep my beliefs to myself because I know beliefs can change by adding/subtracting various variables in life. I do believe however, that the human soul is at the beginning of life, good. I also believe that in order for "good" to exist, there has to be evil. I don't know that evil is tempting, but I do believe that many temptations are physical in nature.

On the other hand, what *physical* needs are met by giving to charity, being loyal to one's spouse, or doing the right thing? Yes, I said *physical* needs. What *non-physical* needs would be sacrificed if you met those needs? Any? I don't know why it doesn't work both ways but the fact that it doesn't, leads me to believe that non-physical needs far outweigh the physical from an importance standpoint. Yes, physical needs can often feel great when satisfied as well as distract us from the truth. The truth being who we really are within and what we really want out of life. Temptations to fulfill physical needs are everywhere. We often self-distract by fulfilling these needs but by doing so, we usually self-destruct. Here is another easy example to help explain what I mean. Let's say that you believe in love but to love is to trust. Based upon having that trust broken in the past, you are now afraid to love and be hurt again. So what might one do? Try and convince themselves that they do not need love? How can one do this? By distracting oneself with someone physically and saying to themselves, "See, I'm happy, I don't need love." Perfect plan right? It is unless your heart and soul truly do need love because physical distraction is only temporary. Eventually you will realize that you have done things/are doing things that your heart does not want or need---regardless of whether or not you care to admit this. Your needs are now in conflict; the physical with the non-physical until you make the necessary sacrifices for the non-physical. Peace will never come if you allow the physical to triumph. Life will consist of hopelessness, sadness, and despair.

Unfortunately most people never know what they want or who they are because life does not slow down long enough for them to figure it out and most continue to live in conflict. Why do you think Buddhist Monks spend years in remote locations that allow them to fully understand who they are? They spend years in these places that have very little in the way of distraction so that they can focus on the non-physical. Who else is willing to spend years away from everything in order to find out who they are/were or want to be? Not many.

There is however, one group of people that often travel a similar path. For many it will be hard to understand what I am about to say and you are free to disregard any or all of what I am about to speak of. I will use Hollywood's portrayal of certain incarcerated individuals. This is one area that Hollywood is pretty spot on with. Think about any prison movie that you have seen. Many are the same with a younger inmate being sent to prison and having a rough time. There is always someone in the movie that decides to take them under their wing and help them out. This person is usually older and is respected by other inmates in the prison population. Who are these older inmates? They are usually *lifers*. Many of them have taken a life, but aren't the serial killer or sexual deviant type. Many of their crimes are ones of passion, with very few of them having extensive criminal records. Many of these men have been incarcerated for twenty, thirty, or forty years and have spent many years in solitary confinement at some point along the way. Over these years, it is difficult not to understand the value of life. You learn that you cannot run from what you did or who you were. There isn't enough sensory distraction to allow one to run from who they truly are. Many years ago I used to say that I had to lose myself before I could find myself. I think this is a true statement. Over years of doing "hole" time, many lifers do find themselves, do find the value in life---in all forms, not just human. Think of the Birdman of Alcatraz. I know many lifers that will not let their cell mate kill a fly or any bug that comes into their cell. I've often wondered about the following irony; there are two groups of people that I believe value life the most. There are those who have been greatly victimized or lost a loved one and those that have taken a life and truly regret doing so. Obviously there are those in each category that do not value life at all. Many killers do not feel any remorse and many victims are so bitter that they hate life and everyone it. The latter is understandable to me for what it's worth. We never know how we will feel if we lose certain people in our lives.

Segregation often forces one's hand, much like the monk that chooses solitude. You can't run from what you have done. There is no distraction and because there isn't, you are forced to realize who you are and all you have done to hurt people. Most people in general would do anything rather than face what they have done. It is brutally hard to do so, to face guilt head on. I understand why so many people are afraid to face what they have done because the guilt can be overwhelming. I will be honest; guilt was the only emotion that made me want to contemplate suicide. I thought that death would have been easier than facing all those that I hurt. Guilt ate at my soul until I could take it no longer. I was forced to value life and evaluate who I was and who I wanted to be. It was guilt that began my journey of self-reflection. I don't know if that was right or wrong but it was my reality. I don't know if guilt should be used to better oneself or not. Two sayings come to mind that lead me in different directions on that question. **1.** It doesn't matter what road you take as long as you reach your destination. (*Destination being self-enlightenment*) **2.** You cannot build a skyscraper on a foundation of sand. (*Guilt being the sand foundation to my enlightened skyscraper*)

Personally I think that guilt can be a powerful motivator to do the right thing, to never victimize again. I also believe however, that guilt can overwhelm and destroy you if care is not taken. I have always liked the fire hose analogy; a fire hose can be used to dash the flames of your burning home, but that same hose can also hurt you badly if you try and use it by yourself. I feel that this is an apt analogy in describing the pros and cons of using guilt to better oneself. I found this out the hard way but I will get into that later.

Back to rock bottom….I was lying on the concrete slab, wondering how I went from the Honor Roll to serving a life sentence so quickly. I was just a Boy Scout and member of the Young Astronauts Program and now I was nothing more than a young punk gang banger with zero potential. I had a great family that loved me greatly and a pregnant girlfriend that would have followed me to the ends of the earth. I threw all of that away in a span of a second and a half. Literally a second and a half was all it took to destroy so many lives. One and a half seconds was all it took for Robert to lose his life, for his family to have their world flipped upside down. What were Roberts's dreams I have wondered for years. What if he were going to cure cancer one day? What if he were going to come up with a cleaner burning fuel that would free us from depending on foreign oil and ending up in so many wars? What if he would have discovered the cure to a disease I will eventually contract? That would be quite the circle of life Karma there wouldn't it?

One and a half seconds took my sons father from him, left his mother abandoned with child, my parent's without a son to make them proud one day. All of these things were racing through my mind as I lay there staring at the ceiling. I felt nauseated, wanting to cry but unable. I had long sense turned off my emotions in order to survive being a kid living within the adult prison system. I couldn't breathe and my eyes began to burn from not blinking. One and a half seconds. One and a half seconds………..

How does one rationalize this? How do you understand this? How does one not give up knowing they are on the short end of a life sentence? Honestly, there are days where I wonder how I am still here, why in a moment of weakness I simply didn't take my own life. After all, what was the point in living now? Really, what was the point? I had no incentive to change. I had no reason to try and make up for my misdeeds. I had hurt everyone that ever loved me, why would they ever forgive me? What is the point?!?! All the

Ambien in the world would not have put me to sleep that night. Life chose to humble me that day and I don't know why. For reasons I am still trying to completely understand, I chose not to give up. Over the next few months, I faced every single thing emotionally that I had been running from for so long. I felt as though my entire world was crumbling down. No longer did I mask what I had done, who I had hurt. I promised myself that I would no longer run from anything. Running had left me in a Supermax prison on administrative confinement serving a life sentence. I had no release date. If I was ever going to be let out of the hole, I would have to work my way out over the next few years with good behavior. This is what can happen if you run from your problems instead of facing them head on.

I had absolutely no idea as to what I was going to do or how I was going to do it. The hole I had dug for myself seemed insurmountably deep. I pondered whether or not I was past the point of no return. Part of me wanted to believe this because if I could convince myself of this, I could give up. If I couldn't convince myself that I was past the point of no return, it meant that I would have to find the strength to fight and claw my way up from rock bottom. After I was released from control status, I was moved to a cell in a different wing of the prison. A couple of cells down from me was an individual that used to belong to the same organization I belonged to at the time. In fact, he was one of the most notorious gang members in Milwaukee prior to him coming to prison for murder. I had looked up to him for years because prior to me coming to prison, I lived a half block from his home. I was friends with a couple of his younger brothers. He was already in prison when I met them, but came to know him through his brothers. They built him up to be this super gang member like younger brothers do. We all looked up to him. I ended up running into him when I first came to prison and just like in the free world, everyone looked up to him in prison as well. He ended up getting transferred to another prison shortly after I arrived though. We ended up meeting again in Supermax when I was moved into a cell a few doors down from his. By then I had made a name for myself. I wasn't that young fifteen-year-old anymore. I was at the wildest point in my incarceration at this time, still struggling to deal with all I had been suppressing for so long. I will never forget two days that would eventually change my life.

It was shower day and officers came around with our clean clothes and towels. The roll I received did not have a towel in it. It was reminiscent of the situation I spoke on earlier when the man next door to me went crazy. I have no reason to lie at this point in my life; the roll honestly didn't have a towel in it. I wasn't trying to keep it to wipe up the water in my cell or anything like that. When I told officers that I did not get a towel, they said that they couldn't help me. Well that was absolutely unacceptable to me at that stage in my life. I once again covered my windows and told them to suit up.

(*Get in riot gear and come get me*) The man I looked up to called me through the vent in the wall and asked me what was wrong. (*We used the ventilation system to talk to one another. It was like an intercom to other cells if you talked loud enough*) I explained the situation to him and he asked why I was going to go through all of this for a stupid towel. I used the excuse of general principle. I'm having this conversation with him all the while officers are yelling for me to uncover my window. I go back and forth from the vent to kick my door and cuss out officers. The man I looked up to kept telling me to calm down, it was just a towel. I then heard him stop an officer and tell him that I could have *his* towel. A towel may seem insignificant to you, but we only get one towel twice a week. We had nothing else to clean up or wipe the floor with. I told him that I wouldn't take his towel because then he would be left without one for the next week. Beyond that, it wasn't even really about the towel anyway. The towel itself was irrelevant. I was using the towel to try and distract myself from all of the emotions that I was experiencing now that I was trying to face all I had done. It was not an easy time mentally.

I couldn't understand why the man I had looked up to cared so much about me not getting into more trouble. It didn't make sense to me. All sorts of things were going through my mind. I asked myself if he was going soft. Before I could find an answer, I heard the guard tell him that he would not give me his towel anyway. I don't know why or how, but two minutes later that same guard came to my cell and gave me a fresh towel. I kid you not. Just like that. Maybe they were tired of suiting up and running in my cell, I don't know. In any event, I uncovered my window and showered without further incident that day.

A few days went by and the man I looked up to called down to me. He asked what I was doing with my life. He wanted to know why I felt as though I had to act out, and what I thought I was proving. He asked me what the organization had to offer me in life. I was confused. Not about the questions, but rather who they were coming from. As I said, he was just a short time earlier, one of the most respected members of our organization, and now he was questioning why I was in a gang. I felt offended at first and he must have sensed it in my tone because he went on to explain what the organization had done to his life. He had gotten snitched on himself by a member of our organization. He explained that he was no longer going to involve himself with a self-destructive lifestyle. He told me how no one looked out for his family after he was sent to prison. His family was retaliated on for what he had done, and I could verify this because I had seen his bullet-riddled house. I lived a half block away. His family stopped putting in new windows because they kept getting shot out. I had heard rumors that people were telling on him but I didn't want to believe it nor did anyone else because if someone was telling on him, who wouldn't they tell on? I couldn't believe what I was hearing. He said that he was done with "this life." He asked me what this life had done for me, for my son, my family. I didn't know what to say.

He never once told me to renounce my gang affiliation or to stop doing what I was doing. Instead he simply made me question what I was doing. A few days later he was moved to another unit for good behavior.

I felt alone, more so than ever before. I think for the first time, I could see through all of the smoke and mirrors. Those of my own creation as well as the gang's creation. I had never been more confused. Now what was I supposed to do? Everything was crashing down on me and before I knew it, I had gone a few weeks without getting into any trouble. I think I was too deep in thought to act out. I was then moved to another unit due to good behavior. I was on this unit for a few weeks when I got word that someone I knew was just transferred to Supermax and was in the receiving unit. This was an individual whom I looked at as my brother. He also received a life sentence at the age of fifteen. He was a member of the same organization that I belonged to. We became so close because no one else could understand what it was like to be so young in the adult prison system. I have personally only met two fifteen-year-olds and one fourteen-year-old in prison other than myself. I wouldn't meet them until later on however, so there was no one else that could really relate to what we were going through. For years he was the only individual that I trusted in the entire prison system. We were cellmates multiple times and were sent to all of the same prisons over the years.

We hadn't seen each other for about two years or so when he arrived at Supermax, so we decided to hatch a plan to meet up in the control status wing. The only way to accomplish this was to make officers suit up and extract us from our cells. We sent coded messages through the mail and set up a time where we would both make officers suit up. The plan worked and we both ended up in control status a few cells apart. There was a comfort in knowing that there was someone who had gone through what I had in this prison system. I cannot put into words what it is like to grow up in here when everyone is older and bigger than you. The only way to understand it was to live it, and he was the only other one that I knew at the time that lived what I had lived through, vice versa for him. We were brothers and I would never go against him and he would never go against me. It made no difference whether we were right or wrong; we were going to ride together.

In control status now, we talked for hours catching up on what we had experienced over the past couple of years. The cell was cold, so unbelievably cold. We had no blankets or sheets, just our underwear. We had to take our mattresses and roll ourselves up in it, creating a makeshift blanket. You don't understand how cold these cells were. I'm sure he'll love that I'm sharing this next part. As I said, we had to roll up in our mattresses to stay warm and in to order to do this, you had to lie on one end and use your body weight to turn over and roll yourself up because the mattresses were so stiff. I remember him yelling that he was stuck. I said, "What do you mean you're stuck? Stuck on what?" While he was rolling himself up, he went to fast and pinned the seam of the mattress underneath him and got trapped next to the wall. His own body weight was preventing him from unrolling himself. You can't move your arms or legs once you are all rolled up because the mattress is to stiff. I remember laughing and laughing because I could hear him struggling to free himself as well as the panic in his voice from being stuck. These cells also had cameras in them so I can only imagine what the officers were thinking. He eventually freed himself after a few minutes. I don't know why I felt it necessary to share that, I just did. I think it was one of those laughing to keep from crying moments in time. We would sit by the vent for hours, sometimes not saying a word. There was a comfort knowing that on the other end of that vent, was another human being that understood what I was feeling.

Imagine when you were a teenager trying to figure life out. Now imagine all of those emotions you were feeling and couple them with growing up in an adult prison. Sometimes I don't know how I feel as I think back to those days. Supermax in a way, was the best thing to ever happen to me even though it was a tremendously difficult place to try and figure life out in. While it was good for me in the long run, I still don't think juveniles belong in the adult prison system. We were left to fend for ourselves. All of the juveniles that I said I had met along the way? All of them ended up going to Supermax. Most of them have not fared so well. My "brother" is still in Supermax. At the time of this writing, he has been in the hole for over a decade. Can you understand what that can do to a human mind? I know many other juveniles that were waived into adult court that are gone mentally. They gave up on life or were not strong enough to make it in this life. Either way, it is a sad state of affairs.

At the end of the day, I committed a crime and deserve to be punished, but I came frighteningly close to ending up like many of the other juveniles that have grown up in the adult prison system. I last got into trouble almost fourteen years ago, but change was not easy. In fact, change nearly broke me mentally.

Going back to when I was in control status, I was moved to a different cell three days later. Over the next few weeks, I ran out of excuses for still being a gang member. The conversation I had with the man I had looked up to was replaying itself over and over in my mind. Deep down inside of me, I knew even before I committed my crime that I no longer wanted to be a gang member, but I feared the repercussions that would befall me if I got out. After coming to prison, I felt as though I had to stay a gang member to make it.

At this point, I only had about five years in on a life sentence. I was worried about being ostracized socially if I renounced my gang affiliation. I had twenty-two years until I was eligible to see parole for the first time to deal with the repercussions from renouncing my gang affiliation. I remember wondering what the hell I had been doing for the past five years. I wasn't raised to act like this, to hurt people, to victimize. Who had I become, or better yet, *what* had I become? This is a terrifying moment to experience. When you finally unveil the mask of what you have been hiding for so many years, your reflection in life's mirror is unrecognizable, at least mine was. For me, there were feelings of despair and hopelessness. How was I going to repair all of this damage? Was it to late to change? Everyone's situation is different, but all who wish to change must find a reason to change for. Think about it, why would an inmate on death row change? I can only think of one logical reason and it relates to the afterlife, whatever afterlife they may believe in. Some may say that one should change simply because it is the right thing to do. True, but if life has gotten to a point where one *needs* to change, odds are that they haven't the mental capacity to simply flip the switch and do so. If it were that easy, everyone who needs to change would change. People don't change because it is extremely difficult to do so. Change in and of itself isn't difficult, but rather the consequences of the decisions one has made that necessitated change.

I looked at my situation; I was now twenty years-old, and over twenty years away from parole. I had rival gang members that wanted to retaliate on me for what I had done, and members of my own organization that would hate me if I decided to renounce my gang affiliation. Correctional officers hated me because I was a young punk that had caused so much trouble, so I had a hard time with them as well. My family was starting to lose hope in me I think. How disappointed they must have been. My son would not have the possibility to have a father until he was twenty-seven years old and his mother both loved and hated me, deservedly so. My appeal had just been denied so this nightmare did not seem to have any end in sight.

I sat there, looking at the past, trying to look into the future. I did not know which one was bleaker. I went to the mirror and stared, wondering whose eyes peered back at me. They were hollow, sad, empty, and forsaken. I couldn't feel my heartbeat. I didn't feel alive. I had an odd moment where I could see my father's reflection in the mirror. This made me want to cry but my eyes felt as dry as the Sahara. I wanted so bad to cry, to let out all of the pain that I had held in for the last five years but to no avail. I can only describe it like this; when you drink too much and you feel nauseated, you know if you throw up you will feel better. This is how I felt, only instead of my stomach feeling nauseated, it was my soul and the vomit my tears. Those tears never did come, seemingly more elusive than finding a reason to change. It's odd, I hated who I had become but I could really not find a reason to change. All of what I have just described was justification to simply give up. Why not? Seriously, why not?

I'm sitting here now, trying to think about what to write next. It scares me as I think back because I came so close to giving up, to throwing in that terrible towel or waving the white flag. I honestly felt as though I had lost all things worth having. I could see no incentive to face life. Had I access to a gun at that moment, I think I would have pulled the trigger.

I guess it came down to two things for me. I didn't know what I was going to do, but I did know that I didn't want to feel like this anymore. Secondly, I feared what God would do to me if I didn't change. I have been hesitant to speak of God because it is my opinion that most of the inmates who say that they believe in God are full of crap. They make me sick as they walk around waiving their Bibles and proclaiming this and that, all the while continuing their illegal activities. It's all for show, both to others and themselves sadly. So many of the Penitentiary Zealots I know have come back to prison. I don't want to be lumped in with them. I do me. Personally, I feel one's relationship with God is the most personal and sacred entity in existence. I don't feel the need to proclaim this or that. I don't care if the next man believes that I have found God. I don't feel the need to try and convince anyone else to find God or force my beliefs on them. I believe you must find God on your own. You cannot force someone to have faith, to believe, but this is only my opinion. I have always found it ridiculous how some of these countries around the world force their people to believe in their God with penalties of death if they do not conform. All religions are guilty of this at some point in time. They then wonder why their people revolt and their countries are in ruins. Religious oppression is one of man's greatest injustices. I have always felt that if one walks upright in righteousness, others will flock to you. They will wonder what your "secret" is, how you cope with life. This is how you bring others into faith. Do as I do, *not* as I say. I believe that I will have to face God one day, and if I do not make some serious changes, I'll know what to expect.

Some time went by, maybe a few more weeks or so when one night I woke up in the middle of the night. I don't know if it was a dream that woke me up or what, but I decided to deal with the situation like a Band-Aid, and rip it off as fast as I could. I promised myself and God, that I was done living a self-destructive life. I renounced my gang affiliation in that moment. I wrote a letter to a member of my organization whom I respected and felt deserved to hear from me that I was done. I was not a member of some little street gang, so there was no way I could simply just "be done" and go about my way. Beyond that, my reputation was at its pinnacle. Everyone knew who I was because I was so young when I came in and had done a lot of things to prove I wasn't just some little fifteen-year-old. I learned another lesson here; to be careful what you wish for. I *thought* I wanted nothing more than for my name to be on the lips of every gang banger in the prison system. I wanted everyone to know who I was, how tough I was. Yea, that philosophy clearly came back to bite me.

As I said, I couldn't just be on my way. There is a process that isn't pleasant. I still had respect for certain individuals as men, so I went about it the right way and wrote to who I needed to write to. I did feel as though I were abandoning some of these individuals, I will not lie. I had been through wars with some of these men, they had put their life on the line for me, and me them. It makes little difference that our cause was not just. In my letter, I explained that I couldn't continue hurting the people that needed me, that I wasn't being true to myself anymore. My son, his mother, and the rest of my family really played a pivotal role in me changing. I often wonder who I would be today if they had given up on me. I fear what or who I would be. I think of those in here that do not have a family and I can sort of understand why they are the way they are. Perhaps I would be just like them had I no family. I explained that I wanted to lead a positive life regardless of my current place of residence. I told him that I knew there would be consequences and I would not run from them. I sealed the letter with my utmost respect, and slid it out of my door to be picked up by guards. I slid it so far out so I couldn't retrieve it if I started to second guess myself. The next chapter in my life was about to begin---alone. Remember how I explained what a soldier might endure if he were to "quit" being a soldier but was forced to still live with the rest of his unit until their tour was up? Well, my journey experiencing millions and millions of those minutes was about to ensue. My only solace was that I had a couple of years left to do in Supermax before I would be sent back to the individuals that I had essentially abandoned---a short stay of execution if you will.

It was about 5:00am in the morning when I slid the letter out of my cell door. It was at the time, the hardest thing I ever had to do in my life. I got on my knees and prayed. I asked God to protect me because I knew I would end up facing many a precarious situation in the future. I knew that the bell would one day toll for me, and I simply asked God to give me the strength to get though it all.

I lay there with eyes wide open, wondering what fate had in store for me. I thought back to other members who had been X'ed out (*Kicked out*) of the organization for various reasons. I had yet to really witness to many individuals that chose to renounce their gang affiliation out of the blue, simply because they wanted to better themselves and their life. I've witnessed many older gang members retire or renounce their gang affiliation because of religious reasons, but never really any younger gang members. I didn't really know what to think. I wondered what the reaction was going to be when my letter reached its destination. I knew it would end up being read by numerous individuals because that is just how things went. I will not even lie to you; I was more than a little worried. Yes, the physical aspects of the consequences I would have to face would hurt, but the thought of having to face the organization I was once a part of left a queasy feeling in the pit of my stomach. At the end of the day however, there was no running from it unless I was going to check into protective custody and that was not an option for me. I made my choices and I had to live with the consequences. I was tired of running from anything hard that I would have to face in life.

What I didn't expect however, was that I felt good. For the first time in my life, I didn't steer clear of the path less traveled. I was proud of myself. It had been years since I had actually been proud of myself and a decision that I made. Perhaps it may seem like no big deal to have renounced my gang affiliation and decide to live a better life, but to me it wasn't an easy choice simply because of what that decision put me in danger of. At that moment in my life, renouncing my gang affiliation was the single hardest choice that I could have made, and I made it. I believe that everyone has a number of choices in their life that they are afraid to make. There is always one that tops the list, one that if made, would be the hardest thing they could possibly face at that moment. Imagine taking that one fear and facing it, no longer letting it dictate your life. Mine at the time was renouncing my gang affiliation. Yours could be anything, from going skydiving to blowing the whistle on a boss who is sexually harassing you. Self-empowerment is I believe, vastly underrated. It can be such a powerful motivational tool, addictive even but in a positive way. When a person finds themselves at a point in life where their own reflection is unrecognizable, odds are that they have been running from tough decisions that need to be faced. These un-faced decisions *will* snowball into an avalanche of inner turmoil and perpetual weakness. I have met so many people that wonder why their lives are in ruin and it's clearly because they are afraid to face tough decisions in their life. Life isn't easy, which you would think should be common sense, but people want to take it day by day. That's a good theory except when one takes it day by day afraid to face what they have done in life. Of course your life isn't going to change if you take it day by day every day.

I promise that if you take that number one fear you have and face it, life will get easier and you *will* get stronger. If you face your number one fear, then your number two and number three fears are nothing because at the end of the day, you faced the number one thing you were afraid to face. Everything else is child's play at that point. You begin to find yourself at this point and realize that there will always be things in life that you are afraid to face but you are no longer afraid to face them.

Today, I look for any possible decision that I feel would be hard to face and I face it. It doesn't matter how small or large the decision, I face it head on. I refuse to let fears and tough choices put a stranglehold on the man I want to be. Yes, sometimes it is difficult, sometimes I wonder if it is worth it to face whatever needs to be faced. At the end of *my* day however, I know that there is nothing that I will not face if necessary. There will always be difficult things that I will broach in life, this cannot be avoided, but I will never be worried that I will be afraid to face these tough phases in life. I know that I will sometimes make the wrong choice and or make mistakes, but that is also life.

Since I faced my toughest choice over fourteen years ago, I have no longer gotten into any trouble. Fourteen years is a long time to go in prison without getting any major negative conduct reports. I'll put it into context. The first four years that I was in prison, I received sixty conduct reports. Most prisoners usually only get a handful during their entire incarceration. I have lived almost my entire free life without getting a major conduct report. That is how powerful facing your innermost fear can be. It is never too late to change. Ask yourself who you have become as a person and whether or not you are proud of whom you have become. If not, why? What choices stand in the way of becoming who you want to be? What is the number one hardest thing you could do right now today that would begin the process of change? Face it! Face it before it is too late. Face it before it gets even more difficult to face. I promise that it will not get easier to face tomorrow because unfortunately life does not work that way. I wish it did, but alas it does not. With each passing day, it will get just a little bit harder to face. You will never know how much harder until the day comes when you lose everything and are forced to change. It is this day when you will lose those you care about the most, forever potentially. You think life is hard now, imagine facing it without those you have taken for granted for so long. You will be destined to live in a world where *no one else exists*. I promise that this is not a world you want to live in.

If you really think about it, what's the worst that can happen? You fail and still hate yourself? Regardless of the outcome, you will not have failed because you faced your number one fear. The outcome is immaterial. Beyond that, the old adage of "Rome wasn't built in a day" again comes to mind. You may not see the fruits of your labor right away, if ever. Fixing the damage you have created for yourself in life can often take many years if not a lifetime. If change were easy, everyone would be who they wanted to be and no one would be afraid to face what they need to. The beautifully tragic aspect to life is that no one can force you to change. It is up to you and you alone. Maybe you are content with hating yourself, with burying your head in the sand hoping it will magically get better. Perhaps you don't mind being a coward when it comes to facing what you need to face, instead choosing to live day by day and caring not of those you are hurting constantly. Like faith with religion, change will come voluntarily or not at all.

A few days went by after renouncing my gang affiliation before I was able to get word to the individual that I considered to be my brother. (*The other individual that received a life sentence at the age of fifteen.*) There was a guard that would relay messages for us if we asked him to. He was one of those guards that treated us all like human beings regardless of what we had done to end up in prison. I told the guard to relay the message that I had "dropped my flags." (*Renounced my gang affiliation.*) He came back about fifteen minutes later telling me that "my brother" did not believe me. He then asked me what dropping my flags meant. I told him. I don't know that he really believed me, but I assured him that I was not joking. It's odd; I never expected to not be believed. It was one of the few surprises that I faced. It makes sense as I look back now, but back then I didn't know why people would think I was just joking. I knew that institutional staff would not believe that I renounced my gang affiliation, but I expected other inmates to believe me. I suppose it came from the fact that during my first five years or so that I was incarcerated; I really tried to make a name for myself. I built a reputation and moved up the ranks while doing so. You will never understand how hard it was doing this while being a Caucasian within a Latino organization. It was not easy and people could not understand why I would throw all of that away when I was just beginning a life sentence.

The next surprise that I faced over the coming weeks was how I felt. I felt as though I was still running from what I had to do and I sort of felt hollow inside. Honestly, I felt angry at God because I had faced what I needed to face, or so I thought. I asked what more he wanted me to do? I renounced my gang affiliation and decided to live life the right way, why do I still feel like I am running? My answer came in the weeks ahead as the one emotion that I had avoided for so long came roaring into focus.

Guilt

I was no longer fast enough to run from it, to hide from it. I examined it with my new "refusing to run" philosophy. I obviously knew that I felt guilty because I was responsible for the loss of a life and for taking from my victim's family, a future spent with Robert. I struggled with this because I couldn't understand how I could make the situation better. It wasn't long before I realized that a million "I'm sorry's" would not bring their loved one back or diminish the pain that I caused all of them. I realized that there was nothing that I could say that would change the past and bring Robert back. No amount of time would ease their pain like so many people like to believe can happen. In the first couple of chapters, I explained how actions supersede want. (*Speak louder than words*) I asked myself how I could *show* my victims that I was sorry and the answer eventually came to me. I realized that while I could do nothing to ever bring Robert back, I could however dedicate my life to make sure that other families do not experience what Robert's did. Simply renouncing my gang affiliation was not enough in my opinion; I had to prevent what I was once a part of. It was the first time in my life that I felt as though I had a purpose, a reason to be in prison, an explanation for why Robert had to lose his life. I know that I will never ask my victims for forgiveness because I don't think that those who have victimized have the right to do so. Would I love to be forgiven? Absolutely, but I think the only way for them to even consider doing so will come after I have spent the rest of my life proving to them with my actions, that I am sorry. I understand that nothing I ever do will bring Robert back or justify what I did on September 26th 1995. I understand and accept that simply because I have no choice in the matter.

I created my own juvenile gang prevention program. I call it, "Council Of Enlightenment—understanding and preventing juvenile gang violence." In short, it aims to connect people in society that might not otherwise normally interact with one another in the hopes of ending the juvenile gang violence crisis. I truly believe that eliminating the juvenile gang epidemic will require former gang members working with social workers, psychologists, youth counselors, parents, and law enforcement.

I knew that from within the walls of a Super maximum prison I would not be able to do much so I used the time to think, formulate potential programs, and visualize what I wanted to accomplish. It was there that I also began writing this book. It has taken me almost thirteen years to write this book, not knowing anything about writing or the publishing world. I had only finished the seventh grade so I had to teach myself much of what I would need to know. I immersed myself in psychology textbooks, trying to understand how the juvenile mind works so that I could come up with various plans of attack to fight juvenile gang membership. I spent so many thousands of hours staring at the ceiling and pacing my cell, trying to come up with ways that I could prevent juveniles from joining gangs while still incarcerated. I had a direction at least. I didn't know what life had in store for me, but if nothing else, I knew I was placed on this earth for a reason and that notion gave me hope. Remember, at this point I was still about twenty-two years away from my first parole hearing. That meant that I would have to spend the next 11,563,200 minutes or so facing the consequences of being an ex-gang member trying to prevent juveniles from joining gangs while still behind bars. I felt like a pebble at the foot of Mt. Everest. I knew it was going to be difficult and I knew that there would be resistance from both inmate and staff but I refused to let it deter me.

I earned my way out of Supermax and was sent back to the prison I came from where I had battered an officer. It was where I had spent four years acting out and being the young punk that led me to Supermax in the first place. I had pissed off a lot of guards over those four years and I had them to worry about as well, not to mention all of my former gang members that I had abandoned. Some were not pleased with me at all. I don't think anyone really quite knew what to make of me. Prison officials really had no incentive to think that I was any different than who I was when I left. Something I also never really thought about while I was an active gang member was being retaliated on by rival gang members for what I had done to come to prison. After all, I had a huge organization behind me to keep retaliators at bay. They no longer were behind me and sure enough, it wasn't long before a rival gang member wanted to retaliate. I don't think I was back for more than two weeks before I found out that I was a target. I faced the situation knowing that it wouldn't simply disappear, understanding that this was only the beginning of what I would potentially have to face due to my earlier actions. I had to face the music so to speak. The past will always find you. The past was born to chase those who fear it, very seldom agreeing to compromise. Our only choice is to face it head on in my opinion, and use it to forge a future. I was a gang member in the past, so now I use my past experiences to keep other juveniles from joining gangs.

It is difficult to prove that you have changed. Many people will refuse to accept it and others couldn't care less if you have. Many rival gang members do not care that I was no longer a gang member; others looked at me as one less enemy they have to keep an eye on.

As far as proving to institutional staff that I had changed, this took time. Many looked at me no differently than they did prior to me being sent to Supermax. I don't blame them, I would have been apprehensive as well. I treated some of them with very little respect when I first was sent to prison, so I couldn't expect them to just respect me now that I had changed. I realized that just because I was young in the prison system and felt a need to act out in order to prove myself, did not give me any right to treat them as I did. My family did not raise me to be like that. Over the next few months, I realized that I had my next quest, my next difficult thing that was going to be hard to do. Because it was difficult, I knew that I had to do it. I went to every single officer that I had disrespected, and apologized to them. Yes, there is supposed to be an us against them mentality in prison, from both perspectives, but I decided that in order to feel like a human being, I had to treat everyone like a human being. This was difficult because there were some guards that treated inmates like animals and it was hard to apologize to them, but I decided that I wasn't going to let others dictate who I was. I had to do what I felt I needed to do, regardless of whether certain guards deserved to be apologized to or not. At the end of the day, I have to look myself in the mirror at night. I can't dictate how they treat people, but I can determine how I act. I remember a saying I heard long ago, "be who you are, not who you are not, because if you're not, you are not who you are." Indeed.

Being "you" under non-hostile conditions is easy, or at least it should be. You really find out who you are however, when the times get tough and you find yourself angry or uncomfortable. This is when one's true colors show.

I didn't really expect officers to believe that I was sorry for my behavior, but over time they all began to see that I was genuine. This came from them witnessing me walk the walk so to speak. They could see that I carried myself different, that I didn't hang around the same people that I used to. My cell was immaculate and I kept it contraband free. I held a steady job and received perfect work performances.

It wasn't long before I was able to join the B.R.I.C.K. program. This was a program where troubled youth were brought into the prison to speak with us about the decisions we had made. I loved it. Finally I was given the opportunity to do what I know I was meant to do. While the apology to my victims began with the renouncement of my gang affiliation, it really began with that program. Eventually I became the coordinator of that program with an emphasis on juvenile gang prevention. I was eventually transferred to a medium security prison due to good behavior and became involved with the Youth Awareness Program. It is a similar program, but instead of troubled youth being brought into the prison for the morning, all community seventh graders are brought in to listen to the choices we have made. Over time, I became the gang coordinator for this program as well.

I completed all of the programs that I am required to complete and also received a culinary arts vocational diploma. I then completed my three year apprenticeship and am now a Journeyman chef. I am currently working on my bachelor's degree so that I will have the credentials to work with troubled youth if I am ever blessed with an opportunity to do so as a free man.

I think back to the little 5' 3" 120 lb fifteen-year-old standing in front of an adult prison, scared to death of what lay in store for him. I honestly thought that my life was over, that there was no hope in tomorrow. That was eighteen years ago and I feel as though I have lived five lifetimes and yet have lived no life at all.

* Change*

Six simple little letters and yet change is one of the most challenging aspects of life depending upon the choices one has made in their life. The road to change is wrought with detours and often times, seems impossible. Nothing about it is easy and quite frankly it is easier to change than to make everyone else believe you have changed. It is frustrating yes, but at the end of the day, you change for you, for your loved ones, and to ensure that you never again create another victim. Many people will not want to believe that you have changed and that is their right and we must accept that. I believe that change can give us the opportunity to show that we are sorry, but I do not believe that it gives us the right to ask for forgiveness.

One can change a moment prior to their final breath if they so choose but it does not mean that they will be forgiven for all of their transgressions. I don't believe that change and forgiveness go hand in hand. Forgiveness I believe, deals with the choices one has made in the past, while change ensures we will no longer need to ask for forgiveness in the future. Change cannot change the past, nothing can. Change can however, shape our future.

It is so much easier to prevent juveniles from joining a gang than it is to get them to renounce their gang affiliation. With that being said, I don't believe that society has a clue how difficult it is to keep certain at-risk youth from joining a gang. Everything is connected. Every aspect of a child's early life has a direct link to eventual gang membership. Their neighborhood, income level, number of parents raising them, hours worked by their parent, quality of school attended, type of friends, extracurricular activities they do or don't participate in, and any positive role models they may have in their lives all play a role. All of these elements are ingredients to a recipe with the final finished product being a gang member.

I hope that over the course of this book I have at the very least, shed a different light on the gang culture. I hope you better understand why it exists, how it began, who it affects, and why we all should have a vested interest in preventing juveniles from joining gangs. I hope you now understand that the gang problem is not solely a minority problem, that gangs aren't solely a product of poverty. The gang crisis is an everyone problem.

This nation's children are killing one another and for what? Because someone wore the wrong colored shirt to school one day or tilted their hat in the wrong direction? These victims will never again walk this earth, breathe another breath. They will forever be all of our victims because we don't want to admit that everything and everyone is connected. We are a society, for better or worse.

Today, we as a society are in the business of manufacturing juvenile gang members.

Hopefully the tears of tomorrow will not be yours that fall, welling up in a pool of "if only."

Appendix A

Council Of Enlightenment

-understanding and preventing juvenile gang violence-

The sole purpose of the Council Of Enlightenment organization is to first gather an accurate understanding of juvenile gang violence and then use that information to aid in the prevention of gang violence committed by juveniles.

The Council Of Enlightenment is a networking platform that connects various groups in society that might not otherwise interact with one another. In one instance, the Council Of Enlightenment might find certain psychologists doing a study on why children from a particular neighborhood are joining gangs, and introduce them to a number of former gang members *from* that community. The psychologist can gather accurate information as to why these particular individuals joined a gang and then possibly be introduced to certain behavioral experts that study juvenile delinquency. The Council Of Enlightenment will then introduce those behavioral experts to youth counselors from the same community in question so that they may begin a dialogue concerning what tendencies those in their community tended to show before they joined a gang. At this point, all parties can begin formulating various prevention measures that will help this particular community.

Deterring juveniles from joining a gang needs to be done on a community by community basis. What works in one community might not necessarily work in another. Gangs in Milwaukee think, act, and recruit differently than those in Oshkosh for instance. The Council Of Enlightenment will also introduce juvenile gang members to willing families that have lost loved ones via gang violence so that they may experience first-hand the potential pain they are inflicting upon their community.

The Council Of Enlightenment will introduce parents to former gang members so that they can be given an opportunity to ask them questions about what they were thinking prior to them joining a gang and what their parents could have possibly done differently. What warning signs they exhibited and what their child might be thinking are other questions that can be answered.

Anatomizing the gang culture

Trying to force a child to get out of a gang is not an effective tactic and will not be employed by the Council Of Enlightenment. An "educate straight" rather than "scared straight" approach will be taken. Juveniles will be given information as to what gang life truly consists of in a respectful and educational manner. There will be no belittling or disrespecting of anyone participating in this program. Our effort is to instill a "want" in the child to never become a gang member. Only then can true gang prevention be effective.

Any inmate or ex-gang member that participates in the Council Of Enlightenment will be put through a screening process conducted by institutional security as well as any other outside law enforcement agency that is involved. This will be done to ensure that their motives are in line with the Council Of Enlightenment's motives.

The war on juvenile gang membership is a war that needs a new approach, an educational approach from people who have been in gangs, working with those that have the authority to implement productive juvenile gang prevention measures.

If this program saves only one child from gang violence,
this program has **failed**.

Appendix A

www.councilofenlightenment.org

adam_procell@yahoo.com

Appendix B

Where parents can

turn

I have included a few services that parents can visit if they are concerned that their child may be hanging around gang members. I initially had a list of about two hundred but decided to only list the nationally recognized websites. From them, you can find links to your particular community.

I have also left some room for you to write down any links you may find from these websites.

1.   NATIONALGANGCENTER.gov

2.   IIR.com –Intergovernmental research

3.   OJJDP.gov—Office of juvenile justice and
      delinquency prevention

4.   NGCRC.com—National gang crime research center

Index

www.ingramcontent.com/pod-product-compliance
Lightning Source LLC
Chambersburg PA
CBHW060232100426

42742CB00011B/1513